MENTOR'S GUIDE

Christian Ministry

Theology *of the* Church

The Church Foreshadowed in God's Plan

....

The Church at Worship

....

The Church as Witness

....

The Church at Work

This curriculum is the result of thousands of hours of work by The Urban Ministry Institute (TUMI) and should not be reproduced without their express permission. TUMI supports all who wish to use these materials for the advance of God's Kingdom, and affordable licensing to reproduce them is available. Please confirm with your instructor that this book is properly licensed. For more information on TUMI and our licensing program, visit *www.tumi.org* and *www.tumi.org/license*.

Capstone Module 3: Theology of the Church Mentor's Guide

ISBN: 978-1-62932-023-6

© 2005, 2011, 2013, 2015. The Urban Ministry Institute. All Rights Reserved.
First edition 2005, Second edition 2011, Third edition 2013, Fourth edition 2015.

Copying, redistribution and/or sale of these materials, or any unauthorized transmission, except as may be expressly permitted by the 1976 Copyright Act or in writing from the publisher is prohibited. Requests for permission should be addressed in writing to: The Urban Ministry Institute, 3701 E. 13th Street, Wichita, KS 67208.

The Urban Ministry Institute is a ministry of World Impact, Inc.

All Scripture quotations, unless otherwise noted, are from The Holy Bible, English Standard Version, copyright © 2001 by Crossway Bible, a division of Good News Publishers. Used by permission. All Rights Reserved.

Contents

Course Overview
- 3   About the Instructors
- 5   Introduction to the Module
- 7   Course Requirements

13   Lesson 1
The Church Foreshadowed in God's Plan

43   Lesson 2
The Church at Worship

79   Lesson 3
The Church as Witness

115   Lesson 4
The Church at Work

149   Appendices

205   Mentoring the Capstone Curriculum
- 213   Lesson 1 Mentor's Notes
- 225   Lesson 2 Mentor's Notes
- 241   Lesson 3 Mentor's Notes
- 253   Lesson 4 Mentor's Notes

About the Instructors

Rev. Dr. Don L. Davis is the Executive Director of The Urban Ministry Institute and a Senior Vice President of World Impact. He attended Wheaton College and Wheaton Graduate School, and graduated summa cum laude in both his B.A. (1988) and M.A. (1989) degrees, in Biblical Studies and Systematic Theology, respectively. He earned his Ph.D. in Religion (Theology and Ethics) from the University of Iowa School of Religion.

As the Institute's Executive Director and World Impact's Senior Vice President, he oversees the training of urban missionaries, church planters, and city pastors, and facilitates training opportunities for urban Christian workers in evangelism, church growth, and pioneer missions. He also leads the Institute's extensive distance learning programs and facilitates leadership development efforts for organizations and denominations like Prison Fellowship, the Evangelical Free Church of America, and the Church of God in Christ.

A recipient of numerous teaching and academic awards, Dr. Davis has served as professor and faculty at a number of fine academic institutions, having lectured and taught courses in religion, theology, philosophy, and biblical studies at schools such as Wheaton College, St. Ambrose University, the Houston Graduate School of Theology, the University of Iowa School of Religion, the Robert E. Webber Institute of Worship Studies. He has authored a number of books, curricula, and study materials to equip urban leaders, including *The Capstone Curriculum*, TUMI's premiere sixteen-module distance education seminary instruction, *Sacred Roots: A Primer on Retrieving the Great Tradition*, which focuses on how urban churches can be renewed through a rediscovery of the historic orthodox faith, and *Black and Human: Rediscovering King as a Resource for Black Theology and Ethics*. Dr. Davis has participated in academic lectureships such as the Staley Lecture series, renewal conferences like the Promise Keepers rallies, and theological consortiums like the University of Virginia Lived Theology Project Series. He received the Distinguished Alumni Fellow Award from the University of Iowa College of Liberal Arts and Sciences in 2009. Dr. Davis is also a member of the Society of Biblical Literature, and the American Academy of Religion.

Terry Cornett (B.S., M. A., M.A.R.) is Academic Dean Emeritus of The Urban Ministry Institute in Wichita, Kansas. He holds degrees from The University of Texas at Austin, the Wheaton College Graduate School, and the C. P. Haggard School of Theology at Azusa Pacific University.

Terry ministered for 23 years as an urban missionary with World Impact before his retirement in 2005. During that time he served in Omaha, Los Angeles, and Wichita where he was involved in church-planting, education, and leadership-training ministries.

Introduction to the Module

Greetings, dearest friends, in the strong name of Jesus Christ!

The Church of God in Jesus Christ is one of the most refreshing and important themes of all the Scriptures. Jesus of Nazareth, through his death, burial, and resurrection, has been exalted as head over his new people, those called to represent him in the earth and bear witness of his already/not yet Kingdom. To understand the Church's role in God's kingdom program is critical to every facet of personal and corporate discipleship; there is no discipleship or salvation apart from God's saving action in the Church. Grasping what God is doing in and through his people empowers God's leader to represent him with wisdom and honor. We invite you with enthusiasm to study the Church in order to fully appreciate the nature of ministry in the world today.

The first lesson, *The Church Foreshadowed in God's Plan,* focuses upon how the Church is foreshadowed in God's exalted purpose to bring glory to himself by saving a new humanity through his covenant with Abraham. You will see how the Church is foreshadowed in the unfolding of his gracious plan of salvation to include the Gentiles in his work in Christ Jesus, and learn of God's intent to create for himself a unique and peculiar people, the *laos* of God. You will also discover the richness and meaning of salvation, what it means to be rescued from the lostness and separation from God caused by sin. Through our union with Christ we become joined to "the people of God" who inherit the Kingdom he promised. United to Christ is to be united to his people, those people whose hope is in God creating a new heaven and a new earth with a new humanity under the rule of God which will completely reverse the effects of sin and death on the world.

In our second lesson, *The Church at Worship*, we'll consider salvation as the foundation of the Church's worship. We'll see that salvation comes by God's grace alone and that human beings can in no way earn or deserve it. Worship, therefore, is the proper response to the grace of God. We will also explore some of the insights from Christian reflection about the Church's worship, including a brief study of the terms "sacrament" and "ordinance" as well as varying views of Baptism and the Lord's Supper applied to the Church's worship. Furthermore, we'll discover the theological purpose of the Church's worship, which is to glorify God because of his solitary holiness, his infinite beauty, his incomparable glory and his matchless works. Approaching the triune God through Jesus Christ, the Church worships through praise and thanksgiving, and through Liturgy, which emphasizes the Word and the Sacraments. The Church also worships God through its obedience and lifestyle as a covenant community.

Lesson three is entitled *The Church as Witness*, and focuses on the mission of the Church. In this lesson we'll cover the most significant aspects of the doctrine of election as it applies to Jesus Christ as the elect of God, to his chosen people Israel and to the Church, and to individual believers. We'll discover Jesus Christ as the Elect of God, the One through whom God saves out of the world a people for himself, and briefly explore the dimensions and definition of the concept of God's chosen people as it is defined both in Israel as the people of God and the Church of Jesus Christ. As God's instrument of his Great Commission, we'll take notice of three critical elements within it: the Church gives witness as she evangelizes the lost, as she baptizes new believers in Christ, that is, to incorporate them as members into the Church, and as she teaches her members to observe all the things Christ commanded.

Finally, in lesson four, *The Church at Work*, we will discover the various dimensions and elements of the Church. Special attention will be given to how we may detect authentic Christian community by concentrating on certain marks which have been proven to be true signs of the Church's actions and lifestyle. We'll consider the marks of the Church according to the Nicene Creed, as well as according to the teaching of the Reformation. We will also look at the Church through the lens of the Vincentian Rule, a helpful guide to understand and evaluate traditions and teachings claiming to be binding upon Christians. We'll end this study by concentrating on the ministry of the Church through various images of the Church mentioned in the New Testament, the image of the household of God (God's family), through the image of the body of Christ and Temple of the Holy Spirit (God's agent of the Kingdom of God). We will also look through the lens of God's army, as the Church does battle in the Lamb's war. These images offer great insight into how we are to understand the Church's identity and work in the world today.

Without question, the Church of Jesus Christ is God's agent for his Kingdom, and the people of his presence. May your study of this material and the Word of God produce in you a deep love and devotion to live for and build up the holy people of God, the Church!

May God richly bless your diligent study of his Holy Word!

- Rev. Dr. Don L. Davis

Course Requirements

Required Books and Materials

- Bible (for the purposes of this course, your Bible should be a translation [ex. NIV, NASB, RSV, KJV, NKJV, etc.], and not a paraphrase [ex. The Living Bible, The Message]).

- Each Capstone module has assigned textbooks which are read and discussed throughout the course. We encourage you to read, reflect upon, and respond to these with your professors, mentors, and fellow learners. Because of the fluid availability of the texts (e.g., books going out of print), we maintain our *official* Capstone Required Textbook list on our website. Please visit *www.tumi.org/books* to obtain the current listing of this module's texts.

- Paper and pen for taking notes and completing in-class assignments.

Suggested Readings

- Allen, Roland. *The Spontaneous Expansion of the Church*. Grand Rapids: Eerdmans, 1962.

- Costas, Orlando. *The Church and Its Mission: A Shattering Critique from the Third World*. Wheaton: Tyndale Press, 1974.

- Green, Michael. *Evangelism in the Early Church*. Grand Rapids: Eerdmans, 1970.

- Richards, Lawrence. *A New Face for the Church*. Grand Rapids: Zondervan, 1970.

Summary of Grade Categories and Weights

Attendance & Class Participation	30%	90 pts
Quizzes	10%	30 pts
Memory Verses	15%	45 pts
Exegetical Project	15%	45 pts
Ministry Project	10%	30 pts
Readings and Homework Assignments	10%	30 pts
Final Exam	10%	30 pts
Total:	100%	300 pts

Course Requirements

Grade Requirements

Attendance at each class session is a course requirement. Absences will affect your grade. If an absence cannot be avoided, please let the Mentor know in advance. If you miss a class it is your responsibility to find out the assignments you missed, and to talk with the Mentor about turning in late work. Much of the learning associated with this course takes place through discussion. Therefore, your active involvement will be sought and expected in every class session.

Attendance and Class Participation

Every class will begin with a short quiz over the basic ideas from the last lesson. The best way to prepare for the quiz is to review the Student Workbook material and class notes taken during the last lesson.

Quizzes

The memorized Word is a central priority for your life and ministry as a believer and leader in the Church of Jesus Christ. There are relatively few verses, but they are significant in their content. Each class session you will be expected to recite (orally or in writing) the assigned verses to your Mentor.

Memory Verses

The Scriptures are God's potent instrument to equip the man or woman of God for every work of ministry he calls them to (2 Tim. 3.16-17). In order to complete the requirements for this course you must select a passage and do an inductive Bible study (i.e., an exegetical study) upon it. The study will have to be five pages in length (double-spaced, typed or neatly hand written) and deal with one of the aspects of the Church which are highlighted in this course. Our desire and hope is that you will be deeply convinced of Scripture's ability to change and practically affect your life, and

Exegetical Project

Ministry Project

the lives of those to whom you minister. As you go through the course, be open to finding an extended passage (roughly 4-9 verses) on a subject you would like to study more intensely. The details of the project are covered on pages 10-11, and will be discussed in the introductory session of this course.

Our expectation is that all students will apply their learning practically in their lives and in their ministry responsibilities. The student will be responsible for developing a ministry project that combines principles learned with practical ministry. The details of this project are covered on page 12, and will be discussed in the introductory session of the course.

Class and Homework Assignments

Classwork and homework of various types may be given during class by your Mentor or be written in your Student Workbook. If you have any question about what is required by these or when they are due, please ask your Mentor.

Readings

It is important that the student read the assigned readings from the text and from the Scriptures in order to be prepared for class discussion. Please turn in the "Reading Completion Sheet" from your Student Workbook on a weekly basis. There will be an option to receive extra credit for extended readings.

Take-Home Final Exam

At the end of the course, your Mentor will give you a final exam (closed book) to be completed at home. You will be asked a question that helps you reflect on what you have learned in the course and how it affects the way you think about or practice ministry. Your Mentor will give you due dates and other information when the Final Exam is handed out.

Grading

The following grades will be given in this class at the end of the session, and placed on each student's record:

A - Superior work	D - Passing work
B - Excellent work	F - Unsatisfactory work
C - Satisfactory work	I - Incomplete

Letter grades with appropriate pluses and minuses will be given for each final grade, and grade points for your grade will be factored into your overall grade point average. Unexcused late work or failure to turn in assignments will affect your grade, so please plan ahead, and communicate conflicts with your instructor.

Exegetical Project

As a part of your participation in the Capstone *Theology of the Church* module of study, you will be required to do an exegesis (inductive study) on one of the following Scripture passages:

- ❐ Romans 12.3-8
- ❐ Galatians 3.22-29
- ❐ 1 Corinthians 12.1-27
- ❐ Ephesians 2.11-22
- ❐ Ephesians 4.1-16
- ❐ 1 Peter 2.9-10

Purpose

The purpose of this project is to give you an opportunity to do a detailed study of a major passage on the Church. As you do an in-depth reading, meditation, and study on one of these passages, our hope is that you will be able to understand as well as show how this passage illumines or makes plain some aspect of God's vision for his people. And of course, in understanding the Church better, our prayer is that you will be more effective to relate these truths to your own personal walk of discipleship, your leadership in your church, and your urban ministry.

This is a Bible study project, and, in order to do *exegesis*, you must be committed to understand the meaning of the passage in its own setting. Once you know what it meant, you can then draw out principles that apply to all of us, and then relate those principles to life. A simple three step process can guide you in your personal study of the Bible passage:

Outline and Composition

1. What was *God saying to the people in the text's original situation*?

2. What principle(s) does *the text teach that is true for all people everywhere*, including today?

3. What is *the Holy Spirit asking me to do with this principle here, today*, in my life and ministry?

Once you have answered these questions in your personal study, you are then ready to write out your insights for your *paper assignment*.

Here is a *sample outline* for your paper:

1. List out what you believe is *the main theme or idea* of the text you selected.

2. *Summarize the meaning* of the passage (you may do this in two or three paragraphs, or, if you prefer, by writing a short verse-by-verse commentary on the passage).

3. *Outline one to three key principles or insights* this text provides on the theology of the Church.

4. Tell how one, some, or all of the principles may relate to *one or more* of the following:

    a. Your personal spirituality and walk with Christ

    b. Your life and ministry in your local church

    c. Situations or challenges in your community and general society

As an aid or guide, please feel free to read the course texts and/or commentaries, and integrate insights from them into your work. Make sure that you give credit to whom credit is due if you borrow or build upon someone else's insights. Use in-the-text references, footnotes, or endnotes. Any way you choose to cite your references will be acceptable, as long as you 1) use only one way consistently throughout your paper, and 2) indicate where you are using someone else's ideas, and are giving them credit for it. (For more information, see *Documenting Your Work: A Guide to Help You Give Credit Where Credit Is Due* in the Appendix.)

Make certain that your exegetical project, when turned in meets the following standards:

- It is legibly written or typed.
- It is a study of one of the passages above.
- It is turned in on time (not late).
- It is 5 pages in length.
- It follows the outline given above, clearly laid out for the reader to follow.
- It shows how the passage relates to life and ministry today.

Do not let these instructions intimidate you; this is a Bible study project! All you need to show in this paper is that you *studied* the passage, *summarized* its meaning, *drew out* a few key principles from it, and *related* them to your own life and ministry.

Grading

The exegetical project is worth 45 points, and represents 15% of your overall grade, so make certain that you make your project an excellent and informative study of the Word.

Ministry Project

The Word of God is living and active, and penetrates to the very heart of our lives and innermost thoughts (Heb. 4.12). James the Apostle emphasizes the need to be doers of the Word of God, not hearers only, deceiving ourselves. We are exhorted to apply the Word, to obey it. Neglecting this discipline, he suggests, is analogous to a person viewing our natural face in a mirror and then forgetting who we are, and are meant to be. In every case, the doer of the Word of God will be blessed in what he or she does (James 1.22-25). | Purpose

Our sincere desire is that you will apply your learning practically, correlating your learning with real experiences and needs in your personal life, and in your ministry in and through your church. Therefore, a key part of completing this module will be for you to design a ministry project to help you share some of the insights you have learned from this course with others.

1 Peter 2:9-10 describes the Church as a race, a nation, an order of priests, and a people. None of these terms allow us to understand our salvation as a purely individual idea. The focus of this ministry project is to help you sharpen your skills in explaining the relationship between salvation and the Church. Please complete each of the following steps: | Planning and Summary

Identify and briefly describe in writing a situation in your past or current experience where a person you know is giving evidence that they do not consider the Church an important part of their spiritual life. (You can use a fictitious name for this person if you would like to keep their identity confidential.) This neglect of the Church may be expressed in their words; "I don't feel like I have to go to church in order to worship God!" Or it may be expressed in their behavior; they claim to have a vital Christian experience but rarely, if ever, attend church. | Step One

Write a sample letter to this person laying out simply in your own words the reasons that you believe they have misunderstood what the Bible teaches about salvation and the Church. The content of this letter should draw from, and demonstrate familiarity with, the theology which you have learned in this course. The point of this letter is to move the theological ideas into practical experience. It is not a "theology paper" but the communication of sound biblical teaching to a person who either misunderstands or deliberately disobeys the Scriptures. | Step Two

Turn in a copy of the letter to your instructor. Then, prayerfully consider whether God might have you approach the person you wrote about (if it is a current situation) and either send them the letter or talk to them in person about their salvation and church life. | Step Three

The Ministry Project is worth 30 points and represents 10% of your overall grade, so make certain to share your insights with confidence and make your summary clear. | Grading

LESSON 1

The Church Foreshadowed in God's Plan

page 213 1

Lesson Objectives

page 213 2

Welcome in the strong name of Jesus Christ! After your reading, study, discussion, and application of the materials in this lesson, you will be able to:

- Explain how the Church is foreshadowed in God's exalted purpose, that is, God's determination to bring glory to himself through a new humanity through the covenant he would make with Abraham.

- Recite relevant Scripture and concepts connected to the Church foreshadowed in the unfolding of his gracious plan of salvation, his goal to unveil the grand mystery of his inclusion of the Gentiles in Christ Jesus.

- Detail and tell how the Church is foreshadowed in God's revealed plan of Scripture, that from the beginning, God's intent was to create for himself a unique and peculiar People, the *laos* of God.

- Give a biblical definition of salvation and understand how it relates to participation in the Church.

- Recite from memory a Bible passage that describes the Church in light of its relationship to the Old Testament people of God.

Devotion

page 214 3

A Holy Nation

Read 1 Peter 2.9-10. The word "church" can bring many images to our mind. For many people the first thing they think of when they hear the word "church," is a building with a cross on top. But that is not how the Apostle Peter thinks about the Church. For Peter the Church is that unique group of people who have been chosen by God to serve him and to represent his name in the earth. In these verses Peter uses the language that God spoke to Israel back in Exodus 19.5-6 when he told them: "Now therefore, if you will indeed obey my voice and keep my covenant, you shall be my treasured possession among all peoples, for all the earth is mine; and you shall be to me a Kingdom of priests and a holy nation. These are the words that you shall speak to the people of Israel." And Peter, knowing that he is talking to a church that includes Gentiles, is quick to add, "Once you were not a people, but now you are

God's people; once you had not received mercy, but now you have received mercy." The Church is God's chosen people, his priests who worship him, and in the midst of all the nations, the Church is now God's nation which lives in the world according to the values of the Kingdom of God. Our task is to live in such a way that whoever wants to know what a world ruled by God will look like, can know simply by looking at the Church. What a remarkable privilege and what a high calling.

After reciting and/or singing the Nicene Creed (located in the Appendix), pray the following prayer:

> *God of Abraham, Isaac, and Jacob, thank You so much for including all of us who have believed in Jesus as children of Abraham and heirs of the promises You made to him. Father, help us to represent You rightly in a sinful world. Help us to be distinct from the nations around us so that we shine like a city on a hill. Help us to do good works that cause people to understand Your heart and give glory to You, our Father in heaven. And most of all help us to proclaim boldly the good news about Jesus so that everyone has the opportunity to be included among Your chosen people. This we pray through Jesus Christ our Lord, who reigns with You and the Holy Spirit, one God, for ever and ever. Amen.*

Nicene Creed and Prayer

page 214 📖 4

No quiz this lesson

Quiz

No Scripture memorization this lesson

Scripture Memorization Review

No assignments due this lesson

Assignments Due

Too Much Time Spent on the Future

After a seminar the pastor was giving on the end times, one of the parishioners commented later in the parking lot, "I don't really understand the need for us to spend so much time on big picture things. That's why the Church is so boring to most folks-we don't know how to focus on the things that are happening today. Everything is pie in the sky, some future paradise, some cosmic purpose about what

page 215 📖 5

God is going to do someday. I truly don't understand why we need to always be talking about 'the big picture' stuff. I need to concentrate on what I need to do today!" What would be your response to a believer who was burdened in this way?"

Identity

 Take out a piece of paper and draw a set of symbols or small pictures on it that would help someone who did not know you understand who you are and what is important to you. Then follow the instructions that your Mentor gives you about sharing these pictures.

page 215 6

Saved and Lost

 The Scriptures can, and often do, talk about people who are "saved" and who are "lost." For a person who has never heard the Gospel, this can be hard language to understand. The natural questions that come to mind are "Saved from what?" and "What do you mean when you say I am 'lost'?" How would you answer someone who asked you these questions?

CONTENT — The Church Foreshadowed in God's Plan

Segment 1

Rev. Dr. Don L. Davis

Summary of Segment 1

The Church is foreshadowed in God's exalted purpose for himself; he has determined to bring glory to himself by redeeming a new humanity through the covenant he would make with Abraham. It is also foreshadowed in the unfolding of his gracious plan of salvation, which includes the wonderful intent to include Gentiles in his kingdom purpose. Finally, the Church is foreshadowed in God's revealed picture of Scripture to create for himself a unique and peculiar people, the *laos* of God.

Our objective for this first segment of *The Church Foreshadowed in God's Plan* is to enable you to see that:

- The Church is foreshadowed in God's exalted purpose to glorify himself through a new humanity which will live with him forever.

- The Church is foreshadowed in God's promise to include the Gentiles in his redemptive purpose for the world.

- The Church is foreshadowed in God's efforts to raise up for himself a people (*laos*) that would live for him as his own peculiar people.

- God is working through human history to draw out of all the nations of the earth a people for himself.

I. The Church of Jesus Christ Is Foreshadowed in God's Exalted Purpose: to Bring Himself Glory through a New Humanity, Based on the Foretelling of the Gospel in the Covenant to Abraham.

Video Segment 1 Outline

page 215 7

  A. God's high purpose is to bring honor to his name.

  1. All creation was done by his will and power and for his glory.

     a. Exod. 20.11

     b. Isa. 40.26-28

     c. Jer. 32.17

  2. The psalmist says that it was for his glory that God chose and worked his plan of redemption for his people Israel and defeated his enemies in his plan, Ps. 135.8-12.

B. God's covenant with Abraham: through him, all the families of the earth would be blessed, Gen. 12.1-3.

This text reveals clearly that:

1. Through Abraham's seed all the families of the earth would be blessed.

2. The promise will be of God's divine working through the lineage of Abraham.

C. This covenant revealed God's exalted purpose to draw out of the earth a people for himself, including Gentiles, all of whom are redeemed through his Son, Jesus Christ, Gal. 3.6-9.

This text has several important implications for the foreshadowing of the Church through the covenant of Abraham.

1. Abraham's faith was counted as righteousness.

2. Believers associated with the promise of God to Abraham.

3. The Scriptures foresaw that God would justify the Gentiles by faith in the Abrahamic covenant.

II. The Church Is Foreshadowed through God's Unfolding Plan: in Jesus Christ, God Has Unveiled His Mystery to All the World of His Intent to Form a People for His Own Glory among Jews and Gentiles.

Three explicit texts point to the revelation of God's mystery to redeem Gentiles through the Abrahamic promise.

A. Text One: the mystery kept secret for long ages is now revealed in the prophets and apostles, Rom. 16.25-27.

This text suggests several critical points:

1. This mystery: the Gospel preaching of Jesus Christ

2. This preaching of Jesus Christ is according to the revealing of the mystery which has been kept secret for long ages.

3. This mystery is being disclosed through the apostles and prophets to all nations for the sake of bringing about the obedience of faith.

B. Text Two: Christ in you, the hope of glory as the revelation of God's mystery, Col. 1.25-29

The critical insights we learn of the mystery are:

1. The mystery hidden for ages and generations has now been revealed to his saints.

2. God has made known among the Gentiles the riches of the glory of this mystery.

3. This mystery is Christ in you, that is, the Gentiles, which is our hope of glory.

C. Text Three: the unveiling mystery of Gentile inclusion in the Church, Eph. 3.4-12.

The mystery of faith in Christ:

page 217 8

1. Was not revealed to past generations but is now revealed to Christ's holy Apostles and prophets by the Spirit

2. Is that Gentiles are fellow heirs, members of the same body and partakers of the promise in Jesus Christ through faith in the Gospel

3. Through the apostolic ministry, God's mystery is brought to light: that through the Church, God would make known to the rulers and authorities in heavenly places this manifold wisdom of God.

III. The Church Is Foreshadowed in the Nation of Israel, through Which God Has Given Us a Picture of His Own Peculiar People, the *Laos* of God, 2 Cor. 6.16 and 2 Thess. 2.13-14.

A. Israel is the vehicle through whom Messiah would come.

1. Israel as the name given to Jacob after the great prayer-struggle with the angel, Gen. 32.28

2. This is the common name given to Jacob's descendants.

   a. The twelve tribes are called the "Israelites."

   b. The "children of Israel," Josh. 3.17; 7.25; Judg. 8.27; Jer. 3.21

   c. The "house of Israel," Exod. 16.31; 40.38

3. This physical lineage of Abraham, elected on the basis of God's covenant faithfulness to Abraham, Deut. 7.6-8

4. God's election and covenant with Abraham, Isaac, and Jacob extended to their descendants. Messiah was to come through the nation Israel, and through him, salvation to the world.

   a. Exod. 19.5-6

   b. Deut. 14.2

   c. Deut. 26.18-19

   d. John 4.22

5. Israel identified as God's people: cf. Exod. 15.13, 16; Num. 14.8; Deut. 32.9-10; Isa. 62.4; Jer. 12.7-10; and Hos. 1.9-10

6. The Gentiles foreseen as God's own people, Rom. 9.24-26

B. The image of Israel as God's people is now applied to the Church as God's covenant kingdom community.

page 218 9

1. The Church, as God's new humanity, both Jew and Gentile, has now become the people of God, 1 Pet. 2.9-10.

   a. God's Church is known not by circumcision but by new creation through faith in Jesus, 2 Cor. 5.17 (cf. Phil. 3.2-3).

b. God's Church relates not on the basis of nationality but a new covenant grounded in faith in Christ, sealed with the indwelling of the Holy Spirit, 2 Cor. 3.3-18.

2. The promises given to Israel have now been given to the Church.

   a. 2 Cor. 6.16-18

   b. Exod. 29.45

   c. Lev. 26.12

3. Though the Church has been given a special place, Israel has been neither abandoned nor her election cancelled.

   a. Just as Zechariah proclaimed the fulfillment of the covenant in Christ, Luke 1.67-79, so Paul insists that God's Word still stands, Rom. 9.6.

   b. God Almighty has not rejected his people, Rom. 11.1.

   c. Israel, which is called by God, will be saved for "the gifts and the call of God are irrevocable," Rom. 11. 25-26, 29.

   d. God's grace ensures that Israel will be saved, Rom. 9.27-29; Isa. 1.24-26.

Conclusion

» The Church is foreshadowed in God's exalted purpose: his determination to bring glory to himself through a new humanity through his covenant with Abraham.

» The Church was foreshadowed in the unveiling of the grand mystery of his inclusion of the Gentiles in Christ Jesus.

» The Church was foreshadowed in God's picture of his people, the *laos* of God.

Please take as much time as you have available to answer these and other questions that the video brought out. To start with, we must be crystal clear about God's intentions to bring glory and honor to himself, and how that relates to his high purpose to redeem a people out of the earth for himself. God gives clear clues about his eternal purpose through his covenant with Abraham, the revelation of the mystery regarding Gentile participation in the Gospel, and the creation of his own people, a picture of the new humanity to come. Be clear and concise in your answers, and where possible, support with Scripture!

Segue 1

Student Questions and Response

page 218 📖 *10*

1. In what way did God covenant with Abraham in order that, through him, all the families of the earth would be blessed?

2. What is the testimony of Scripture regarding God's high purpose for himself in regards to his creation, his revelation of himself, and his redeeming of others to him? Why did God make the universe?

3. What is the nature of the mystery spoken of in Romans 16, Ephesians 3, and Colossians 1 regarding God's purpose of redemption?

4. What does God reveal concerning his purpose with the Gentiles as it relates to his purpose to draw out of the earth a people for himself? How is this purpose seen in the covenant God made with Abraham?

5. In what way is Israel the instrument and vehicle of God to Messiah into the world? How does Israel reveal in its relationship with God a clear picture of the people of God, the Church?

6. How do the apostles apply the promise of Israel to the Church of God in Jesus Christ? Give examples.

7. The Church through Christ has been given special place in God's salvation plan. What now, then, is Israel's place as God's people? Has God abandoned Israel or cancelled its election? Explain.

The Church Foreshadowed in God's Plan

Segment 2: Salvation: Joining the People of God

Rev. Terry Cornett

Summary of Segment 2

page 219 11

Because of sin, every human being is in a seemingly hopeless position. We desperately need to be saved from sin and its effects, but our sinful nature keeps us from desiring God's salvation or having any means by which to be reunited to him. Remarkably, God did not choose to leave us as his enemies. The Apostle Paul teaches that while we were still bound up in sin, Christ died for us. The Gospel is the good news that God offers saving grace that can do for us what we cannot do for ourselves. Understanding this grace is the basis for recognizing the Church's responsibility to be a community of worship.

Our objective for this segment, *Salvation: Joining the People of God*, is to enable you to:

- Give a theological definition of salvation.

- Explain the consequences of being separated from God.

- Explain the benefits that come to us through our union with Christ.

- Understand how the Exodus serves as a model (type) of Christian salvation.

- Grasp that incorporation into the Church (God's people) is not something extra which is added following salvation but which is central to the meaning of being saved.

I. What Is Meant by Salvation?

Video Segment 2 Outline

A. The Greek word usually translated salvation in the New Testament is *soteria*. It means to rescue or to deliver or to make someone safe.

1. Rom. 1.16

2. 1 Thess. 5.9

3. 1 Pet. 1.9

B. A definition of salvation: For me as an individual, to be saved means that I am:

Rescued from the lostness and separation from God caused by sin by being *united to Christ* and therefore *joined to "the people of God"* who inherit the Kingdom he promised.

II. Biblical Salvation Means that We Are Rescued from the Lostness/Separation Caused by Sin.

A. Sin has separated humanity from God.

1. Gen. 3.8

2. Isa. 59.2

3. Col. 1.21

B. The separation from God caused by sin means that human beings are lost.

Human beings are no longer where they are supposed to be but have wandered away from God like lost sheep. In Luke 15, Jesus described the human condition that resulted from sin completely in terms of lostness. He tells stories in which human beings are said to be like a:

1. Lost son

2. Lost sheep

Luke 19.10
For the Son of Man came to seek and to save the lost.

3. Lost coin

C. The three consequences of separation from God are death, bondage, and judgment.

1. Because God is the source of all life, this lostness/separation caused by sin has the consequence of death as the story of Adam and Eve makes clear.

    a. Gen. 2.16-17

    b. Luke 15.24

    c. See also Rom. 5.12, Eph. 2.1

2. Because God is the source of freedom and protection, our lostness/separation from him leads to our enslavement by sin and the devil.

a. John 8.34

b. Rom. 6.20-21

c. Col. 1.13

3. Because God is the source of all goodness, our lostness and separation from him and our resulting evil actions have the additional consequence of punishment and judgment.

a. Rom. 2.5-6 (see also Eph. 2.3)

b. John 3.36

III. People Can Be Saved Only by Being United to Christ and through Him to God the Father.

A. Union with Christ

page 220 12

1. 2 Cor. 5.17

2. John 15.5

3. Gal. 2.19b-20

4. Rom. 6.5

page 221 📖 13

B. Union with Christ has a legal (judicial) dimension: God placed his wrath and judgment on Christ who died in our place. Through union with Christ, we share in his death on the cross and therefore, God considers our sins to be paid for and graciously forgives them.

1. Isa. 53.5

2. Heb. 9.28

3. Col. 2.13-14

Since faith is a believing in and union with Christ, this imputation of righteousness is by no means a pretense or make-believe, as if God declares about us what really is not so. Rather, by virtue of our union with Christ through faith (Christ thereby living in us), God declares what really is true. Yes, God does justify the ungodly, but only as they are believers in Christ and thereby united with him. Hence, Christ's righteousness does clothe the sinner and he is in some sense thereby constituted righteous, but this occurs through the faith that unites one to Jesus Christ. . . . This does not mean that we are no longer sinner, for indeed in ourselves we are. But in Christ, we are wholly righteous!

~ J. Rodman Williams. **Renewal Theology**. Vol. 2. Grand Rapids: Zondervan, 1996. p. 74.

C. Union with Christ has a spiritual dimension: because our spirit is joined with his Spirit, Jesus' life flows through us overcoming corruption and death.

1. Rom. 8.10-11

2. Col. 3.3-4

D. Union with Christ has a deliverance dimension: because we are joined to the conqueror of Satan, we can no longer be overpowered by the Evil One. Christ frees us from slavery to evil.

   1. John 8.34-36

   2. Luke 11.20-22

   3. Col. 2.15

   4. James 4.7

IV. **Salvation Means that We Are Joined to "the People of God" Who Inherit the Kingdom He Promised.**

For more information on this critical point see the Appendix titled "Salvation as Joining the People of God."

   A. Because Christ is the Son of God, our union with him joins us to the family of God.

   1. Eph. 1.5.

   2. Heb. 2.11-13

   3. Gal. 4.6

   B. Some of the things that God has promised his people include:

   1. A Kingdom that cannot be shaken

    a. Luke 12.32

    b. Heb. 12.27

2. A new heaven and earth where there is no evil or pain

    a. 2 Pet. 3.13

    b. Rev. 21.1-5

3. A new body that is uncorrupted and that will live forever

    a. Luke 18:29-30

    b. 1 Cor. 15:50-57

4. The right to dwell in God's presence in the New Jerusalem

    a. Rev. 21:2-3

    b. Rev. 22:3-4

5. The right to reign with God in the new order

    a. 2 Tim. 2.12

b. Rev. 22.5

6. Rewards for faithfulness in this present life

   a. 2 Tim. 4.8

   b. James 1.12

   c. Rev. 2.10

7. Unimaginable new wonders that defy description or comprehension

   a. 1 Cor. 2.9

   b. 1 John 3.2

C. Both Paul and Peter describe salvation as becoming part of the "people of God."

   1. 1 Pet. 2.10

   2. Eph. 1.18-23

To be saved in the biblical sense is to share in these experiences as a part of the people of God who are chosen to receive them. The new heaven and earth are to be inhabited not by isolated individuals but by the new community that God has called out of the earth. Anyone who does not take up their place among God's people as they inherit these blessings is understood to be "lost."

> *Thus, God is not just saving individuals and preparing them for heaven; rather, he is creating a people for his name, among whom God can dwell and who in their life together will reproduce God's life and character. This view of salvation is thoroughgoing in Paul.*
>
> ~ Gordon D. Fee. **God's Empowering Presence**.
> Peabody: Hendrickson, 1994. p. 872.

D. The Old Testament Scriptures laid the foundation for us to understand that salvation is being joined to the people of God.

page 221 📖 14

Perhaps the very best image of salvation in the Bible is the story of the Exodus in which the children of Israel are freed from slavery in Egypt. From very early times in Church history, the story of the Exodus was understood to be a story which explained the Christian understanding of salvation. Notice how the Exodus story paints a picture of what it means to be saved.

1. Salvation from Egypt (the Exodus):

   a. A slave people living in misery without hope (Israelites in Egypt)

   b. Are called out by God's gracious choice through a champion he sends (Moses)

   c. Are saved from God's wrath through the application of the blood (Passover lamb)

   d. Are liberated from an evil tyrant through God's mighty power (defeat of Pharaoh and his armies).

   e. Are delivered by passing through water (Red Sea)

   f. Are formed into a holy nation (Israel) who obey God's will (Law)

   g. Are given the responsibility of being a witness to the nations (Exod. 19.5-6)

h. And are finally brought into a promised land (Canaan) with a glorious capital city (Jerusalem) where they live in peace under a great King (David)

2. Salvation from sin:

   a. A slave people living in misery without hope (every human being under sin)

   b. Are called out by God's gracious choice through a Champion he sends (Jesus)

   c. Are saved from God's wrath through application of the blood (Jesus, the slain Lamb of God)

   d. Are liberated from an evil tyrant through God's mighty power (defeat of Satan and his demonic forces)

   e. Are delivered by passing through water (baptism)

   f. Are formed into a holy nation (Church) who obey God's will (Christ's commands)

   g. Are given the responsibility of being a witness to the nations (Matt. 28.18-20)

   h. And are finally brought into a promised land (new creation) with a glorious capital city (New Jerusalem) where they live in peace under a great King (Jesus)

3. What did it mean to be saved in the Exodus?

4. What did it mean to be saved in the New Testament?

   a. Rom. 8.20-25

   b. 2 Pet. 3.13

Conclusion

» To be saved means to be rescued from the lostness and separation from God caused by sin by being united to Christ and therefore joined to "the people of God" who inherit the Kingdom he promised.

» This salvation always involves being rescued from God's judgment on sin and freedom from the bondage that sin brings in the life of a person.

» Salvation and Church are really two sides of one coin because to be saved, by definition, means to become a part of God's people. Individuals experience salvation but no one is saved by themselves. To be united with Christ always involves being united to his people.

» The Church is part of the larger story of God that will result in a new heaven and a new earth with a new humanity under the rule of God which will completely reverse the effects of sin and death on the world.

» To call people to be saved is to invite them to participate in this new world through faith in Jesus who will rule over it.

Segue 2

Student Questions and Response

The following questions were designed to help you review the material in the second video segment related to the meaning of salvation. As you answer the questions, focus on ideas that make it clear what the Bible means when it speaks about "salvation." Remember that these questions are not trying to define how Jesus accomplished salvation or how people become saved (those ideas will be discussed in other Capstone modules) but rather to help us be clear about what salvation is. Be clear and concise in your answers, and where possible, support with Scripture!

1. What are the three results of sin that human beings need to be saved from?

2. What do Jesus' parables about lost things, in Luke 15, teach us about salvation?

3. Why is "union with Christ" the key to salvation?

4. Why is it important to understand that salvation always involves being incorporated into the Church?

5. Why can a Christian believer say "I have been saved" and "I will be saved" and know that both statements are equally true?

CONNECTION

Summary of Key Concepts

page 221 15

This lesson focuses upon God's sovereign design to redeem a people out of the earth that would belong to him forever. The Church is foreshadowed in the covenant God made to Abraham, in the mystery revealed now concerning the Gentiles, and through the pattern of the people of Israel. God has saved his people for his own glory, uniting them to himself through their faith in Jesus Christ. To be saved individually is to be united by faith to Christ, and in him, to his redeemed community.

- God's high purpose, his ultimate intention, is to bring himself glory and honor through his creation and through his people in the person of Jesus Christ. All things exist by his will and for his glory.

- The Church of Jesus Christ is foreshadowed in God's statement of his exalted purpose. From the beginning, God has determined to bring glory to himself by redeeming from among humanity a people that would belong to him forever. He accomplished this through his covenant with Abraham.

- The Church was foreshadowed in the unveiling of the grand mystery of his inclusion of the Gentiles in Christ Jesus. Through the apostles and the prophets, God has made known to this generation and to the principalities and powers his intent to save Gentiles by faith in his Son, and to include them in his family forever.

- The Church was foreshadowed in God's picture of his people, the *laos* of God. Through the people of Israel, God has given us a sign of the one new humanity to come, which includes both Gentile and Jew.

- Even though God has given to the Church a special place as his people, he has neither abandoned Israel as his own, nor cancelled their calling and election. Once God has brought Gentile salvation to the full, he will then save the remnant Israel, as is mentioned in Romans 9-11.

- Salvation, *soteria*, means to rescue or to deliver or to make someone safe.

- Sin separates us from God and causes us to be lost, that is "cut off" from experiencing God's love, protection, and truth.

- The consequences of being "lost" from God are: physical and spiritual death, bondage to sin, and judgment/punishment.

- Union with Christ (through faith in his life, death, and resurrection) is the means by which God restores us to relationship with himself.

- Union with Christ remedies the three problems caused by sin. Christ's death pays the legal debt we owed for breaking God's law since Christ bore our punishment and judgment on the cross. Christ's victory over Satan frees us from bondage to sin. And Christ's victory over death guarantees us eternal life because we are joined to his life.

- By being united to Christ, a person is joined to the whole people of God who will experience life in the new Kingdom. The Christian's identity is rooted in the fact that he or she is now a part of the Church which is the chosen people of God.

Student Application and Implications

page 222 📖 16

Now is the time for you to discuss with your fellow students your questions about the concept of this lesson, the Church foreshadowed in history and Scripture. In order to appreciate the richness of the concept of the Church, it is important to understand that God's desire to draw out the earth a people for his name is both ancient and passionate. For you, as students, to grapple with God's great cosmic plan is the purpose of this section. What particular questions do you have in light of the material you have just studied? Maybe some of the questions below might help you form your own, more specific and critical questions.

* Why would it be significant for a church leader to understand and be able to explain that the Church is foreshadowed in God's exalted purpose to glorify himself in his people? What is the relationship of your local congregation to God's desire to raise up a new humanity which will live with him forever?

* What are some of the practical implications of the idea that God intended to include even the Gentiles in his redemptive purpose for the world? What does this say about God's intention for his local congregations to be open, free from bigotry, prejudice, and partiality?

* If all those who believe in Christ belong to his people, how ought we to look at even the humblest gathering of believers, even the tiniest store front church where Jesus is worshiped and glorified? How can tiny, little urban churches claim to be a part of the people (*laos*) that God promised to raise up for himself as his own peculiar people?

* Why does it appear that certain groups among the people of God seem to carry more weight and prestige than others do? How does this common tendency among Christian groups undermine the idea God is working to draw out of all the nations of the earth a people for himself?

* Why might it be important for a leader within a church to understand that God has been working to gather his people together for many centuries? What kind of lies might the enemy tell a discouraged, despairing leader that his or her efforts to build the Church will never work?

* Why might it be important for an urban minister to understand God's deep desire to make the Church a place for everyone, even for Gentiles, i.e., those in the Bible associated with immorality, idolatry, and sin? What might this suggest for those on the outside of society today?

* Why might it be necessary for a committed Christian worker to affirm God's purpose to bring together a people? Does that mean we ought to work any less to make disciples for Christ?

"Israel Is No Longer the People of God."

page 222 17

Recently in a well-attended adult Sunday school class, several members engaged in a heated discussion about the status of Israel in God's work. Some argued that since the Jews were involved in Jesus' death, they are no longer accepted by God as his people. Others said that God has not abandoned Israel as his people, but that they no longer have the place of favor they once had, because they failed to believe in Christ. Another small group suggested that Israel remains the people of God and will be recognized to be so when Jesus returns at the Second Coming. One group believes that the question is not even important, stating that we shouldn't worry much about Israel, the issue is Christ and being saved by faith in him. What would you advise the teacher if s/he came to you for help?

"Who Needs Church?"

A friend of yours claims to be a committed Christian who loves God, reads the Bible, and seeks to live a life of good deeds. However, this person never attends church or involves herself in the life of the body of Christ. Whenever you invite her to come to church she says, "I don't believe you need to be a part of a church to be a Christian, besides I worship God better out in nature than I do in a church building." What would you say to this person about her view of Christianity?

Preaching the Whole Bible

The title of the lesson "The Church Foreshadowed" suggests that there is a relationship between the Old Testament people of God and the Church, an idea that the Apostle Paul explores in 1 Corinthians 10.1-11 - "I want you to know, brothers, that our fathers were all under the cloud, and all passed through the sea, and all were baptized into Moses in the cloud and in the sea, and all ate the same spiritual food, and all drank the same spiritual drink. For they drank from the spiritual Rock that followed them, and the Rock was Christ. Nevertheless, with most of them God was not pleased, for they were overthrown in the wilderness. Now these things took place as examples for us, that we might not desire evil as they did. Do not be idolaters as some of them were; as it is written, 'The people sat down to eat and drink and rose up to play.' We must not indulge in sexual immorality as some of them did, and twenty-three thousand fell in a single day. We must not put Christ to the test, as some of them did and were destroyed by serpents, nor grumble, as some of them did and were destroyed by the Destroyer. Now these things happened to them as an example, but there were written down for our instruction, on whom the end of the ages has come."

Suppose a young preacher finds that the vast majority of his sermons come from the New Testament Scriptures. He confesses, "I just don't know how the wars and commands and stories in the Old Testament relate to my church congregation." How would you help him understand that the history of the Old Testament people of God (Israel) serves as the foundation for understanding what God is doing with his New Testament people (the Church)? How does thinking about the Church as "the people of God" help us in making this connection?

"Our Church is the Right Church."

In sharing their faith with neighbors, a youth group encountered a home where the people were believers, but argued with the young ministers that the church which they attended was not the best. "There are many practices you guys are involved in which started in pagan nations–Christmas, Easter, and especially issues your church allows–rock music, movie-going, dancing, and other things which show you guys to be less than holy!" At hearing this, some of the young people were greatly discouraged, with some even thinking that they were not really Christians. The youth minister wants to instruct his students about the nature of God's grace and being united with Christ, without making it seem as if he is against the believers the youth contacted. What should he say about the Church that would clear up this problem regarding whose church and congregation is best?

Christian salvation means that a person is rescued from the lostness and separation from God caused by sin by being united to Christ and therefore joined to "the people of God" who inherit the Kingdom he promised. The Church of Jesus Christ is foreshadowed in God's carrying out of his exalted purpose, that is, God determined centuries ago to bring glory to himself through a new humanity through the covenant he would make with Abraham. This intent is a significant part of the unfolding of his gracious plan of salvation, that is, the grand mystery of his inclusion of the Gentiles in Christ Jesus. In the people of Israel, God has given us a picture of his unique and peculiar People, the *laos* of God, the Church, as it represents God and his Kingdom today.

Restatement of the Lesson's Thesis

Resources and Bibliographies

If you are interested in pursuing some of the ideas of *The Church Foreshadowed in God's Plan*, you might want to give these books a try:

> Chapter 6 in Fee, Gordon D. *Paul, the Spirit, and the People of God*. Peabody, MA: Hendrickson Publishers, 1996.
>
> Snyder, Howard A. *Kingdom, Church, and World: Biblical Themes for Today*. Eugene, OR: Wipf and Stock Publishers, 2001.
>
> ------. *The Problem of Wineskins: Church Structure in a Technological Age*. Downers Grove: InterVarsity, 1975.
>
> Wallis, Jim. *Agenda for Biblical People*. New York: Harper and Row, 1976.

Ministry Connections

page 223 ☐ 18

Now is the time to try to nail down this high theology to a real practical ministry connection, one which you will think about and pray for throughout this next week. What in particular is the Holy Spirit suggesting to you in regards to the idea of the Church foreshadowed in God's covenant with Abraham, with the revelation of the mystery of Gentile participation in salvation? What particular situation comes to mind when you think about the connection between personal faith in Jesus and in the body of Christ? How might you personally apply the truth of the teaching that to be one with Christ is to be one with his people? Are there individuals who need to hear this truth for the first time, or those who might need to have it further clarified right now? Give time to meditate on your personal situation of life and ministry, and ask the Holy Spirit to bring the appropriate individuals or situations to mind for your application of these truths and principles.

Counseling and Prayer

page 223 ☐ 19

To fully appreciate the place and importance of the Church in God's plan we need the teaching and leading of the Holy Spirit. Paul said that the revelation of the mystery of Gentiles in God's family came through God's teaching through the prophets and the apostles (cf. Rom. 16.25-27; Eph. 3.3ff.). Only God the Spirit can adequately show us how dear and precious the people of God are to Christ, and how important it is for us to give ourselves to serve and build up the people of God. Ask God to forgive you, if you have entertained low or unworthy opinions about the Church. Pray to him for new insight into the role of the Church in his kingdom business, and ask him to provide you with new energy, wisdom, and resources as you serve him by serving his people.

Scripture Memory

1 Peter 2.9-10

Reading Assignment

To prepare for class, please visit *www.tumi.org/books* to find next week's reading assignment, or ask your mentor.

Other Assignments

page 224 20

Your work begins in earnest for the next lesson, so do not procrastinate or seek to cram your work at the last minute. Give yourself enough time to concentrate on the reading so you can glean the concepts we will consider next week. Furthermore, stay up on your memorization work, and review carefully the materials from this week in preparation for your upcoming quiz. Again, your quiz next session will concentrate upon *the actual video content and outline covered in this lesson*. So, make certain that you spend time covering your notes, especially focusing on the main ideas of the lesson.

Please read the assigned reading, and summarize each reading with no more than a paragraph or two for each. Keep your summary concise and simple; please give your best understanding of what you think was the main point in each of the readings. Do not be overly concerned about giving detail, but rather write out what you consider to be the main point discussed in that section of the book. Please bring these summaries to class next week. (Please see the "Reading Completion Sheet" at the end of this lesson.)

Looking Forward to the Next Lesson

In this lesson we talked about God's eternal plan to call a people out of the earth for himself who will live forever with him in the New Jerusalem. In the next lesson, we will talk about the grace of God that enables sinners to become part of his chosen people and how that grace causes us to respond with worship and praise. The next lesson is, in fact, entitled "The Church at Worship" and reminds us that one of the most important reasons the Church exists is to give God the glory he deserves!

This curriculum is the result of thousands of hours of work by The Urban Ministry Institute (TUMI) and should not be reproduced without their express permission. TUMI supports all who wish to use these materials for the advance of God's Kingdom, and affordable licensing to reproduce them is available. Please confirm with your instructor that this book is properly licensed. For more information on TUMI and our licensing program, visit *www.tumi.org* and *www.tumi.org/license*.

Capstone Curriculum

Module 3: Theology of the Church
Reading Completion Sheet

Name _____

Date _____

For each assigned reading, write a brief summary (one or two paragraphs) of the author's main point. (For additional readings, use the back of this sheet.)

Reading 1

Title and Author: _____ Pages _____

Reading 2

Title and Author: _____ Pages _____

LESSON 2

The Church at Worship

page 225 📖 *1*

Lesson Objectives

Welcome in the strong name of Jesus Christ! After your reading, study, discussion, and application of the materials in this lesson, you will be able to:

- Defend the idea that salvation comes by God's grace alone and that human beings can in no way earn or deserve it.

- Recognize that worship is the proper response to the grace of God.

- Explain the difference between the terms "sacrament" and "ordinance" and describe the theological perspective that lies behind each term.

- Understand the meaning of baptism and the Lord's Supper and discuss the key differences in the way Christians think about their meaning.

- Recite the primary purpose of the Church's worship of God, to glorify God because of his solitary holiness, his infinite beauty, his incomparable glory, and his matchless works.

- Articulate that the Church worships the Triune God through Jesus Christ. We worship Yahweh God alone, through Jesus Christ, in the power of the Holy Spirit.

- Know and apply how the Church worships through praise and thanksgiving, through liturgy, which emphasizes the Word and the sacraments, and through our obedience and lifestyle as a covenant community.

Devotion

We Bring the Sacrifice of Praise

page 226 📖 *2*

Read Romans 12.1-2, Hebrews 13.15, and Habakkuk 3.17-19. One of the most common ideas associated with the Old Testament form of worship was the idea of sacrifice. In general public worship, as was connected to the services in the temple, those who draw near to God were in every case to bring sacrifices, whether during ordinary times of worship, or especially at important events like the dedication of the temple. At this high moment, the blood of the animals flowed greatly as the worshipers expressed their thanksgiving to God for his great blessing in the establishment of his house (2 Chron. 7.5). What is so amazing is that no one was to come before the presence of God without offering to him something to be sacrificed on his behalf. God deserves our best, highest, and most important offerings, and above our gifts and things, he deserves our very selves. We are to offer to him our highest praise, not merely during those times when we are most refreshed and most able, but even during the times of deepest hardship and greatest trial. Our God is impervious to change; he is worthy to be worshiped however things are going in our lives and ministries. Exalted high above all creation, he is the Lord God, deserving of our best and most focused energies, out best songs, our liveliest dancing, our greatest service, our most aggressive response. The Church at worship always provides to God a sacrifice fitting to his holiness and worthy of his acknowledgment. He is truly worthy to be worshiped, to be offered our praise.

Habakkuk the prophet illumines the way for us in terms of offering to God the sacrifice of praise:

> Hab. 3.17-19 - Though the fig tree should not blossom, nor fruit be on the vines, the produce of the olive fail and the fields yield no food, the flock be cut off from the fold and there be no herd in the stalls, [18] yet I will rejoice in the Lord; I will take joy in the God of my salvation. [19] God, the Lord, is my strength; he makes my feet like the deer's; he makes me tread on my high places.

Let us, therefore, heed the words of the writer to the Hebrews:

> Heb. 13.15 - Through him then let us continually offer up a sacrifice of praise to God, that is, the fruit of lips that acknowledge his name.

After reciting and/or singing the Nicene Creed (located in the Appendix), pray the following prayer:

Nicene Creed and Prayer

> *Eternal God, our Father, God and Father of our Lord Jesus Christ, You alone are worthy of all praise, and as such, You require that we give You honor and glory and praise. We approach You in the name of Your beloved Son and our Savior, Jesus Christ, asking that You grant us the power of the Spirit in order to glorify You with our whole hearts in joyful worship in all of our meetings, in all our relationships, in all our actions, and in all our ministries. Receive all that we say and do as an acceptable sacrifice offered to You as the Lord our God, worthy of praise and glory, in Jesus' name we pray, Amen.*

Quiz

Put away your notes, gather up your thoughts and reflections, and take the quiz for Lesson 1, *The Church Foreshadowed in God's Plan*.

Scripture Memorization Review

page 227 📖 3

Review with a partner, write out and/or recite the text for last class session's assigned memory verses: 1 Peter 2.9-10.

Assignments Due

Turn in your summary of the reading assignment for last week, that is, your brief response and explanation of the main points that the authors were seeking to make in the assigned reading (Reading Completion Sheet).

Grace

page 227 📖 4

I heard a story about a person who was doing an experiment in human behavior. This person stood by the pumps at a gas station in a big city and tried to give away twenty dollar bills to the people who pulled up to the station. To his amazement, no one would take the money. Those of us who live in cities are probably not so surprised at this response. Most people in big cities have learned the hard way that "you don't get something for nothing" and that anyone who appears to be giving away something valuable for free is probably not to be trusted. We urbanites recognize that if something seems too good to be true, then it almost always is. It is natural for us to be suspicious of things that are free. Today's lesson is about worship as a response to the grace of God. The Gospel is the good news that everything we need and could not have is being given to us by God as a free gift of grace. Like the people at the gas pumps, most of us probably did not recognize at first that the grace of God is a completely free gift. When did you first realize that the gift of salvation could never be earned and comes only as a gift to be received?

Going a Little too Far

page 227 📖 5

If your church had to answer this question, how would it do so: "All forms of worship and praise are enjoined to give to God, but as far as we are concerned, engaging in (X) is taking worship a little too far." What might it mean in some of our church contexts to go beyond the acceptable boundaries of the way worship is understood in your congregation? Should there be boundaries to our expression of worship, and if so, what ought the standards be to hold such boundaries in conjunction with our freedom in Christ, and our desire to express our love to God in new and unique ways?

Liturgy Is So Boring - Does God Like Us to Be Depressed?

At the dinner table, one of the children of a church family commented on their view of the church service. In her 13-year-old opinion, church services were too formal, too similar, with a lot of language and activity that didn't mean anything to her. She wondered why the songs were so old, and the music was kinda like going to a funeral home. The whole atmosphere seemed sad and depressing; she didn't know why they had to chant, and sing at certain times, stand up sometimes, and read at other times. It all seems so boring and old-fashioned. She asked her folks why can't church be more exciting, like game shows on TV, or the excitement at athletic events. "Does God like us to be depressed?" she asked. What would you say to the 13 year old about her worship experience at her church, and how God wants her to understand and perceive worshiping together?

The Church at Worship

Segment 1

Rev. Terry Cornett

The grace of God comes before all human decision or effort–only his grace can enable people to respond to him. It is because of this grace that the Church can worship God and all of the Church's worship, especially the Lord's Supper and baptism, is meant to be a testimony to, and an experience of, the grace of God.

Our objective for this first segment of *The Church at Worship* is to enable you to:

- Give a definition of grace.
- Distinguish between grace and mercy.
- Identify and answer the Pelagian heresy.
- Explain the difference between the term "sacrament" and the term "ordinance."
- Name and briefly explain the four major Christian views about the Lord's Supper.

Video Segment 1 Outline

Rev. 22.21
The grace of the Lord Jesus be with all. Amen.

page 228 📖 6

I. ***Sola Gratia* (Grace Alone)**

   A. Grace is an essential attribute of who God is.

      1. Exod. 34.6-7

      2. John 1.14

      3. Eph. 1.6

      4. Heb. 10.29

   B. Grace is undeserved favor. When God is gracious he acts lovingly toward us even though we have no reason to claim or expect that kindness.

   C. The difference between "grace" and "mercy"

      1. Mercy is God withholding what we actually deserve.

      2. Grace is God giving us what we don't deserve.

      3. In the New Testament Scriptures, grace means that God acts toward us just as he does toward his Son Jesus. Therefore, grace is truly unmerited and undeserved favor.

D. What do we mean when we insist that everything we have is *Sola Gratia*, by grace alone?

1. First of all, we mean that every human being who has ever lived comes into the world locked up under sin and is in a completely hopeless position, Rom. 3.10-12.

    The Pelagian error or heresy, is the belief that a person is not born with a sinful nature and can seek and believe in God completely out of their own free will. The Church has rejected the Pelagian error and taught from the Scriptures that a person can come to God only because the grace of God is already working in them.

    If anyone says that the grace of God can be conferred as a result of human prayer, but that it is not grace itself which makes us pray to God, he contradicts the prophet Isaiah, or the Apostle John who says the same thing, "I have been found by those who did not seek me; I have shown myself to those who did not ask for me"... The sin of the first man has so impaired and weakened free will that no one thereafter can either love God as he ought or believe in God or do good for God's sake, unless the grace of divine mercy has preceded him.

    ~ The Council of Orange (529 A.D).

page 228 7

2. Secondly, we mean that because salvation comes only through faith it cannot ever be earned by anyone. Salvation can only be received as a free gift, not deserved through acts of goodness. Salvation is completely a gift of God's grace.

    a. Eph. 2.8-9

    b. Acts 20.24

page 229 8

c. Gal. 2.21

   d. Any good work or righteous act we do is a result of God's grace working in us. Good works are the result of salvation not the cause of it. No good work gains us any extra favor with God. No one can be good enough to earn a relationship with God or eternal life with him in his Kingdom. We have his grace poured out on us because of Christ and what his work has done for us. Our good works are a response to the grace that God has given. Again, as the Apostle John says, "we love him because he first loved us," 1 John 4.19.

II. **Worship Is the Church's Response to the Grace of God.**

Worship is always the single most important responsibility of the Church because it is the starting point for living by grace. In worship, we acknowledge that as James wrote in his Epistle, "Every good gift and every perfect gift is from above, coming down from the Father of lights," James 1.17a.

   A. Two pivotal events in Christian worship (the meal and the bath)

   In every Christian tradition, the Lord's Supper and baptism are important parts of the way in which we experience the grace of God at work among us. Christians differ, however, as to how these acts of worship demonstrate God's grace in the Church. Some churches call the Lord's Supper and baptism "sacraments" and understand them as a "means of grace" while others refer to them as "ordinances" and understand them as a testimony to the grace of God. Let me explain the difference.

   B. The meaning of "sacrament"

   1. A sacrament is usually defined as "an outward and visible sign of an inward and spiritual grace." Those who use the term sacrament would see baptism and the Lord's Supper as a means by which the grace of God comes to us.

2. Although Catholics and Eastern Orthodox Christians have many sacraments, Protestants have usually reserved the term sacrament only for baptism and the Lord's Supper. These two sacraments have a special place in the history of the Church as a particularly important "means of grace" because they were directly instituted by the command of Jesus. Those who define the Lord's Supper and baptism as sacraments would argue that when they are received in faith, God is graciously at work in us to fulfill his promises.

page 230 11

C. The meaning of "ordinance"

1. There are many church traditions which understand the Lord's Supper and baptism as ordinances, rather than sacraments. The word "ordinance" means an "authoritative command" and so the Lord's Supper and baptism are done in obedience to the command of Christ. Rather than being a means by which God's grace comes to us, these churches argue that in baptism and the Lord's Supper we remember and testify to the grace of God which we have already received.

page 230 12

2. Exod. 12.14 - This is a day you are to commemorate; for the generations to come you shall celebrate it as a festival to the LORD - a lasting ordinance.

3. The focus of most Old Testament ordinances was to help people remember to obey by means of a command or religious ceremony. In the New Testament, baptism and the Lord's Supper serve as public testimony to the grace that God gave to us through Jesus' life, death and resurrection and reminds us that the Church exists and lives through this grace.

III. Baptism: How Is Baptism Related to Salvation?

A. Those who see baptism as a sacrament see it as a means by which God's grace becomes effective for salvation. In sacramental theology, baptism is important for regeneration.

1. Scriptural support for baptism as a sacrament or means of grace:

    a. Acts 2.38

    b. Acts 22.16

    c. Mark 16.15-16

    d. 1 Pet. 3.20-22

    "The Thirty-Nine Articles of Religion" which is the core creed of churches in the Methodist and Episcopal tradition describes the sacramental doctrine of Baptism like this. "They that receive Baptism rightly are grafted into the Church; the promises of the forgiveness of sin, and of our adoption to be the sons of God by the Holy Ghost, are visibly signed and sealed; Faith is confirmed, and Grace increased by virtue of prayer unto God."

    ~John H. Leith, ed. **Creeds of the Churches**.
    Louisville: John Knox Press, 1983. pp. 275-76

2. It is important to understand that those who see baptism as a sacrament are *not* teaching baptismal regeneration.

Baptismal regeneration is the false belief that baptism by itself will save a person simply because the act of baptism has been performed. At times in the past, the Catholic Church seemed to teach something very close to this, but today both Catholic and Protestant teaching agree that the key element of baptism is faith. The Church father Gregory of Nyssa emphasized that if a person is baptized but does not combine it with genuine repentance then, "in these cases the water is but water, for the gift of the Holy Ghost in no way appears in him who is thus baptismally born."

B. Those who define baptism as an ordinance see it as a symbol by which a person declares their identification with Christ and his Church. Baptism is important for incorporation into the Church.

1. Scriptural support for baptism as an ordinance or symbol:

   a. Acts 10.47

   b. 1 Cor. 1.14-17

2. The key motivation for baptism is obedience.

   The Holman Bible Dictionary, which represents the Baptist tradition, says: "Baptism is not a requirement of salvation, but it is a requirement of obedience. Baptism is a first step of discipleship. Although all meanings of baptism are significant, the one that most often comes to mind is water baptism as a picture of having come to know Christ as Lord and Savior. Baptism is never the event but, rather, the picture of the event. So the pattern of obedience is to come to Christ in trust and then to picture that through the symbol of baptism."

   ~ Trent C. Butler, Gen. ed. **Holman Bible Dictionary** (electronic ed.). Nashville: Holman Bible Publishers, 1991.

page 230 📖 14

C. Baptism is equally important in both sacramental and ordinance traditions.

Baptism is given and commanded by Christ himself. It is never optional or dispensable. Therefore, both for those who see it as a sacrament and those who see it as an ordinance, baptism is the defining mark that a person has committed themselves to the lordship of Jesus Christ.

page 231 📖 15

IV. The Lord's Supper

> *There is in the Lord's Supper a constant renewal of the covenant between God and the Church. The word 'remembrance' (anamnesis) refers not simply to man's remembering of the Lord but also to God's remembrance of his Messiah and his covenant, and of his promise to restore the Kingdom. At the Supper all this is brought before God in true intercessory prayer.*
> ~ R. S. Wallace. "Lord's Supper." *Evangelical Dictionary of Theology*. Walter A. Elwell, ed. Grand Rapids: Baker, 1984. p. 653.

A. Common terms:

1. The Lord's Supper is a common name for this act of worship.

2. You may also hear it called the *eucharist* (which means "thanksgiving meal"), Communion, or the Lord's Table.

   The Lord's Supper was given to the Church by Jesus himself on the night before he was arrested.

B. Established by Jesus Christ

1. Matt. 26.26-29

2. 1 Cor. 11.23-26

C. Observed regularly from the earliest days of the Church onward

All the early evidence . . . indicated that while the elements of the service [of the early Church] had no fixed sequence, the climactic event of the weekly service on the Lord's Day was the sacrament of the Lord's Supper.

~ R. G. Rayburn. "Worship in the Church."
Evangelical Dictionary of Theology.
Walter A. Elwell, ed.
Grand Rapids: Baker, 1996. p. 1193.

The [Lord's Supper] might be celebrated in the most becoming manner, if it were dispensed to the Church very frequently, at least once a week. . . . We ought always to provide that no meeting of the Church is held without the word, prayer, dispensation of the Supper, and [collecting money for the poor].

~ John Calvin. **Institutes**. 4.17.43-44.

A second reason why every Christian should [take communion] as often as he can is, because the benefits of doing it are so great. . . . The grace of God given herein confirms to us the pardon of our sins, by enabling us to leave them. As our bodies are strengthened by bread and wine, so are our souls by these tokens of the body and blood of Christ. This is the food of our souls: This gives strength to perform our duty, and leads us on to perfection. If, therefore, we have any regard for the plain command of Christ, if we desire the pardon of our sins, if we wish for strength to believe, to love and obey God, then we should neglect no opportunity of receiving the Lord's Supper; then we must never turn our backs on the feast which our Lord has prepared for us. We must neglect no occasion which the good providence of God affords us for this purpose. This is the true rule: So often are we to receive as God gives us opportunity. Whoever, therefore, does not receive, but goes from the holy table, when all things are prepared, either does not understand this duty, or does not care for the dying command of his Savior, the forgiveness of his sins, the strengthening of his soul, and the refreshing it with the hope of glory.

~ John Wesley. "Sermon 101: The Duty of Constant Communion."
The Works of John Wesley. Vol. 7-8. p. 148.

D. The Lord's Supper is to be eaten in repentance and faith.

page 231 📖 16

1. One of the reasons that Protestant reformers first broke away from Catholic churches was because they felt that the sacraments were being viewed as a magic action rather than as the grace of God received by faith.

2. The Lord's Supper is not like a magic ritual which causes grace to be given just by participating in the action.

*The early Protestant reformers objected to the Catholic doctrine which was known as **ex opere operato**. (This is a Latin phrase that means "by the very fact of the action's being performed.") This meant that if the sacrament was given it produced the desired effect whether or not the person offering it or the person receiving it were acting in faith. Reformers objected that this had caused people to view the sacraments as magic: that getting baptized or taking the Lord's Supper made you into a Christian. Their response was that a person becomes a Christian and grows as a Christian "by faith alone."*

*Catholics continue to teach **ex opere operato** but have nuanced their teaching to reemphasize that receiving the sacraments in faith is not just a Protestant idea but is necessary to the Catholic view as well by saying that "[the sacraments] presuppose faith" and that, "celebrated worthily in faith, the sacraments confer grace."*

~ **Catechism of the Catholic Church**.
Liguori, MO: Liguori Publications, 1994. pp. 291-293.

E. There are four basic Christian views on the Lord's Supper (see Appendix 17).

page 231 📖 17

1. *Transubstantiation* is the belief that the bread and wine become the literal body and blood of Jesus Christ. This is the view of the Lord's Supper held by Roman Catholic Christians.

a. Matt. 26.26

b. John 6.53-60

By the miracle of the loaves and the fishes and the walking upon the waters, on the previous day, Christ not only prepared his hearers for the sublime discourse [of John 6] containing the promise of the Eucharist, but also proved to them that he possessed, as Almighty God-man, a power superior to and independent of the laws of nature, and could therefore, provide such a supernatural food, no other, in fact than his own Flesh and Blood.

~ Joseph Pohle. "Eucharist." **Readings in Christian Theology.** Vol. 3. Millard Erickson, ed. Grand Rapids: Baker, 1973.

2. *Consubstantiation* is the belief that the bread and wine become the literal body and blood of Jesus without ceasing to be bread and wine. This is the view of the Lord's Supper held by Lutheran churches.

    This view accepts the basic idea discussed above that the real body and blood of Jesus is present in the Lord's Supper but has a different explanation of how they are present together.

3. The third view is the *Reformed* view. Presbyterian and Reformed churches teach that the body and blood of Christ are given to us in the Supper, not physically, but spiritually through the power and presence of the Holy Spirit.

    This tradition would point out that in the John 6 passage that as Jesus teaches about eating his flesh, he goes on to emphasize this as a spiritual truth:

    John 6.60-63 - On hearing it, many of his disciples said, "This is a hard teaching. Who can accept it?" Aware that his disciples were grumbling about this, Jesus said to them, "Does this offend you? What if you see the Son of Man ascend to where he was before! The Spirit gives life; the flesh counts for nothing. The words I have spoken to you are spirit and they are life."

In this sacrament Christ is present not bodily but spiritually. . . . His people receive him not with the mouth, but by faith; they do not receive his flesh and blood as material particles, but his body as broken and his blood as shed. The union thus signified . . . [is] a spiritual and mystical union due to the indwelling of the Holy Spirit. The [effectiveness] of this sacrament as a means of grace is not in the signs nor in the service, nor in the minister, nor in the word, but in the attending influence of the Holy Ghost.

~ Charles Hodge. **Systematic Theology**. Abridged edition. Grand Rapids: Baker, 1992. pp. 496-498.

a. Col. 3.1

b. John 16.7

Although most Pentecostal traditions are Memorialist, the Pentecostal scholar Gordon Fee defends a similar view to Calvin's when he says: "Indeed, one would not be far wrong to see the Spirit's presence at the Table as Paul's way of understanding the real presence. The analogy of Israel's having had 'Spiritual food,' and 'Spiritual drink' in 1 Corinthians 10.3-4 at least allows as much."

~ Gordon Fee. **Paul, the Spirit and the People of God.** Peabody, MA: Hendrickson Publishers, 1996. p. 154.

4. The *Memorialist* view believes that the bread and wine only symbolize the body and the blood of Christ and help us to remember what he had done for us.

    a. Unlike the first three views which all see the Lord's table as a sacrament, the Memorialist view sees the Lord's table as an ordinance.

> *The Lord's Supper has no regenerative power, it possesses no sanctifying grace. There is nothing magical or mystical about its nature. It is a symbol of the relation of the believer to Christ, who alone does the sanctifying. The outward tokens devised by Christ himself are the symbols of the atoning power and forgiving love of his great sacrifice, which was once and for all efficacious.*
>
> ~ Williams Stevens. "The Lord's Supper." **Readings in Christian Theology**. Millard Erickson, ed. Grand Rapids: Baker, 1973.

    b. Luke 22.19

    c. 1 Cor. 11.23-24

F. What all the differing views about the Lord's Supper share in common:

  1. Every part of Christian theology believes that the Lord's Supper is:

    a. An essential part of Christian worship

    b. A direct command of Christ to his Church

    c. A time that draws us closer to God and to our fellow believers

    d. A time that allows us to grasp hold of God's grace and respond to him with gratitude and praise

    e. Meant to be received in faith and to help us place our complete faith in the work of Christ

f. A time in which sins can be dealt with and placed under God's forgiving mercy

2. We may disagree on how the Lord's Supper causes these things to happen but those disagreements should not cause us to lose sight of the fundamental importance of the Supper in our life of worship. It is a gift of God's grace to his Church.

Conclusion

» Worship is the response of the Church to the grace of God.

» Salvation comes completely by the grace of God and there is no human being that can say that they have earned their salvation by what they have done.

» Baptism and the Lord's Supper are especially significant parts of Christian worship.

» The Church differs on how to understand the Lord's Supper and baptism. Some believe that they are sacraments, that is a means by which the grace of God comes to us while others believe that they are ordinances which symbolize and testify to the grace of God.

Segue 1

Student Questions and Response

page 232 19

Please take as much time as you have available to answer these and other questions that the video brought out. These questions were designed to help you review the material in this first segment related to God's grace as the basis of the Church's worship. As you answer these questions, try to form clear convictions about what the Scriptures teach in regard to the grace of God. Since Bible believing Christians differ about *how* the grace of God comes to us in the Lord's Supper and baptism, please listen closely and respectfully to those in the class who may disagree with you. Be clear and concise in your answers, and where possible, support with Scripture!

1. What does *sola gratia* mean and why is it important?

2. What is the Pelagian heresy?

3. What is the difference between Christian traditions that describe baptism and the Lord's Supper as *sacraments* and those that think of them as *ordinances*?

4. What are the main biblical arguments for and against seeing baptism as a "means of grace"?

5. What are the four major views about the Lord's Supper?

6. Why is baptismal regeneration (the belief that being baptized causes salvation) an unscriptural doctrine? How is this different from a sacramental view of baptism?

7. Why did the Protestant reformers disagree with the Catholic doctrine of *ex opere operato*?

8. What role does faith play in our experience of the sacraments/ordinances?

The Church at Worship

Segment 2: The Vocation of the Church

Rev. Dr. Don L. Davis

The vocation of the Church proper is to worship Almighty God. We glorify God in our worship because of his perfect character–his solitary holiness, his infinite beauty, his incomparable glory and his matchless works. The Church worships the true God, the Triune God through Jesus Christ. We worship Yahweh God alone, through Jesus Christ, in the power of the Holy Spirit. In addition, the Church worships God through its praise and thanksgiving, through liturgy, which emphasizes the Word and the sacraments, and through our obedience and lifestyle as a covenant community.

Our objective for this segment, *The Vocation of the Church*, is to enable you to see that:

- We worship to glorify God because of his solitary holiness, his infinite beauty, his incomparable glory and his matchless works.

Summary of Segment 2

- We worship the Triune God through Jesus Christ. We worship Yahweh God alone, through Jesus Christ, in the power of the Holy Spirit.

- We worship through praise and thanksgiving, through liturgy, which emphasizes the Word and the sacraments, and through our obedience and lifestyle as a covenant community.

Video Segment 2 Outline

page 233 20

I. The Central Reason Why the Church Worships Is the Purpose of Glorifying the One, True, and Almighty God, Yahweh.

Like Israel of old, the Church exists for God's ultimate glory and pleasure, and all that she is and does is to be done in order to glorify him in all things. Paul makes this point numerous times in the New Testament, suggesting, for instance:

> "And whatever you do, in word or deed, do everything in the name of the Lord Jesus, giving thanks to God the Father through him." (Col. 3.17)

> "Everyone who is called by my name, whom I created for my glory, whom I formed and made," and again in verse 21, "the people whom I formed for myself that they might declare my praise." (Isa. 43.7)

> "But you are a chosen race, a royal priesthood, a holy nation, a people for his own possession, that you may proclaim the excellencies of him who called you out of darkness into his marvelous light. Once you were not a people, but now you are God's people; once you had not received mercy, but now you have received mercy." (1 Pet. 2.9-10)

Specifically, then why ought we worship our great and glorious God? The answers are rooted in his solitary holiness, his infinite beauty, his incomparable glory, and his matchless deeds.

A. We worship God because he is *solitary in holiness*.

1. Isa. 6.3

        2. Rev. 4.8-9

        3. Rev. 15.3-4

    B. We worship God because he is *infinite in beauty*.

        1. Ps. 29.1-2

        2. Ps. 96.6-8

        3. Ps. 113.3-6

    C. We glorify God in worship because of *his incomparable glory*.

        1. Exod. 15.11

        2. Ps. 57.11

        3. Ps. 99.1-3

        4. Ps. 97.9

    D. We worship God because of *the mighty character of his deeds*.

        1. The Church marvels at God's work in his creation, Ps. 104.1-5.

2. The Church extols the Lord because of his wonderful salvation, Ps. 103.8-13.

   The Church is motivated by gratitude to God, for his love in Jesus Christ, and the glorious salvation he has supplied to us in him.

The Church worships the triune God through Jesus Christ

E. The Church worships God alone: the Triune God, Father, Son, and Holy Spirit will not share his glory with another, and alone is deserving of our highest and best praise.

   1. Jesus teaches us that the Father looks for his people to give him a particular kind of worship, John 4.21-24.

   2. The God whom the Church worships will not share his glory with another.

      a. Isa. 48.11

      b. Isa. 42.8

      c. John 5.22-23

F. The Church worships and extols God *through Jesus Christ*.

   1. His shed blood on the cross allows the Church to enter into God's presence, Heb. 10.19-20.

2. His blood cleanses our consciences from dead works to worship and serve God in truth and faith, Heb. 9.13-14.

3. We do not approach God on our own righteousness and honor. Rather through the high priestly ministry of Jesus, we can now draw near to our holy God with full assurance of faith, Heb. 10.21-22.

G. Set free in Jesus, we have been given *the Holy Spirit* to provide us with the power to bring acceptable worship to God.

1. First, the Spirit makes us ministers of the new covenant, a covenant of faith in Jesus and not in the works of the Law, 2 Cor. 3.4-6.

2. As we are filled with the Spirit, the high worship and praise of God is expressed in the assembly of believers, Eph. 5.18-20.

II. How the Church Practices its Worship to God

page 234 📖 21

A. Through our services and lifestyle of Praise and Thanksgiving

Based on the pattern of God's people Israel, the Church is exhorted to celebrate in its worship and praise of God. The Scriptures are filled with specific instruction and encouragement on how we ought to show our love and gratitude to Almighty God through our praise and thanksgiving.

1. Above all forms of worship, we are to worship God in the freedom that Christ has provided for us, Phil. 3.2-3.

   We have been set free in Christ from trying to please God in our own power, and now we worship him from the heart, filled with gratitude and joy. How are we to worship God when we gather together?

2. We are to worship God *in our songs*, Eph. 5.18-19.

3. We are to worship God *in the skillful playing of musical instruments*, Ps. 33.2-3.

4. We worship God *as we give him thanks*, Ps. 100.3-4.

5. We worship God as we give to him *shouts of praise*, Ps. 66.1-2.

6. We worship God as we *come before his presence with silence and meditation*.

    a. Ps. 46.10

    b. Hab. 2.20

7. God desires free, expressive, and creative praise, *in full and free physical expression*.

    a. Through our *clapping*, Ps. 47.1-2

    b. By *lifting up our hands*, Ps. 28.2

    c. By *dancing before the Lord*, Ps. 150.4

    d. By *bowing down prostrate before him*, Ps. 5.7

e. By *kneeling before God*, Ps. 95.6-7a

B. Through our liturgy

page 235 📖 22

Definition: Liturgy = those particular order of services where we declare the Word of God and celebrate together at the Lord's table.

When we look at the evidence of early Christian worship, we see that it differed from religions in the Roman world in that it claimed no cult statues, temples, or regular sacrifices. It was oriented around the Word, like its close historical connection to synagogue Judaism. Yet early believers did gather and practice particular kinds of rituals. Believers met to fellowship, to eat, and to celebrate the Lord's Supper, to hear the Scriptures read and preached, to pray and sing hymns of praise and thanksgiving to God, as well as to baptize new believers and to pray for healing. These practices were not tied to any particular place, and were done informed by the Christian story. The word "liturgy," is the term given to the service calendar that congregations use as they worship together.

1. When the Church gathers, we worship God through the preaching of the Word of God.

    a. The liturgy, or worship schedule and calendar, reenacts and rehearses the great works of God in history.

    b. The Church through its liturgy recalls and reflects upon the one, true, and great story of God in Scripture.

    c. And as we preach and teach the Word of God as God's story, we are led to worship God, to express our wonder and celebration at what God has accomplished through his people and through Jesus Christ.

2. We also worship God when we eat together at the Lord's table, (called the Lord's Supper or the eucharist).

The New Testament sources of our knowledge of the institution of the eucharist are fourfold, a brief account thereof being found in each of the Synoptic Gospels and in Paul's First Epistle to the Corinthians (Matt. 26.26-29; Mark 14.22-25; Luke 22.14-20, and 1 Cor. 11.23-26).

a. The Lord's Supper is also called the "eucharist," which is derived from the Latin term *eucharisteosas* ("to give or gave thanks"). This term was the most widely used term in the early Church, and was applied to the whole service, as well as to the consecration of the bread and wine or to the consecrated elements themselves.

b. The heart of the Lord's Supper is patterned on Christ's celebration of the Passover. At the close of the paschal supper, Jesus took the bread and cup, and "gave thanks" over them, as a thank offering to God.

(1) He broke the bread, and distributed the cup among the disciples, asking them to "Take, eat," and "Drink all of it," respectively.

(2) Jesus declared of the bread, "This is my body given for you," and of the cup, "This is my blood of the covenant," or, "This is the new covenant in my blood which is poured out for you," "unto remission of sins."

(3) Jesus then gives the purpose of this celebration: to do this in remembrance (in memorial) of him.

c. As we gather and eat the Lord's Supper, we remember what he accomplished on the cross, and receive his grace and peace as we serve him joyfully and look forward to his soon return.

C. Through our obedient lifestyle, as members of God's covenant community:

1. Our life together as believers can be an act of worship, as can be our fellowship together in Christ, Heb. 10.24-25.

2. As we care for one another in love as family, and seek to do his will, our very lives as his people can become an act of worship to God.

   a. Rom. 12.1

   b. 1 Cor. 10.31

Conclusion

» The Church worships in order to glorify God because of his solitary holiness, his infinite beauty, his incomparable glory, and his matchless works.

» The worship of God relates to the persons of the Trinity: we worship Yahweh God alone, through Jesus Christ, in the power of the Holy Spirit.

» The Church worships God through praise and thanksgiving, through liturgy, which emphasizes the Word and the sacraments, and through our obedience and lifestyle as a covenant community.

The following questions were designed to help you review the material in the second video segment. As you rehearse the principal truths of this segment, you will want to make certain that you grasp and understand the basic ideas associated with the Church's vocation of worship. Especially concentrate on the purpose behind our worship of God, and look for connections between the purpose of worship and function of worship. Be clear and concise in your answers, and where possible, support with Scripture!

Segue 2

Student Questions and Response

page 236 23

1. According to this segment, what is the central and critical reason the Church of Jesus Christ engages in worship as it most important activity and true vocation?

2. How does the fact that God made all things for his honor, glory, and pleasure influence the Church's motivation in its worship of God?

3. Explain the fact that the Church worships God because of the majesty of his character and his deeds? What particular attributes in God demand and call us to worship him?

4. Why is it important to understand that the Church only approaches God in worship through the person and work of Jesus Christ? Could it be otherwise? Explain your answer.

5. How does the Holy Spirit enhance and empower the worship of the Church as it seeks to glorify God in its praise? How does the Church access the Spirit's power as she gives God glory?

6. What are the ways in which the Church may worship God: In its obedience and lifestyle? In its liturgy, especially in the preaching of the Word and observing the ordinances (sacraments)? In its forms and expressions, both physically and musically?

7. How does the expression of love and care within a church affect the worship of God through the church to God? Can a church worship God if the relationships amongst its members are tense and frayed? Explain.

Summary of Key Concepts

page 237 24

This lesson focuses upon the foundational approach we as members of the Church have with God, that is, on the grounds of grace alone through faith in Christ, and how the experience of this grace expresses itself in authentic praise, adoration, thanksgiving and worship to God through Jesus Christ. In one sense, understanding these foundational concepts are at the heart of what it means to serve the Church as one of its leaders, and helps us to discern when a congregation is healthy or sick, depending on its experience of God's unmerited favor and grace in Christ, and the active expression of its gratitude through its way of life in worship. Below are some of the foundational concepts associated with worship, the Church's true vocation.

- Salvation is completely a free gift of God to be received by faith and cannot be earned or deserved.

- Human beings are so enslaved by sin that they cannot desire the right things unless the grace of God works in them first.

- God always is the first to act in bringing someone to salvation. "We love him because he first loved us."

- Because the Church is a community of people who have experienced the grace of God, worship is both the duty and the joy of the Church.

- The "meal and the bath" (Lord's Supper and baptism) are part of the way in which we experience and remember the grace of God. They are key elements of Christian worship.

- A sacrament is a means by which the grace of God is given to us while an ordinance is an action that acknowledges grace through obedience and remembrance. Both types of theology emphasize that participation in the Lord's Supper and baptism is helpful only if it is combined with repentance and faith.

- Christian leaders must study the Scriptures and decide whether it is best to understand the Lord's Supper and baptism as sacraments or as ordinances.

- The central vocation of the Church is worship of God, and the key reason why the Church worships is for the purpose of glorifying the one, true, and Almighty God, Yahweh.

- The Church worships God because of the matchless nature of both his supreme character and mighty deeds through creation and salvation. As such, God is always worthy to be worshiped and praised by members of the Church.

- Because all things exist by God's good will and for his pleasure, worship of God is the one activity that all beings and matter share in their goal. The telos (ultimate goal) of every thing that exists is to praise and honor God for who he is and what he has done.

- The Church worships God through its services of praise and thanksgiving, and, as priests and priestesses of God, she gives him glory in a variety of means and methods, including song, dance, kneeling, silence, clapping, shouting, etc.

- Liturgy is the Church's particular order of services where it declares, regardless of tradition, the preaching and teaching of the Word of God and celebrates together at the Lord's table when all assemble.

- All forms of expression of the Church in its worship should be influenced by the leading of the Holy Spirit under the guidance of the Word of God. Each culture of the Church is free and responsible to define its music, style, and form of worship, consistent with the principles and truths of Christ.

Student Application and Implications

page 237

Now is the time for you to discuss with your fellow students your questions about the Church at worship. To comprehend the strategic role of grace in establishing a relationship between God and the worshiping community, as well as the freedom and responsibility the Church has to exalt God is foundational to being a leader for God today. It may arguably be said that until a person understands and can articulate these truths with one's words and deeds, one cannot exercise effective leadership in the Church. Go over these questions to see if you fully grasp both the facts and implications of the material, and how it relates to you and your relationships in ministry. What particular questions do you have in light of the material you have just studied about your own understanding of these truths? Maybe some of the questions below might help you form your own, more specific and critical questions.

* Although most people have never heard of the "Pelagian heresy," there are many people who commit it. How would a person who misunderstood salvation in this way talk about what it means to become a Christian?

* Does your church (or denomination) understand the Lord's Supper and baptism to be sacraments or ordinances? Why?

* How often should a church take the Lord's Supper together? Why?

* To what extent does your worship team at your church fully grasp the facts and implications associated with worship as the Church's vocation?

* How free is the expression of your church's worship in terms of the physical and psychological expressions exhorted in the Bible? How much are these injunctions to shout, clap, and dance "cultural expressions" versus biblical mandates for worship? Explain your answer.

* What is the nature of your church's "liturgy," in other words, how your church organize its services and celebrations in order to "retell the story" in its worship services? What prevents this from being more effective in your church?

* How does one shift the cultural climate of a congregation from stiff, familiar worship to dynamic and life-giving praise? What are the steps to such a situation?

CASE STUDIES

Showing Off Unnecessarily

In a local congregation which has more than its fair share of gifted musicians and singers, the church has begun to grow through its dynamic and remarkably excellent worship services. Some have begun to complain, however, because the music minister has made it more difficult for so-called "ordinary" worshipers to be on the worship team or the praise band. All singers must be auditioned for their vocal quality and ability to read music, and no musicians are allowed to participate on the praise band who cannot read sheet music and accompany the beautiful (but difficult) arrangements selected for the songs. The minister of music is strong in his opinion that God is excellent and therefore our worship should be as excellent as possible. What would your counsel be to the music minister if he asked you to comment on the direction the worship was taking in this congregation?

page 238 26

You Can't Make Me Worship

The new worship leader in church has been emphasizing the need for active, physical expression during the worship service. He is very strong in his opinion that we ought to employ all the different means Scripture speaks of in expressing our love to God–clapping, lifting and waving our hands, shouting, dancing, kneeling, being silent, lying prostrate, making joyful noise–we ought to show our love to God with our bodies. A small but determined group in the church is dead set against all of this motion and commotion, and wants to end this emphasis on all this bodily expression. After all, this isn't a pro football game, but the worship of Almighty God. Conflict is brewing among the members about what is most appropriate for this church. How would you help them resolve this issue?

Grace Alone

 A pastor is witnessing to a young woman about Jesus and invites her to attend church. The woman replies, "I'm not really good enough right now to be doing that. I'm interested in religion and stuff but I want to get my life together first. Once I clean some things up, then I'll come to church." What should the pastor say to this young woman?

Getting Down for the Lord

A new jazz-funk-rock praise band has emerged from the church who call themselves *Selah*. They are determined to bring praise and worship to a whole new level of intensity and power in the congregation, but are doing it with an "in your face" kind of volume and showmanship that has many members of the church, even some of the staff, concerned about them. Selah is experiencing real popularity in their Saturday evening concerts, and have been used of the Lord greatly in some of the evangelistic outreaches around town. Yet, when you hear them, they sound exactly like secular bands. As a matter of fact, many of their songs use the melody of popular pop music songs set to Christian lyrics. Some people have admitted they come to their concerts to dance! How would you advise Selah as it attempts to give full expression to their love for God in worship, while continuing to, as the drummer says, "get down for the Lord?"

Restatement of the Lesson's Thesis

There is nothing we can do to desire or obtain salvation that is not given to us as a free gift by the grace of God. This experience of God's grace causes the Church to become community whose duty and delight is to worship God. We glorify God in our worship because of his perfect character–his solitary holiness, his infinite beauty, his incomparable glory and his matchless works. Through the grace of God in Jesus Christ, we have been set free to worship the true God, the Triune God in the power of the Holy Spirit. In addition, the Church worships God through its praise and thanksgiving, through liturgy, which emphasizes the Word and the sacraments, and through its obedience and lifestyle as a covenant community.

Resources and Bibliographies

If you are interested in pursuing some of the ideas associated with the themes brought up in this lesson, *The Church at Worship*, you might want to give these books a try:

Boschman, Lamar. *The Rebirth of Music*. Shippensburg: Destiny Image, 2000.

Bridges, Jerry. *Transforming Grace: Living Confidently in God's Unfailing Love*. Colorado Springs, CO: NavPress, 1993.

Engle, Paul E. *Baker's Worship Handbook*. Grand Rapids: Baker Book House, 1998.

Hill, Andrew E. *Enter His Courts With Praise!* Grand Rapids: Baker Book House, 1993.

Oden, Thomas C. *The Transforming Power of Grace*. Nashville: Abingdon Press, 1993.

Webber, Robert. *Planning Blended Worship*. Nashville: Abingdon, 1998.

Ministry Connections

Now is the time in the lesson to discover what facets of this biblical theology is most applicable to your personal life. Where might the Holy Spirit be calling you to most readily apply in your current ministry situation these teachings on the grace of God, and the worship that a full understanding of that grace leads to in our personal and church lives? Making clear and dynamic ministry connections is a major skill of any qualified leader, and now is an opportunity for you to practice this skill, especially in connection to your own life. Meditate on these truths and see which one(s) you might need to think about and pray for throughout this next week. Be open to how the Holy Spirit might want you to emphasize these truths as you minister to those under your care this week, and ask him for wisdom as you apply these truths to your particular situation.

Counseling and Prayer

Pray to God for yourself and those whom you serve, that you might specifically come to understand and appreciate the power of the transforming grace of God in your life and the lives of those whom you disciple and teach. Ask the Holy Spirit to make Christ's love more real in your personal life, and seek his power as to how you might become more free in expressing your praise and thanksgiving to God for all he is and has done in your life. Especially ask the Lord for insight into those things,

page 238 27

areas, habits, or practices in your life which might hinder you from giving more and better praise to God, consistent with our vocation to bring maximum pleasure and honor to God.

Scripture Memory

Hebrews 10.19-22

Reading Assignment

To prepare for class, please visit *www.tumi.org/books* to find next week's reading assignment, or ask your mentor.

Other Assignments

Please read carefully the assignments above, and as last week, write a brief summary for them and bring these summaries to class next week (please see the "Reading Completion Sheet" at the end of this lesson). Also, now is the time to begin to think about the character of your ministry project, as well as decide what passage of Scripture you will select for your exegetical project. Do not delay in determining either your ministry or exegetical project. The sooner you select, the more time you will have to prepare!

Looking Forward to the Next Lesson

The Church of Jesus Christ are all those who through faith in Christ have experienced and been transformed by the grace of God. This transforming grace opens them up to worship and praise their mighty God of love, but it equally burdens them with a passion to share with others this marvelous story of Jesus and his love. In our next lesson we will focus on the Church's mandate to give witness to Christ and his Kingdom through its actions and proclamation, and how God equips the Church to be his agent and representative in the world by his Spirit.

Capstone Curriculum

Module 3: Theology of the Church
Reading Completion Sheet

Name _____

Date _____

For each assigned reading, write a brief summary (one or two paragraphs) of the author's main point. (For additional readings, use the back of this sheet.)

Reading 1

Title and Author: _____ Pages _____

Reading 2

Title and Author: _____ Pages _____

THEOLOGY OF THE CHURCH  Capstone Curriculum / 7 9

LESSON
3

The Church as Witness

page 241   1

Lesson Objectives

Welcome in the strong name of Jesus Christ! After your reading, study, discussion, and application of the materials in this lesson, you will be able to:

- Outline the most significant aspects of the doctrine of election as it applies to Jesus Christ as the Elect Servant of God.

- Describe how God's election relates both to his chosen people Israel as well as to the Church.

- Explain the relationship of God's election of individual believers "in Christ," that is, in connection to Christ as they cling to him by faith.

- Articulate how the Great Commission provides an overall outline for the Church's threefold witness in the world to make disciples.

- Recite how the Church fulfills Christ's commission by obeying Jesus' call to evangelize the lost, by baptizing new believers in Christ (incorporating them as members into the Church), and by teaching true converts to observe all the things Christ commanded.

Devotion

Preach the Gospel

page 242   2

Read Mark 16.14-20. There is something very significant about last words. What do you say to a person when you are seeing them for the last time? Surely your instructions are chosen with great care. In the last words that Jesus spoke to his disciples prior to ascending into heaven, he was very clear. Your most important priority, he tells them, is to preach the good news about Jesus to everyone in the world. And then, knowing that they will face persecution and disbelief, he adds that as they preach the Gospel they should depend on the Holy Spirit (cf. Acts 1.8) to protect them and to verify their preaching by visible displays of God's power. The Church has taken those last words to heart. Every century since Jesus ascended the Gospel has been taken to new parts of the world— to new groups of people, to new languages and cultures—and has resulted in the steady and often spectacular growth of the Church so that today more people name Jesus as Lord than at any point in human history. We can thank God for what has happened, but our task is not fulfilled until we preach the Gospel "to every creature." Let's make sure that the Church in our generation doesn't falter in the task, but that we redouble our efforts to make sure that everyone hears the Good News and sees the power of God at work among us to confirm the truth of our message.

After reciting and/or singing the Nicene Creed (located in the Appendix), pray the following prayer:

> *Spirit of God, we pray that You would come upon us in power and make us witness about Jesus to the ends of the earth. Help us to find the lost and to persuade them of the truth of the Gospel. Help us to witness to those near to us, our families and friends, but also help us to witness to those who are far away, who are different from us because of where they live, the language they speak, or the culture they grew up in. Help us to truly preach the Gospel "to every creature" and not become weary in this task as we wait for the appearing of our Lord and Savior Jesus Christ. This we pray in the name of the Father, and the Son, and the Holy Spirit. Amen.*

Nicene Creed and Prayer

Put away your notes, gather up your thoughts and reflections, and take the quiz for Lesson 2, *The Church at Worship*.

Quiz

Review with a partner, write out and/or recite the text for last class session's assigned memory verse: Hebrews 10.19-22.

Scripture Memorization Review

Turn in your summary of the reading assignment for last week, that is, your brief response and explanation of the main points that the authors were seeking to make in the assigned reading (Reading Completion Sheet).

Assignments Due

God Playing Favorites?

In a discussion of Church history, one person commented in discipleship class that it appears that God plays favorites. Some nations seem so wealthy and prosperous, while others constantly struggle for food, and are traumatized by horrible weather and war. Some churches seem to be growing, with plenty of staff, much money, and

page 242 3

a ton of activity, while other churches, equally or even more godly, struggle just to stay afloat. Some ministries seem to get all kinds of attention and resources when they do not appear to be as biblical and faithful as others we know, which are functioning on the barest of budgets. Some of the students began to agree with this line of thinking. How would you've responded to this line of argument about God and his "playing favorites?"

Election

In our world, we use the word "election" to describe the process by which we choose our political leaders and to be "elected" means to be chosen by the voters for a special position of responsibility. Both the Old and New Testaments use this word when they speak about God's people as being "elected." How is the Scriptures use of the word "elect" like or unlike our modern use of this word?

Testimony

None of us are born as Christians. We have to be "born again" in order to receive the Kingdom of God. What did God use to convince you to become a Christian?

The Church as Witness

Segment 1

Rev. Dr. Don L. Davis

Summary of Segment 1

page 243

The Lord God, as a sovereign and authoritative God, has called and elected certain persons to certain ends and status. Above all else, God has elected Jesus of Nazareth to be his Elect, Suffering Servant. In his person, God has elected to bring about salvation to all humankind, to everyone who clings to him by faith in his death, burial and resurrection. God has also elected Israel to be the instrument through which he would bring Messiah into the world, and by which he would provide us with a clear picture of his salvation given to both Jew and Gentile in Jesus Christ. Individual believers are elected "in Christ," through their union and association with him. God's election is based on his sovereign purpose and grace, given to the base and weak of the world in order that no one should boast in his presence. God's election is effective and secure, so we can be certain of our eventual salvation in Jesus Christ.

Our objective for this first segment of *The Church as Witness* is to enable you to see that:

- The Lord God, as a sovereign and authoritative God, has called and elected certain persons to certain ends and status.

- Above all else, God has elected Jesus of Nazareth to be his Elect, Suffering Servant. In his person, God has elected to bring about salvation to all human-kind, to everyone who clings to him by faith in his death, burial and resurrection.

- God elected Israel to be the instrument through which he would bring Messiah into the world, and by which he would provide us with a clear picture of his salvation given to both Jew and Gentile in Jesus Christ.

- Individual believers are elected "in Christ" through their union and association with him.

- God's election is based on his sovereign purpose and grace, given to the base and weak of the world in order that no one should boast in his presence.

- God's election is effective and secure, so we can be certain of our eventual salvation in Jesus Christ.

I. In Order to Understand God's Elective Purpose, We Must Affirm that Jesus Christ Is the Elect of God.

Video Segment 1 Outline

Of all elements of the doctrine of election as it relates to the Church in its witness, no element is as important as what the Bible says about the person of Jesus Christ.

A. Yes, Jesus possesses titles which prove that he is the Elect Servant of Almighty God.

1. Jesus is the Chosen One (*elektos*) of God, Matt. 16.16.

2. Jesus as God's Precious Stone, the Capstone of God's Building; he is God's stone, chosen and precious, the stone rejected by the builders which God has made the very Capstone.

   a. 1 Pet. 2.4

   b. Ps. 118.22-23

3. Furthermore, Jesus is God's only begotten and beloved Son, the one whom we should hear and in whom we should believe.

   a. John 1.34

   b. Luke 9.35

   c. cf. John 6.35

4. Those who scorned him while on the cross ironically ridiculed him with the name of "the Christ of God, the Chosen One of God," Luke 23.35.

B. Jesus also is the Servant of Yahweh, chosen to represent him both in revealing his glory and redeeming the world.

   1. The Servant Songs of Isaiah (cf. Isa. 41.8-9 with Isaiah 42.1)

2. Matthew 12.18 paraphrase of Isaiah 42.1

3. The Servant Songs of Isaiah are predictions about the coming and ministry of Jesus of Nazareth.

    a. Jesus associated directly with the Suffering Servant of Isaiah, the one through whom Yahweh would save his people, Matt. 8.17 (cf. Isa. 53.7–8).

    b. Jesus is the Suffering Servant of Yahweh, the One Chosen to redeem the world on behalf of the holy God Yahweh.

        (1) Acts 3.13

        (2) Acts 4.25, 27, 30

        (3) Acts 8.32–33

C. Jesus is also the Messiah, the One elected by God himself to die for the sins of all humankind, appointed to rise from the dead, and elected eventually to reign over the entire creation.

    1. The often-used Pauline phrase "in Christ" is shorthand in the New Testament for understanding how God brings about the election of his people.

    2. According to the New Testament, Jesus was chosen to fulfill the divine plan, that the Messiah would suffer and die, rise again, and rule over creation.

        a. Acts 3.20

b. Eph. 1.9–10

c. 1 Pet. 1.20

d. Rev. 1.5-8

3. Jesus affirms his role as God's anointed Messiah in his testimony about himself to the travelers on the Emmaus road, and to the apostles after his resurrection, Luke 24.25-27, 44-48.

4. God's election is always in Christ, and all spiritual blessings we receive we receive by virtue of our union with and faith in Christ.

a. Eph. 1.3

b. 2 Pet. 1.3-4

II. Next, God Has Chosen for Himself a People from Which Messiah Would Be Born, through Which the Promise of Salvation Would Be Given.

A. The nation Israel is the sign and precursor (i.e., the forebearer) of the chosen people of God.

1. The nation of Israel has been elected as a possession for God and as a witness to him throughout the earth, Deut. 7.6-8.

2. This same emphasis is also perceived in other critical Old Testament texts.

a. Deut. 10.15

b. Deut. 14.2

c. Ps. 105.6, 43

d. Isa. 41.8

e. God's election of Israel to select and represent him is linked directly to his demand that they be holy, for they as God's elect nation must reflect his own righteous character.

3. Notice that the Old Testament does not woodenly suggest that the people of Israel are the elect of God simply due to genetics and the physical lineage of Abraham.

   a. Within the larger nation there exists God's own holy and elect remnant.

   b. God recognizes some of the Israelites as his chosen, a remnant which forms a distinct group within greater Israel, Isa. 65.8-9.

   c. Isa. 10.20-23 and Isa. 14.1. The Lord God will "again choose Israel."

4. Rom. 9-11. Even though the Gospel has been rejected by a majority of Jews, God's chosen people, God will deliver his remnant, as spoken in the Old Testament.

a. Israel is made up of two distinct classes:

   (1) Those unbelieving descendants of Abraham

   (2) The elect believing remnant who will be spared from destruction by God's mercy

b. This elect remnant of Israel (which is of his own physical lineage) is coming to God through faith in Christ by the Gospel.

   (1) Rom. 11.1-2

   (2) Rom. 11.7

c. According to Paul, this remnant within Israel is both "chosen by grace" (Rom. 11.5) and was foreknown (Rom.11.2).

d. After the Gentiles enter salvation, Paul boldly suggests that "all Israel will be saved" (Romans 11.26, a quotation of Isaiah 59.20-21). For Paul, Israel will be cherished and elected by God on account of their beloved patriarch and thus will be included in the final elect of God (Rom. 11.28–29).

B. God has also elected his chosen people the Church to salvation, both Jew and Gentile, through faith in the finished work of Jesus on the cross.

The teaching of Scripture is clear that God has elected both Jews and Gentiles to be saved through faith in Jesus Christ.

1. Gentiles who believe in Jesus Christ are included in God's saving election.

   a. We who believe are blessed along with Abraham, the man of faith, Gal. 3.7-9.

b. This election of the Gentiles was a mystery kept secret for generations but now is made known to us through the apostles and prophets.

   (1) Rom. 16.25-27

   (2) Eph. 3.8-11

   (3) Col. 1.25-27

2. Correspondingly, God is now making a universal invitation and offer to all humankind to be saved by faith in Jesus Christ. God is inviting all people to himself, initiating true reconciliation through his sovereignty and grace.

   a. Titus 2.11 and 1 John 2.2

   b. John 3.16

   c. Acts 17.30-31

   d. 1 Tim. 2.3-6

   e. 2 Pet. 3.9

   f. God beckons all men and women, boys and girls everywhere to respond to him.

      (1) Isa. 55.1

      (2) Matt. 11.28

g. Ezek. 33.11

page 244 📖 5

3. God personally elects individuals to salvation, ensuring forever their certain and blessed redemption.

   a. God has guaranteed the salvation of his own through his foreknowledge and predestination to life, Rom. 8.28-30.

   b. God has elected those who believe in Jesus Christ to salvation, to be his own recipients of eternal life, Eph. 1.4-6.

   c. All those whom the Father gives to Jesus will come to him, John 6.37; and no one can come to Christ unless the Father draws him, John 6.44.

   d. He chose us and appointed us to bear fruit that remains, John 15.16.

page 244 📖 6

C. Certain principles emerge from this discussion of God's elective purposes.

page 246 📖 7

1. First, God's mercy is given not on the basis of human initiative and merit, but on the basis of God's lovingkindness and grace alone, Exodus 33.19 is quoted in Romans 9.15-16.

2. Next, God's election is made on the basis of his own sovereign purpose in order that no one can boast in their own righteousness or holiness, Eph. 2.8-9.

3. Third, God chose the base, the weak, and the foolish to bring to shame the wise and powerful in this age, 1 Cor. 1.26-31.

4. Fourth, no one can call into question God's elective choice of Jesus, Israel, or the Church. God's election flows from his own sovereign purpose and choice, and is neither conditioned nor determined by external manipulation.

   a. Indeed, God does according to his own pleasure in all things, Ps. 135.6.

   b. Rom. 9.18-24

5. Fifth, God's election is absolutely effective to the salvation of those whom he calls.

   a. Rom. 8.38-39

   b. Rom. 11.29

6. And lastly, the vivid description of the lostness of humankind is set against the plain and ready invitations that God gives to us to be saved. God's election is God's affair.

   a. John 5.24

   b. John 6.40

   c. We present the good news of salvation to all, knowing that those who repent and believe are God's chosen and elect, Acts 13.48.

III. Let Us Summarize this Important Segment with Several Observations Regarding the Deep Meaning and Implication of God's Election.

A. The first implication is that God's elective choice highlights the glory of his sovereignty and lordship in the world. As in all things, God is Lord, even in regards to salvation.

1. The Lord has made everything for its purpose, even the wicked for the day of trouble, Prov. 16.4.

2. God's sovereign purpose for us will be accomplished, so our salvation is sure and secure, Rom. 8.31-34.

3. When none are found worthy to take the scroll from him who sits on the throne, a Lamb as if freshly slain takes the honor, and the heavenly creatures declare his worthiness to open the scroll, Rev. 5.9-10.

4. God's election of Christ, Israel, the Church, and the saints reveals his sovereign choice and holy character. He is Lord alone.

B. Another implication of God's election is that his election reveals the wonders of God's grace.

1. 2 Tim. 1.9-11

2. In God's electing purpose, he reveals the richness of his lovingkindness to us, a love which was given us before the ages began but now is revealed to us in the person of Jesus Christ.

C. A third implication of God's election is that evangelism and missions are essential, even in the face of the sure hope we have in God's electing grace.

page 246 □ 8

1. While God Almighty knows those who are his, we don't! In obedience to the Great Commission, we are to proclaim the Good News to the very ends of the earth, making disciples of all nations, teaching them to obey Christ's teaching, Matt. 28.18-20.

2. Empty and wrongheaded speculation about whether or not God predestines the lost to damnation is foolish distraction from the plain revealed will of God to make disciples till he comes.

D. A fourth and final implication suggests that God's election provides God with certainty regarding those who belong to him.

page 247 □ 9

1. God knows those who belong to him, 2 Tim. 2.15-19.

2. We need never feel guilty for those who reject Jesus. We are to declare Jesus as Lord, and leave the rest with his Spirit.

3. Rather than argue about issues which can only be settled in the mind of God we ought to embrace our role as believers, affirming the mystery of God's elective purpose, and the limits of our reason. We may never know all those whom we have touched, or the reasons within God's heart for his sovereign choices. We can affirm, however, that God has instructed us to share the Good News with all, and that every one who believes will inherit eternal life in Jesus Christ.

Conclusion

» Jesus Christ is the Elect Servant of God, the one through whom God saves out of the world a people for himself.

» God has elected a nation to be the vessel through whom Messiah would come, the nation Israel, and a community of faith made up of both Jews and Gentiles, the Church of God in Jesus Christ.

» God's election underscores the glory of his sovereignty, the wonder of his grace, the critical nature of evangelism, and the certainty of our salvation.

Segue 1

Student Questions and Response

page 248 10

Please take as much time as you have available to answer these and other questions that the video brought out. Undoubtedly, the concept of God's election is difficult and complex, but all is made clearer when one realizes that God has elected Christ to represent him, and elects us in him. Still, many valid questions remain about the nature of God's foreknowledge, his elective purpose, and just how God works out all things together for the good of those who believe on him, those called according to his purpose. Seek to understand the critical concepts associated with this theme, especially underscoring the important role that Christ plays in all discussion of God's election. Be clear and concise in your answers, and where possible, support with Scripture!

1. In what sense do the Scriptures teach us that Jesus Christ is the Elect Servant of God, the one through whom God saves out of the world a people for himself?

2. What titles are given to Jesus by the apostles and prophets which reveal a unique and unrepeatable relationship between Jesus of Nazareth and Yahweh God?

3. How are we to understand the relationship of those elected to salvation and Jesus Christ? In what way can we say that the elect are elected by virtue of their union with Jesus, who himself is the true Elect Servant of God?

4. In what ways does Israel serve as a sign and precursor of God's elect people? According to the Scriptures, what are some of the reasons God elected Israel as a nation through his covenant with Abraham?

5. In what ways today can we say that God has also elected the Church to be his agent and representative in the world? What is the significance that God has elected both Jews and Gentiles to be members of the Church of God in Jesus Christ?

6. What are some of the implications that arise from a biblical understanding of God's election of Jesus, Israel, and the Church?

7. How might the doctrine of election underscore for us our understanding of the glory of God's sovereignty, the wonder of his grace, the critical nature of evangelism, and the certainty of our salvation? Give answers for each.

The Church as Witness

Segment 2

Rev. Dr. Don L. Davis

The mandate from Jesus for his Church to be his witness is summarized in the Great Commission. This Commission can be easily outlined according to three critical elements, which constitute the mission of the Church in the world today. The first element involves the task to "go and make disciples of all nations" which instructs the Church to evangelize the lost. Next, the Church gives witness by "baptizing them in the name of the Father, Son, and Holy Spirit," that is, we are called to baptize new believers in Christ incorporating them as members into the Church. Finally, the Church gives witness through "teaching them to observe all things I have commanded you;" in others words, the Church of Jesus Christ teaches its members to observe all the things Christ commanded.

Summary of Segment 2

> Matt. 28.18-20 - And Jesus came and said to them, "All authority in heaven and on earth has been given to me. Go therefore and make disciples of all nations, baptizing them in the name of the Father and of the Son and of the Holy Spirit, teaching them to observe all that I have commanded you. And behold, I am with you always, to the end of the age."

This divine command outlines the dimension of the Church's witness to Christ and his Kingdom in this present age. We will divide Christ's command into its various parts, and briefly look at each facet of Jesus' mandate.

Our objective for this second segment of *The Church as Witness* is to enable you to see that:

- The mandate from Jesus for his Church to be his witness is summarized in the Great Commission.

- This Commission can be easily outlined according to three critical elements, which constitute the mission of the Church in the world today.

- The first element is that the Church gives witness as she goes: the Church of Jesus Christ is called to evangelize the lost.

- The second element is that Church gives witness through baptism: the Church is called to baptize new believers in Christ, that is, to incorporate them as members into the Church.

- The third element is that the Church gives witness through its teaching: the Church of Jesus Christ teaches its members to observe all the things Christ commanded, and so grow to maturity in him.

Video Segment 2 Outline

page 248 11

I. **The First Element of the Great Commission Is Jesus's Command to Go. We as the Church Give Witness to Jesus by Going into the World. We Give Witness as We Respond to the Call to Evangelize.**

   A. The call to witness is a call to share the Good News, a call to evangelize, to go into the entire world and preach the Gospel.

   1. The tense of the Greek verb in Jesus' commission gives the sense of 'to be continuously going.' According to Jesus, the Church is 'to be going into the world;' evangelism is the business of the Church.

   2. We are to go into all the world and preach the Good News to every person, Mark 16.15-16.

3. The global nature of this call to witness is made explicit again by Christ himself in Acts 1.8 (i.e., Jerusalem, Judea, Samaria, and to the uttermost parts of the earth).

4. This constitutes a charge to go into every nation, state, among every culture and clan to declare plainly the good news of the Kingdom to those who have yet to hear of God's love in Jesus Christ, Rom. 15.20-21.

B. The call to evangelism is directly related to the charge to be ministers of reconciliation, 2 Cor. 5.18-21.

1. God was in Christ reconciling the world to himself.

2. God has given to the Church the ministry of reconciliation and now, through us, calls the world to be reconciled to him through Christ.

3. Finally, as the ambassadors of Jesus Christ, we bear witness in the world of God's saving grace in Christ, inviting all to receive God's mercy and escape his judgment through his Son, Jesus Christ.

C. Moreover, the New Testament tells us what mode and manner we are to go. As we are going into the world to share the Gospel, we are to become all things to all people in order to save some, 1 Cor. 9.19-23.

1. Communicate the truth of the Gospel in ways that the lost can comprehend it, using our freedom in Christ to make the Good News plain and clear.

2. We are not permitted to alter the message; we are to contextualize the message without changing or augmenting it, Gal. 1.8-9.

3. The Church bears witness to Jesus as she goes into the world, with creative freedom, evangelizing the lost by preaching the Gospel of Christ.

II. The Second Element of the Great Commission Is Baptism: We Witness by Baptizing.

As members of the Church we are called to baptize new believers in Christ, that is, to incorporate and establish them as members into the Church.

A. First, we are commanded to baptize new believers into the faith, Mark 16.15-16.

1. The biblical formula for baptism:

    a. We are to baptize in the name of the Triune God, Matt. 28.19.

    b. This is tantamount to being baptized in the name of Jesus Christ. While some argue that this is different from the triune formula, Paul's statement in Ephesians 4.5 that "there is only one baptism" suggests that baptism in the name of the Father, Son, and Holy Spirit is equivalent to being baptized "in the name of Jesus Christ," or into Jesus Christ. Peter says to Jews of Pentecost in Acts 2.38, "Repent and be baptized every one of you in the name of Jesus Christ for the forgiveness of your sins, and you will receive the gift of the Holy Spirit."

Confession of Christ must inevitably lead to association with his people. If a professing Christian refuses to identify with God's people, it might indicate that they have not truly repented and believed. Where there is no commitment to the Church, there is probably no salvation in Christ. All believers are incorporated into Christ's body through baptism. When we baptize new believers in the Lord Jesus, we introduce them to our faith community, and we must then establish them in the foundational, first truths of the faith, and incorporate them as vital members into Christian assembly.

2. The rite of baptism derives its significance from its association of the believer's repentance and faith in the Lord Jesus.

   a. Baptism is an outward sign and confirmation of a believer's inward confession and faith in the person of Jesus Christ as Savior and Lord. Through faith and baptism, the believer now becomes the property of Jesus as Lord of all.

   b. Paul speaks of the new relationship through faith and baptism with Christ in terms of ownership.

      (1) 1 Cor. 1.12

      (2) Gal. 3.27

      (3) cf. 1 Cor. 3.23

   c. Baptism appears to have always followed a faith confession in the apostles' ministry, Acts 8.12.

   d. Paul makes plain that while he baptized a few in Corinth, God did not call him to baptize but to preach the good news of Jesus Christ. Baptism is not the *cause* but the *result* of saving faith in Jesus Christ.

      (1) 1 Cor. 1.13-17

      (2) Acts 16.14-15

3. True faith commitment ought to be accompanied by being baptized in water as a sign of one's allegiance and identification with Christ and his people.

4. A significant effect of baptism is how it identifies the new believer with Jesus Christ in his death, burial, resurrection, and new life.

a. Placed into the body of Jesus Christ by the Holy Spirit, 1 Cor. 12.13

b. Through baptism, we become directly identified with Jesus in his death and resurrection, Rom. 6.3-5.

c. Baptism, therefore, is a sign of union with Christ: we are buried with him in baptism, and raised with him through faith, Col. 2.12.

B. A part of baptism is establishing new believers in the first truths of Jesus Christ.

1. 1 Pet. 2.2

2. Col. 2.6-7

3. Heb. 5.12-6.2

   What are the implications of this teaching?

   a. Milk must be given to new believers, to get them established in the truth in the midst of godly Christian assembly and fellowship.

   b. This milk, introductory teaching, is critical as a foundation for the ongoing growth toward maturity in Christ.

C. Finally, newly baptized believers are to be brought in and incorporated into a local church where they can grow and serve in Jesus Christ.

1. Every new believer must associate directly with an assembly of believers, which becomes for them their body and their household, Heb. 10.24-25.

2. Every believer, as a part of this body, must come to know and submit to the godly Church leaders who will provide care and training for their life and service, Heb. 13.17.

   a. They guide the Church's worship and growth.

   b. They encourage the Church's witness of the good news of Christ.

   c. They coordinate the Church's work of service and mission to the world.

      (1) 1 Thess. 5.12-13

      (2) 1 Tim. 5.17

III. The Third Element of the Great Commission Is Teaching: the Church Gives Witness by its Teaching.

Jesus commanded us to teach his disciples to observe all that he commanded them. This effort centers on the preaching and teaching of the Word of God in the assembly, and through that teaching, to equip believers to become more like him and to do his work in the world.

A. First, we are called to witness by preaching and teaching the Word of God in the Church assembly.

1. Of all the critical elements in the Church's witness, she must be committed to preaching and teaching the Word of God, 2 Tim. 4.12.

2. The centrality of preaching and teaching the Word of God with zeal and clarity in the Church can be seen for several reasons.

   a. First, the Word of God is able to feed and nurture the spiritual growth of the body, 2 Tim. 2.15.

   b. Next, it equips God's people in the Church for every good task that the Holy Spirit calls them to do, 2 Tim. 3.15-17.

   c. Finally, it equips members to engage and defeat the enemy in spiritual warfare as the Spirit's Sword, Eph. 6.16-17.

B. Next, as we teach the Word of God, we will help individual members of our assemblies identify their gifts and callings as God-endowed members of his people.

   1. All believers are endowed with gifts of the Holy Spirit to be used on behalf of the Church, to 1 Cor. 12.4-7.

   2. God has given specially gifted men and women to the Church to equip the believers for the work of the ministry, Eph. 4.11-13.

   3. Every member contributes their part for the overall growth and outreach of the body, to God's glory, Eph. 4.15-16.

   4. As we teach new Christians to do all that Jesus provides and commanded, new Christians will identify their gifts, learn to use them for the benefit and edification of fellow members of the Church, Rom. 12.4-8.

C. One marvelous result: increasing depth and Christlikeness experienced by members of the Church.

1. The goal of the Church's witness is that the Church will grow in both number and maturity, resulting in members who become more like Christ in their individual lives and service to the world.

2. Goal of spiritual activity: the reproduction of Christ's life in the Church. Christlikeness is the goal of all discipleship.

   a. Great Commission focus: teach the new believers to observe and follow everything that Jesus commands.

   b. This focus on Christ and his Word is key to biblical discipleship in the Church. Above all else, becoming like Jesus in his life, death, and resurrection is the explicit goal of the Christian's life.

   c. Phil. 3.8

   d. Gal. 4.19

   e. Rom. 8.29

   f. 2 Cor. 3.18

   g. 1 John 3.2-3

3. Thus, the call to witness is a call to experience and to demonstrate in our lives the character and passions of Jesus Christ, loving each other as he has loved us.

   a. We are the body of Jesus together in this world, 1 Cor. 12.27.

   b. Making disciples is taking the yoke of Christ upon us and learning of him, Matt. 11.28-30.

   c. We are to visibly demonstrate the love with which Christ has loved us, John 13.34-35.

4. And as we go, baptize, and teach, we will be better able to represent Jesus in the world and reveal to the lost the glories of his person and rule through our words, conduct, and actions, 2 Cor. 2.14-17.

Conclusion

» The witness of the Church is summarized in the Great Commission, which has three distinct elements of responsibility for body.

» The Church gives witness by going: the Church of Jesus Christ is called to go into all the world and to evangelize the lost.

» The Church gives witness by baptizing: the Church is called to baptize new believers in Christ, and through baptism, to incorporate them into Christ's Church.

» The Church gives witness by teaching: the Church of Jesus Christ teaches its members to observe all the things Christ commanded. In so doing, the members of the Church grow to maturity, even to Christlikeness.

Segue 2

Student Questions and Response

The following questions were designed to help you review the material in the second video segment. A thoroughgoing study of the elements of the Great Commission is critical for Church men and women to understand the Church's relationship to the world, and its call to proclaim the good news of salvation to the lost in it. The three elements of going, baptizing, and teaching make up the heart of our corporate calling to give witness to Christ and his Kingdom, and the Church is called to be ever vigilant in following through on each of these three dimensions of its life and ministry. Make sure that you comprehend and can articulate the basic tenets of each element, and can relate that element to the Church's role as witness. Be clear and concise in your answers, and where possible, support with Scripture!

1. What is the nature of the statement "Great Commission," and what are the three elements emphasized within it which summarize the responsibility of the witness of the Church?

2. What is the meaning of the phrase in the Great Commission, "Go into all the world and make disciples?" What is the relationship of disciple-making to evangelism and missions?

3. What is the nature of the scope of the commission to go into all the world, in other words, whom has Jesus asked us to make disciples of, and where are we to make them?

4. What is the nature of baptism in the witness of the Church? What is the relationship of water baptism to saving faith in Jesus Christ? If baptism does not directly save us, what are the reasons why every new believer ought to be baptized?

5. How is baptism related to incorporating new believers into a church? Why is it impossible for a believer to thrive and prosper if they are never incorporated into a local body of believers?

6. How is our union with Christ demonstrated through our baptism? Why is demonstration of this union so important for Christian growth and maturity?

7. How does the phrase "teaching them to observe all things I have commanded you" fill out our understanding of the Great Commission? Who has been given the task to proclaim and teach the Word of God in the Church?

8. What has God promised to those who feed on the Word of God through the teaching ministry of the Church? How does the goal of Christlikeness relate to the goal of observing the teaching of Jesus in the midst of the Church?

9. What promise does Jesus make to us in the Great Commission about himself while we obey this mandate to make disciples throughout the entire earth?

CONNECTION

Summary of Key Concepts

page 249  *12*

This lesson focuses upon the doctrine of election as it applies to Jesus as God's Elect Servant of God, and God's election of Israel and the Church as witness to his grace and as his agent in the world. We also covered in detail the various elements of the Great Commission (going, baptizing, and teaching) as it relates to the Church's witness in the world. Again, the importance of the Christian leader to be at home with and be completely familiar with these ideas is plain. Without understanding the role of the Church's witness, the Christian leader will neither be able to train others to witness effectively nor be an effective witness himself or herself. Make sure you understand the basic ideas and Scripture associated with the concepts below on the Church as witness.

- The Lord God, as a sovereign and authoritative God, has called and elected certain persons to certain ends and status, all for his glory.

- Above all else, God has elected Jesus of Nazareth to be his Elect, Suffering Servant. In his person, God has elected to bring about salvation to all humankind, to everyone who clings to him by faith in his death, burial and resurrection.

- God has also elected Israel to be the instrument through which he would bring Messiah into the world, and by which he would provide us with a clear picture of his salvation given to both Jew and Gentile in Jesus Christ.

- Individual believers are elected "in Christ," through their union and association with him. God blesses his people as they are associated with Christ through their faith and allegiance.

- God's election is based on his sovereign purpose and grace, given to the base and weak of the world in order that no one should boast in his presence.

- God's election is effective and secure, so we can be certain of our eventual salvation in Jesus Christ.

- The mandate from Jesus Christ for his people to be his witnesses is summarized in the Great Commission.

- The Great Commission contains three critical elements, which constitute the mission of the Church in the world today: going and making disciples, baptizing in the name of the Triune God, and teaching these believers everything that Jesus commands.

- The first element of the Great Commission is that the Church gives witness as she goes: the Church of Jesus Christ is called to evangelize the lost (i.e., make disciples of all nations).

- The second element of the Great Commission is that the Church gives witness through baptism: the Church is called to baptize new believers in Christ, that is, to incorporate them as members into the Church.

- The third and final element of the Great Commission is that the Church gives witness through its teaching: the Church of Jesus Christ teaches its members to observe all the things Christ commanded, and so grow to maturity in him.

Student Application and Implications

page 250 13

Now is the time for you to discuss with your fellow students your questions about the nature of the doctrine of election, and our obedience to the Great Commission. These topics represent two deep strands of teaching regarding the Church's witness, and coming to grips with their meaning is critical for your own maturity as well as your ability to win others to Christ and see them grow to maturity in him. Many tough questions are associated with these topics, especially with the doctrine of election, so you ought to take adequate time to think carefully through your questions and seek clear, biblical answers to them. What particular questions do you have in light of the material you have just studied? Maybe some of the questions below might help you form your own, more specific and critical questions.

* Does God elect some to be saved and others to be lost? Is there any such idea as God elected people to be lost?

* In what sense does God elect individuals to salvation, or should we concentrate on God electing his people in Christ?

* Since Israel failed to trust in Christ as a group, does that mean that God has abandoned them as his people? Is the nation Israel still the people of God, and if so, how?

* If salvation is due to God showing mercy and not our own initiative, what precisely was our role in coming to Jesus?

* Can anyone who wants to be saved come to Christ, or only the elect?

* Are all believers commanded to go and make disciples, or is this a special calling for a particular group of believers in the Church? How do we know if we have been called to go, baptize, and teach?

* What is the relationship between world evangelization and being a Christian? What am I supposed to do about lost people overseas, if I live in the city and have no way to reach them?

* What role does the Holy Spirit play in sharing the Good News with others? How does the message of the Great Commission relate to the other places where Jesus commands his apostles to go and be witnesses of him?

* What makes a person a valid witness? Can you be God's witness even though you don't go to Bible college or seminary? Who is qualified to go, baptize, and teach for God?

Only the Elect Will Come to Jesus

page 250   14

In discussing the doctrine of election with other students, one happened to mention that he believes that Christ died only for the elect; those who are not elected to salvation were not included in God's plan for salvation. He argued that if God wants you saved, you will be saved. It is clear that not everyone is going to be saved, so God does not intend on saving everyone, but only some. Christ died, therefore, just for those whom God wants to save. What do you make of this line of reasoning? Is this argument persuasive? Why or why not?

God Has Elected You to Damnation

After reading a book on Reformed theology, one student is particularly troubled about an idea he encountered in the book. The idea simply put is this; the fact that God elects some to be saved means also that God has elected some to go to hell.

There are some people, the book suggested, who will not and could not come to Christ because they were not chosen to be saved; God overlooked them, and therefore they will die, without Christ and without hope. This idea troubles the student, but it seems to make logical sense. Doesn't choosing some and not choosing others say that God is playing favorites? Did those he never chose even have a chance at salvation? Aren't we hypocrites asking people to come to Jesus when we know that some of them could never come, no matter how hard they wanted to? How would you help this dear student resolve these issues?

All Evangelize, but Only a Few Are Evangelists

In a cell group focused on studying missions, a discussion breaks out among the members about whether or not everyone is meant to obey the Great Commission. Some suggest that no matter how hard we might try, we could never win souls like Billy Graham or the Apostle Paul. They were gifted by God to do their task, we are only called to share the Good News in the circle of our friends and family. Others protest, saying, the Great Commission is a fresh word for every generation of Christians. All believers are to find ways that they are to go, baptize, and teach, for Jesus commanded us to do it. No one is exempt; all must respond. How would you address these contradictory arguments?

Lordship Salvation

Completely discouraged and disgusted by people who pretend to believe but don't really, one little storefront church is now saying that in order to be saved you must confess Jesus as Lord. This isn't anything new, that is, after all, what Romans 10 teaches. Yet, they have tried to take it to another level. Because so many people will claim to belong to Jesus but show no sign of commitment to him, the pastor has begun to ask people to not merely believe the facts about the resurrection, but make a personal commitment to live for and obey the commands of Jesus in order to be saved. Some of the elders are concerned; they think the pastor is teaching a works salvation that will drive people away from the Lord. Others welcome the teaching as a needed and refreshing alternative to the weak, anemic preaching which seems to be so prevalent in churches today. How would you weigh in on this dilemma?

Restatement of the Lesson's Thesis

Jesus of Nazareth has been made according to God's sovereign election the Elect Servant of God, the One through whom God would save the world, and the One in whom all the saved find their redemption. Israel is a sign and precursor of God's chosen people, through whom the Messiah came, who died, rose, and reigns as God's chosen Lord. The Church, made up of all believing Jews and Gentiles, are elect and chosen "in Christ," that is, in connection to Christ as they cling to him by faith. The Great Commission provides an overall outline for the Church's threefold witness in the world to make disciples. The Church gives witness by going and making disciples (evangelizing the lost in the world), by baptizing (incorporating new believers into the assembly of believers), and by teaching (instructing disciples to do everything Jesus commands and so grow to maturity in him).

Resources and Bibliographies

If you are interested in pursuing some of the ideas of *The Church as Witness*, you might want to give these books a try:

Arn, Win, and Charles Arn. *The Master's Plan for Making Disciples*. 2nd Edition. Grand Rapids: Baker Books, 1988 (1982).

Coleman, Robert. *The Master Plan of Evangelism*. 30th Anniversary Edition with Study Guide by Roy J. Fish. Grand Rapids: Fleming H. Revell-Baker Books, 1993 (1963).

Phillips, Keith. *The Making of a Disciple*. Old Tappan, New Jersey: Revell Books, 1981.

Snyder, Howard. *Kingdom, Church, and World: Biblical Themes for Today*. Eugene, OR: Wipf and Stock Publishers, 2001 (1985).

Ministry Connections

page 251 📖 15

The wonder of being chosen by God in Christ, and called by God to be a disciple maker is a sweet and deeply moving truth for us as believers. We are chosen in Christ, elect, called to go into the entire world to make disciples, baptizing them in the name of the Triune God, and teaching them Christ's holy Word. These truths have direct bearing on your life and ministry as a disciple; you cannot fulfill your responsibility as a leader if you fail to appreciate and understand your union with God in Christ, and Jesus' mandate on his Church to fulfill what is commonly called the Great Commission. Now it is time for you to assess how these truths have come to influence and affect your life. Have you been able to integrate within your life so far the truth that God has elected you in his Son–how does this truth impact your thinking or change the way you pray or relate to other believers, or unbelievers? Do you sense a deep commitment to the Great Commission? What is God calling you to be and do to make the maximum contribution you can to fulfilling it, right where you live and minister today? Spend some time asking the Holy Spirit to speak to you about these and other truths, and how God might want you to respond personally to them. Your life and ministry are open to being touched by this teaching, if you will be sensitive to search just where these truths can directly impact your life. Set aside time this week to spend meditating on the truths in this lesson, and ask God for insight in applying them. Be prepared to return next week ready to share your insights with the other learners in your class.

Pray and ask God the Holy Spirit to give you insight into the breadth and the depth of the apostolic teaching on the nature of the doctrine of election, and how this truth can revolutionize and impact your life. Perhaps there are some specific needs which the Holy Spirit has surfaced through your study and discussion of this material. Be open to the Lord in prayer; find a partner in prayer who can share the burden and lift up your requests to God. Further, ask God to renew his vision for you in the Great Commission mandate. Ask him again to confirm to you your role in making disciples–is he asking you to go, to make disciples here, to plant a church, to pastor, to mentor and train young Christians, to change jobs, to move? Seek the Lord, and he will give you specific input as to what he wants you to do. Of course, your instructor is extremely open to walking with you on this, and your church leaders, especially your pastor, may be specially equipped to help you answer any difficult questions arising from your reflection on this study. Be open to God and allow him to lead you as he determines.

Counseling and Prayer

ASSIGNMENTS

Matthew 28.18-20

Scripture Memory

To prepare for class, please visit *www.tumi.org/books* to find next week's reading assignment, or ask your mentor.

Reading Assignment

Other Assignments

page 251 📖 16

Make certain you set aside ample time to carefully read the upcoming textbook assignment, as well as respond to the material by filling out your worksheet containing your summary of the reading material for the week. Also, by this time in your study you should have selected the text for your exegetical project, and have turned in your proposal for your ministry project. If you have not, please do so as soon as possible.

Looking Forward to the Next Lesson

Our next lesson is directly related to the theme of lesson three. Our next study is entitled, "The Church at Work," and its aim is to understand the various dimensions and elements of the Church, and how we may detect authentic Christian community through the Church's actions and lifestyle. We will use the marks and definitions which arise from the Nicene Creed, the teaching of the Reformation, and the rule of St. Vincent to understand and evaluate claims of true congregations from untrue. We will also look at the works of the Church through different images which we will use as lens to understand what the Church is to do in its life and mission. These images will include the household of God, the body of Christ, and temple of the Holy Spirit, the ambassadors of Christ, and the army of God.

Capstone Curriculum

Module 3: Theology of the Church
Reading Completion Sheet

Name _____

Date _____

For each assigned reading, write a brief summary (one or two paragraphs) of the author's main point. (For additional readings, use the back of this sheet.)

Reading 1

Title and Author: _____ Pages _____

Reading 2

Title and Author: _____ Pages _____

Lesson 4: The Church at Work

page 253  *1*

Lesson Objectives

Welcome in the strong name of Jesus Christ! After your reading, study, discussion, and application of the materials in this lesson, you will be able to:

* Articulate the various dimensions and elements of the Church, and be able to say how we may detect authentic Christian community through the Church's actions and lifestyle.

* Discern the marks of the Church according to the Nicene Creed.

* Recognize the dimensions and definition of Church according to the teaching of the Reformation.

* Recite the standard of doctrinal unity through the lens of the Vincentian Rule, a helpful guide to understand and evaluate traditions and teachings claiming to be binding upon Christians.

* Describe the character of the Church's works in the world by exploring various images of the Church mentioned in the New Testament.

* Provide insights into the Church's nature and function through the lens of the household of God, the body of Christ, and temple of the Holy Spirit, through the ambassadorship of the Church as the agent of the Kingdom of God, as well as God's army, the Church's work as doing battle in the Lamb's war.

Devotion

page 253 *2*

Learning to Represent God

Read 2 Corinthians 5.18-21. Of all the images of the Church that move and challenge, the image of being an ambassador of the Lord is one of the richest and most suggestive. Paul speaks to the Corinthians as an ambassador of Christ, one who represents the interests, policies, and leaders of a distant land, and whose essential task is to simply carry out the edicts and instructions of the home country. Throughout the Scriptures, God envisions his people as belonging to a different land, looking for a new and different city whose maker and builder is God, whose citizenship is in heaven, who set their affections on things above where Christ sits at the right hand of God. We belong to the Lord; we have no certain place here. We are aliens, strangers, and sojourners, representing the interests of the Kingdom of God which, miraculously, has been revealed and inaugurated in the person and passion of Jesus Christ. To be a Christian is to be an ambassador of Jesus Christ, and to be a congregation is to be an outpost, an embassy of the Kingdom of God in a particular community. Our role is to represent the "home country," to get orders from the Prime Minister of heaven, and to declare to the powers that be in this realm his Word and will. To be a Christian is to learn to represent good, to be the kind of representative that is faithful, clear, and unmoved.

Are you the kind of man or woman who represents the interests and instructions of the home country well? Can the living Lord of the new city-to-come count on you to stand for him, where you are, with integrity? Stand up for Jesus as you stand for the Kingdom to come.

After reciting and/or singing the Nicene Creed (located in the Appendix), pray the following prayer:

> *Eternal God and Father of our Lord Jesus, I thank You for Your goodness, mercy, and grace that allows us to represent You in the world. You have promised that Your Spirit will empower us and enable us to accomplish Your will with excellence. Give us the power and direction in order that we may stand for You in all that we say and do–in our homes, our jobs, our neighborhoods, and our churches. We desire to be the kind of disciples You find trustworthy, those whom You can use to glorify Your name in a world that neither knows nor respects You. Only You can make us the kind of representatives worthy of Your name and Your Kingdom. Make us like Your Son, who fulfilled Your will completely, and humbled himself in order that You might be glorified in him. Conform us to his image, for Your name's sake, in Jesus' name, Amen.*

Nicene Creed and Prayer

Put away your notes, gather up your thoughts and reflections, and take the quiz for Lesson 3, *The Church as Witness*.

Quiz

Review with a partner, write out and/or recite the text for last class session's assigned memory verse: Matthew 28.18-20.

Scripture Memorization Review

Turn in your summary of the reading assignment for last week, that is, your brief response and explanation of the main points that the authors were seeking to make in the assigned reading (Reading Completion Sheet).

Assignments Due

Not a Real Church Service

page 254 📖 *3*

1. In a recent meeting in a cell group meeting of a new church plant in an urban neighborhood, a discussion arose about whether or not meeting in homes only is enough to be a real church. Some of the members who went to traditional church services have felt a little awkward meeting in homes and calling those meetings with believers "church service." This discussion has grown into a larger discussion about what makes a church service a legitimate one. If you were a part of this discussion, what would you say regarding the true marks of a "real church service?"

Full, Fuller, and Fullest Gospel

2. In all of the various divisions and denominations which speak about what constitutes a "full gospel" fellowship, many criteria are being used to say what a whole church is. Based on what your understanding is now, if you could only suggest five characteristics of a true church, what would they be? Think for a moment. Why did you choose these five? What, if anything, might be left out of your list?

We Alone Are Jehovah's Organization

3. After a difficult discussion with some Jehovah's Witnesses one morning, a dear Christian sister is troubled about the conversation. The Witnesses claimed two things that stayed in her mind.

First, they claimed that God could only really have one legitimate and true Church–all of these bodies claiming to be God's organization cannot all be correct. Second, they claimed that because of the great division and confusion in the doctrines and practices of the churches (Catholic, Protestant, Anglican, and Orthodox), they cannot be true. Only the clean and understandable positions of the Jehovah's Witnesses, along with their non-racial and non-institutional practices makes sense. How would you answer this dear sister as she tries to make sense of all the differences among the various traditions all claiming to represent God and to be Christian?

The Church at Work

Segment 1

Rev. Dr. Don L. Davis

Historically, believers have identified and argued for certain criteria by which to understand the various dimensions and elements of the Church, and how we may detect authentic Christian community through the Church's actions and lifestyle. Three sources have been especially helpful to make sense of the biblical vision of the Church. First, the marks of the Church according to the Nicene Creed emphasize its oneness, holiness, apostleship, and universality. The definition of Church according to the teaching of the Reformation emphasize the preaching of the Word, the observance of the sacraments and the right order of discipline. In regard to doctrinal truth, the rule of St. Vincent emphasizes those things which have been believed everywhere, always, and by all. These marks are helpful in discerning right practices and doctrines of the Church.

Our objectives for this first segment of *The Church at Work*:

- Our aim is to understand the various dimensions and elements of the Church, and how we may detect authentic Christian community through the Church's actions and lifestyle.

- We will look at the marks of the Church according to the Nicene Creed.

- We will briefly explore the dimensions and definition of Church according to the teaching of the Reformation.

- We will look at the Church through the lens of the Vincentian Rule, a helpful guide to understand and evaluate traditions and teachings claiming to be binding upon Christians.

Summary of Segment 1

Video Segment 1 Outline

I. **The Marks of the Creedal Standard: the Church according to the Nicene Creed: "We Believe in One, Holy, Catholic and Apostolic Church."**

The original Nicene Creed was the product of perhaps the first worldwide gathering of Christian bishops at Nicaea in Bithynia (what is now Isnik, Turkey) in the year 325. The teachings of this first gathering were confirmed and extended at a later meeting in 381. The original convocation sought to undermine a heresy called Arianism (which called Jesus' deity into question, and claimed that he was God's greatest creation). The meeting also sought to refute the idea that the Holy Spirit was not God (i.e., not of the same substance as the Father). A council of 150 bishops of the Eastern Church were gathered in 381 at Constantinople (modern day Istanbul, Turkey), where they confessed again that Jesus was fully God, and extended the first's councils language to include an explicit paragraph which expressed the deity and work of the Holy Spirit. The second, expanded version of the original 325 Nicene creed is known today as "The Nicene Creed." Seen to be one of the first truly foundational confessions of Christian belief, this creed is universally acknowledged by all traditions and denominations.

Regarding the Church, the Creed affirms "We believe in one, holy, catholic, and apostolic Church." Let's look briefly at these creedal marks respectively.

page 254

A. To begin with, according to the Nicene Creed, the Church is one.

1. Notice how this unity is stated in Jesus' high priestly prayer, John 17.20-23.

2. This insight is reaffirmed by Paul in Eph. 4.4-6.

3. Jesus's teaching on the oneness: one sheepfold on his people, John 10.14-16.

B. Next, the Church of Jesus Christ is holy.

page 255 5

The Church has been sanctified, made holy, through the ministry of Jesus Christ.

1. The Church is made holy, sanctified, and set apart by the blood of Jesus Christ, Heb. 10.10-14.

2. The Church is made holy through the presence and ministry of the Spirit.

   a. 1 Cor. 3.16-17

   b. This connection with God through the Spirit is made the basis for the Church's obedience and purity, 1 Cor. 6.19-20.

3. The Church is also made holy, sanctified, and set apart for God's possession and use through its obedience to the will and Word of God, John 17.15-19.

C. Again, the Church is catholic.

page 256 6

1. The Church is both multi-cultural and trans-historical: that is, it embodies believers from diverse cultures from all eras and ages. It is not limited by culture, or language, or clan, or country.

   a. Rev. 5.8-10

   b. Rev. 7.9-10

2. The Church is catholic in its inclusiveness, being made up of all who place their faith in Jesus Christ, whether Jew or Gentile, bond or free, living, dead, or still yet to be born.

   a. Col. 3.11

   b. Gal. 3.28

page 256 □ 7

D. Finally, and perhaps most importantly, the Church is apostolic.

   1. The Church's faith and practice is rooted in the apostles' election by Jesus Christ, (cf. John 17.6-9).

   2. The Church has been given the high mandate to be accurate and zealous defenders of the apostles' teaching, the apostolic doctrine and tradition.

      a. 2 Thess. 3.6

      b. Jude 1.3

   3. Also, the Church of Jesus Christ functions as those who bear the impress and guard the core of the apostolic authority.

      a. As guardians of the apostolic testimony, the Church is named the "pillar and foundation of the truth," 1 Tim. 3.15-16.

      b. The Church is apostolic, birthed through their testimony and defenders of their doctrine.

The Church of Jesus Christ, as the Nicene Creed affirms, is one holy, catholic, and apostolic Church.

II. The Reformation Marks of the Church: "The Church Exists Where the Word Is Rightly Preached, the Sacraments Are Rightly Administered, and Discipline Is Rightly Ordered."

Reformation theologians were those churchmen in the seventeenth century who argued for such classic doctrines of salvation by grace through faith alone and the sufficiency of the saving power of Jesus Christ. They also wrote extensively on the nature of the true Church, which they took to mean three things: "The Church exists where the Word is rightly preached, the sacraments are rightly administered, and the discipline is rightly ordered."

A. The first Reformation marker of the true Church is "Where the Word is rightly preached."

1. This mark is related to the Reformation idea of *sola Scriptura*: This doctrine suggests that no *magesterium*, creed, or council may exercise final authority for the Church's faith and practice over Scripture. The Word of God is our only infallible rule of faith (for what we believe) and practice (for what we are called to do).

2. To feed upon and teach the whole counsel of the Word of God is the duty of both believers and leaders of the Church. In all things, the Scriptures are to be given critical priority in the life and practice of the Church.

3. Affirming *sola Scriptura* (Scripture alone), of course, does not mean that we should not consult the tradition of the Church, or ignore the role that the Holy Spirit plays in understanding the Bible's teaching. It is not either/or, but both/and.

Once the Bible has been constituted as the Scripture of the Church, it becomes its main written authority, within the Church and not over or apart from it. Everything in the Church is judged by the Bible. Nothing in the Church may contradict it. Everything in the Church must be biblical; for the Church, in order to be the Church, must be wholly faithful to and expressive of that reality to which the Bible is itself the scriptural witness.
~ Thomas Hopko, quoted in Theodore G. Stylianopoulos. *The New Testament: An Orthodox Perspective.* Vol. 1. Brookline, Massachusetts: Holy Cross Orthodox Press, 1997. pp. 55-56.

B. The second mark of the true Church according to Reformation teaching is "Where the sacraments are rightly administered."

A true church is an assembly where the sacraments (sometimes called "ordinances" in some traditions) are mandated by Jesus Christ and practiced regularly as a part of the Christian community life. Two sacraments universally recognized in denominations are baptism and the Lord's Supper.

According to the Reformers' reading of Scripture, what constituted a sacrament?

1. First, it had to be established (or ordered) by Jesus himself.

    a. For instance, Jesus submitted to and instituted baptism as a token of salvation. In Mark 16.15-16 Jesus tells his apostles to go into all the world and proclaim the Gospel to the whole creation. He said that those who believed and were baptized would be saved.

    b. Jesus also inaugurated the Lord's Supper through his celebration of the Passover with his disciples before his death, see 1 Cor. 11.23-26.

2. Next, true sacraments should be seen as a token of saving faith of those who have joined God's covenant community.

    a. Baptism was for those who have repented and believed in Jesus Christ, those who had turned from sin and turned to God in Christ.

    b. The Lord's Supper was intended for believers as seen in the face of Paul's teaching where he exhorts the Corinthians to eat the bread and drink from the cup worthily, that is, in full fellowship with Christ, 1 Cor. 11.

3. Also, true sacraments were seen to be an act of lived faith, a means to proclaim publicly one's commitment and allegiance to the truth of God in Jesus Christ.

   a. Baptism affirms our identification with Christ in his burial, death, and resurrection, Rom. 6.3-4.

   b. The Lord's Supper bears witness of the sufficiency of Jesus' death and our looking for his soon return for our ultimate salvation.

4. True sacraments must be spiritually beneficial and edifying to those who partake of them.

   a. Baptism reveals our confession of faith and gives evidence to other believers of our commitment to live as bondslaves of Jesus Christ.

   b. Again, the Lord's Supper provides grace and assurance as we wait steadfastly in hope for Christ's return.

5. In surveying different Christian traditions, it is clear that denominations hold widely varying views regarding the sacraments. In discussing the issues, several critical questions arise:

   a. *Which suggested rites are the true sacraments?* While baptism and the Lord's Supper are universally recognized as sacraments instituted by Jesus himself, traditions hold conflicting views about other rites which might be considered sacraments. For instance, the Catholic Church has recognized a number of sacraments in addition to baptism and the Lord's Supper or eucharist, including such things as confirmation, marriage, and last rites.

b. *What actually do the sacraments accomplish?* Among Christians there is disagreement as to whether or not sacraments are merely signs, pointing to spiritual realities, or whether or not God actually supplies the Christian with unique and empowering grace and blessing in association with it.

c. *Who is free to administer the rites?* In certain traditions and denominations, only specially ordained or recognized leaders are permitted to administer the sacraments, while in others, any believer in good fellowship may administer the rites, as opportunity permits.

d. *Who are the appropriate recipients?* Virtually all Christian traditions would suggest that baptism and the Lord's Supper should be practiced by believers, for baptism as a sign of one's identification with Christ, and the Lord's Supper relates to the believer's union and celebration of Jesus' death on their behalf.

C. The final Reformation mark of the Church is "Where the discipline is rightly ordered," which deals with the life and structure of the assembly under the leadership of its own pastors and elders through the Holy Spirit.

1. The right order of discipline refers to the life structure among the body members. All forms of order exist for the upbuilding and edification of the Church.

   a. John 13.34-35

   b. 1 Cor. 10.23-24

2. The Church is to maintain credible testimony before outsiders: believers are called to live in accordance with the tenets and standards of the Kingdom of God.

   a. Matt. 5.14-16

   b. 1 Cor. 5.9-13

3. Right order of discipline relates to proper government of the Church. God has ordained that godly leaders provide oversight to church's affairs, and give instruction, care, and nurture to the assembly.

   a. Heb. 13.17

   b. 1 Thess. 5.12-13

4. What about dealing with heresy, immorality, and schism in the Church? These are to be dealt with sensitively and biblically in the assembly.

   a. 1 Cor. 5

   b. 1 John 2.19

   c. Matt. 18

   d. Gal. 6.1-3

The marks of the Reformation hold to Scripture: A true church exists where the Word is rightly preached, the sacraments rightly administered, and where discipline is rightly ordered.

III. The Marks Regarding Tradition and Faith, or the Vincentian Rule - "What Has Been Believed Everywhere, Always, and by All."

The Vincentian Rule gives a way whereby we can determine whether some teaching or practice conforms to the teaching of the "Great Tradition" of the one, true Church of Jesus Christ.

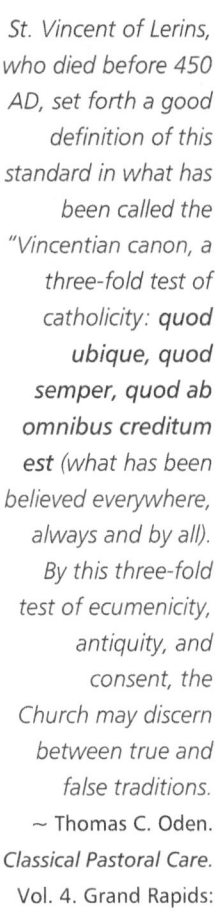

*St. Vincent of Lerins, who died before 450 AD, set forth a good definition of this standard in what has been called the "Vincentian canon, a three-fold test of catholicity: **quod ubique, quod semper, quod ab omnibus creditum est** (what has been believed everywhere, always and by all). By this three-fold test of ecumenicity, antiquity, and consent, the Church may discern between true and false traditions.*
~ Thomas C. Oden. *Classical Pastoral Care*. Vol. 4. Grand Rapids: Baker Books, 1987. p. 243.

A. The rule establishes that the ground for true tradition is "What has been believed everywhere."

1. This is the *ecumenical standard* (i.e., that which is everywhere believed): the Church is a faith community which has held historically to a core of confessions grounded in the person of Christ.

2. Christian faith is anchored in the person and work of Jesus Christ as Lord and Savior, and this anchor has been believed by all Christians from the beginning.

B. Next, the rule expands the standard to include "What has been believed everywhere *always*."

1. This is the *standard of antiquity* (i.e., that which is from the beginning): the Church has held to this core of confessional truth grounded in Jesus throughout the ages, starting with the apostles' generation.

2. The essential core has been confessed always, since the beginning: the salvation of God in Christ is the ground on which all Christian faith and practice are built.

C. Finally, the rule summarizes the principles with "What has been believed everywhere, always, and *by all*."

   1. This is the *standard of consent*: all branches of the Church have held to this same core of confessional truth.

   2. The essential core has been confessed always by all: heresy, by definition, is that which innovates or changes the meaning of that which has "once for all been delivered to the saints," Jude 3.

In this wonderfully simple statement we have a certain and sure rule for detecting true teaching from false teaching regarding Christian belief. We may consider a teaching to be authoritative and binding on the Church if it can pass the test of being "what has been believed everywhere, always and by all."

Conclusion

We have considered three sets of marks of the Church:

» The Nicene Creed: One, holy, apostolic, and catholic Church.

» The teaching of the Reformation: Word rightly preached, sacraments rightly administered, discipline rightly ordered.

» The Vincentian Rule: That which has been believed everywhere, always, and by all.

Segue 1

Student Questions and Response

page 258 9

Please take as much time as you have available to answer these and other questions that the video brought out. Understanding how the Church has defined the criteria of authentic assembly can help us in every phase of our ministry in the Church. While these marks of the Nicene Creed, the Reformation, and the Vincentian Rule are not explicitly organized around specific Scripture, they are all based on clear teachings of Jesus and the apostles, and offer us an invaluable aid to understand the nature of the Church. Make certain, then, that you understand the various dimensions that these criteria represent. As always, be clear and concise in your answers, and where possible, support with Scripture!

1. Briefly describe each of the four criteria mentioned in the Nicene Creed regarding the nature and function of the Church. How does each one help us understand the work of the Church in its relationship to God and the world?

2. Why is the Nicene standard of Church so critical for us to understand and defend today?

3. Of all the various criteria mentioned in the Nicene Creed, do you believe that one of them is predominant over the others? If so, which one(s)?

4. How did the Reformers understand the nature of authentic Christian assembly–what are the three criteria they recognized to be central in identifying true Church life?

5. As you meditate on the three Reformation marks of the Church, how ought we to understand them relating to each other? How do these marks relate to the marks of the Nicene Creed?

6. State clearly the tenets of the Vincentian Rule for evaluating the truthfulness of theological claims for the Church. Why would it be important for the Church to have such a rule to evaluate the various conflicting claims regarding its belief and practice?

7. How does the Nicene criteria of apostolicity relate to the Vincentian Rule? Why ought these two rules always inform and be related to one another in order to do justice to what the Church has historically believed?

8. Who in our congregations ought to be most concerned about applying these rules and criteria within our churches? How might we come to use them most effectively in urban churches?

The Church at Work

Segment 2

Rev. Dr. Don L. Davis

The character of the Church's works in the world can be understood by exploring various images of the Church mentioned in the New Testament. Each of the images provide us with a different set of concepts to reflect upon the Church's role and mission in the world. We see the Church's intimate relationship with God through the images of the household of God, the body of Christ, and temple of the Holy Spirit. We comprehend the Church as agent of the Kingdom of God through the lens of the Church as ambassador of Christ. Finally, we see the Church as doing battle in the Lamb's war as God's engaging army.

Our objectives for this second segment of *The Church at Work*:

- To concentrate on the character of the Church's works in the world by exploring various images of the Church mentioned in the New Testament.

- To look at the works of the Church through the lens of the household of God, the body of Christ, and temple of the Holy Spirit.

- To explore the works of the Church through the lens of ambassadorship, the Church as the agent of the Kingdom of God.

- To look at the Church through the lens of God's army, the Church's work as doing battle in the Lamb's war. These images offer great insight into how we are to understand the Church's identity and work in the world today.

Summary of Segment 2

page 258 📖 *10*

I. **The Primary Work of the Church Is to Give Evidence of God's Work in its Community Life: the Church's First Work Is to Declare the Excellencies of God in its Life and Relationships.**

The primary work of the Church is to be something, not to do something; the Church, as God's people, is called to display a quality of life that reflects the glory of him who created her in the first place.

The New Testament provides us with many images of the Church, all of which give us insight into the nature of the works that we must do in order to glorify God as his people.

Video Segment 2 Outline

According to Paul in Titus 2.14, Jesus sacrificed himself on behalf of his people, the Church in order to "redeem us from all lawlessness and to purify for himself a people for his own possession who are zealous for good works." Yes, we are to be zealous for the good works for which, according to Ephesians 2.10, we were created to do. And Peter makes plain in 1 Peter 2 that the primary motive behind these works is to show forth God's excellencies and character. We are his possession, to proclaim the excellence of his character in the world. "But you are a chosen race, a royal priesthood, a holy nation, a people for his own possession, that you may proclaim the excellencies of him who called you out of darkness into his marvelous light" (1 Pet. 2.9).

A. To begin with, as the household of God, we are to live as brothers and sisters in unity as God's own dear family.

1. Scripture declares that we are the children of God, members of God's household and family, Eph. 4.1-3.

2. We are to also do the works that make for cooperation and collaboration in testifying of the good news of the Gospel of Jesus Christ, Phil. 1.27-28.

B. Next, as Christ's body in the world, we are to incarnate Jesus' life in our relationships with each other and among our neighbors.

1. It is the right and responsibility of every Christian and every local church to represent and contribute to the work of Jesus in the world, Rom. 12.4-6a.

2. Paul affirms that there is only one body, one faith, and one hope of our calling. In light of this unity, we are to repent, therefore, of every selfish tendency to think our tradition or movement is more important to God than others. It is immoral to ignore or overlook the contributions of other believers, and we must seek to align ourselves with them in order to accomplish God's purposes in the world, Eph. 4.1-6.

C. Finally, as the temple of the Holy Spirit, we are to pursue the works of holiness and obedience as a sacred place where God's name is known and glorified.

1. In all our deeds together as believers, we are to do the works and live lives which reveal God's purity and our obedience, Heb. 12.14.

2. As God's very own dwelling place, members of the Church must individually pursue lifestyles which display God's purity, for this is our primary work as the people of God, 2 Cor. 6.16-7.1.

These images of the Church in the New Testament, the family of God, the body of Christ, and the temple of the Spirit, enable us to understand our work to display God's own excellencies. Before anything else, we are to demonstrate our unity in mission, our mutual cooperation in doing God's will, and our pursuit of holiness in our actions and activities.

II. The Church Is to Display the Kingdom's Righteous Rule through Our Works of Freedom, Wholeness, and Justice, as Christ's Ambassadors.

2 Cor. 5.18-21 - We are to live and work as Christ's ambassadors, representing Christ's Kingdom and asking all people to be reconciled to God. We are in this world, but not of this world.

Phil. 3.20-21 - We are the citizens of heaven through faith in Jesus Christ.

1 Pet. 2.16 - We are aliens and strangers upon the earth, sojourning toward our true home, the New Jerusalem.

As ambassadors, we engage in works which reveal the freedom, wholeness, and justice of the Kingdom.

A. First, as ambassadors of Christ, we work to display the freedom of the Kingdom.

1. Jesus' ministry and Isaiah 61: the Year of Jubilee, his ministry to proclaim good news to the poor, liberty to the captives, and recovery of sight to the blind.

2. This same emphasis on freedom underlies much of the work of God's people in the Old Testament, Deut. 15.12-15.

3. As those who have been set free by God, we therefore are to stand against all things that produce oppression and bondage, especially those spiritually corrupt practices which reveal the devil's will and commitment to destroy and enslave. As God's agents, we are to do the works which make for the liberation of the orphan and the oppressed, Ps. 10.15-18.

4. As ambassadors of the Kingdom we are to pursue works that promote the release and deliverance from ungodly oppression and bondage, whether it is economic, cultural, political, or social.

    a. As advocates of Christ's freedom we must promote creative responses to bondage, and affirm the inherent value of human beings as unique and special, made in the image of God, worthy of being cherished and cared for.

    b. We must strive to support those individuals and causes which coincide with God's mandate of peace and freedom among human beings, Prov. 24.11-12.

B. Second, as ambassadors of Christ, we engage in works to display the Kingdom's wholeness.

    1. Without question, the God and Father of our Lord Jesus is a God who longs to establish wholeness among the broken and despised of the world, Ps. 146.

    2. As ambassadors of Christ, those who have been made whole in Christ, we now stand against all things which produce discord, sickness, disease, suffering, and misery to other human beings everywhere.

a. We produce works against physical disease, malnutrition, and the lack of adequate care for human beings made in the image of God.

b. Furthermore, we as believers stand against human suffering and the numberless causes of that suffering, regardless of where we find persons who are oppressed.

3. We are assured as those called to promote the wholeness of the broken, that God himself will recognize our works, Ps. 41.1-2.

C. Finally, as ambassadors of Jesus Christ, we practice activities to display the Kingdom's rule of justice.

1. God instructs his people of true worship and authentic sacrifice, Isa. 1.16-18.

2. As ambassadors of Jesus, we work actively to stand against injustice and unfairness at whatever level, wherever we find it among persons.

3. Conditions in urban America and cities around the world today show signs of deep injustice, Eccles. 4.1.

    a. As ambassadors of Jesus' just rule, we are to cry out against all forms of political, social, religious, and personal oppression.

    b. We stand for those who are unable to stand for themselves, and speak up for those who lack any voice to represent their rights as human beings, Prov. 31.8-9.

c. We are to refuse to be silent regarding any inequality and discrimination against the weak or the poor which undermines their ability to live free, whole, and just, Deut. 27.19.

4. We work for just and fair dealings between people at all levels, persons, in families, between cultures, and among the nations.

   a. No authentic worship and praise without genuine efforts toward justice and righteousness, Amos 5.23-24.

   b. We are Christ's ambassadors. In all things, therefore, we should seek to do justice in his name for the poor and oppressed, expressed in practical, concrete ways like:

      (1) The administration of justice for them in our legal system, Amos 5.10-15

      (2) In economic affairs which tend to exploit them, Lev. 19.35-36

      (3) In ways in which our laws can easily ignore the needs of the most vulnerable, Isa. 10.1-4

As the ambassadors of the Kingdom of God, the Church is to display the Kingdom's righteous rule through our works of freedom, wholeness, and justice.

page 259 11

III. The Church Is to Battle as God's Army, Doing Battle in the Lamb's War, Proclaiming God's Truth, Destroying the Devil's Work, and Overcoming Evil with Good.

Paying the penalty for our sin on the cross of Calvary, Jesus rose victorious as *Christus Victor*, and through his death destroyed the works of the devil and his minions, Col. 2.15, 2 Cor. 2.14.

A predominant image of the Church, therefore, is the army of God, which battles not against flesh and blood but against spiritual forces in high places (Eph. 6.12-13). Though Jesus won the victory, we still must do battle in this present age, until he returns to consummate his work at the Second Coming. How are we to fight the good fight of faith in our age today?

A. First, we do battle as soldiers of God by proclaiming the truth of God in Christ.

1. We are called to expose the lies and false notions of the enemy wherever they are found. The nature of spiritual warfare revolves around God's truth, Rom. 3.4.

    a. The devil's key weapons are lies and deception, John 8.44.

    b. Moreover, the devil through lying accusation and manipulation deceives the entire world, which lies under his limited, malevolent control, 1 John 5.19.

    c. And in Revelation 12.9-10 we see that the devil is the arch deceiver and accuser of the entire world.

2. The Church proclaims the victory of Jesus Christ, unashamedly declaring the victory won through Jesus' death on the cross.

    a. Jesus defeated the principalities and powers through his death on the cross, Col. 2.15.

    b. We declare God's victory in Jesus Christ, 1 Cor. 15.57-58.

    c. We proclaim Jesus Christ as Lord, him whose name is higher than all others, who must reign until all enemies are placed under his feet, 2 Cor. 4.3-5.

d. The Church is about the works of proclamation. Through our efforts of evangelism, teaching, publishing, church planting, and ministry we bear witness that the rule and reign of God has now come in Jesus, and that God is commanding all to repent and receive his grace in Christ, Acts 17.30-31.

B. Next, as soldiers of the Lamb, we labor to destroy the devil's work.

1. Again, I would argue that the general testimony of the New Testament bears witness to the great fact that the Church in this current age is the Church Militant, doing battle with God's enemies to frustrate and destroy the devil's work.

   a. Eph. 6.12-13

   b. 1 John 3.8

   c. 1 John 4.6

   d. John 14.12

How do we frustrate and destroy Satan's work in the world?

2. We destroy his work by boldly presenting the Good News to the lost.

   a. According to Romans 1.16-17, the Gospel is the very *dunamis* or power of God to save all those who believe, yes, even to break the power of the devil's deception over their lives.

b. The Holy Spirit can illumine the minds of those who do not believe in order that the light of the Good News might shine upon them.

   (1) 2 Cor. 4.3-4

   (2) John 16.7-11

3. We destroy his work by appropriating God's delivering power over evil.

   a. We have Christ's promise that God will confirm his dynamic Word with power and signs which give testimony to its veracity, or truth.

      (1) Mark 16

      (2) Heb. 2.3-4

   b. As we proclaim God's truth, we are assured that the Holy Spirit will confirm the Word of God through miracles and acts of power, Rom. 15.18-19.

C. Finally, as soldiers in God's army we are to do battle in the Lamb's war as we overcome evil with good.

In the same spirit that our Lord Jesus demonstrated, we are to overcome the malevolent and vicious evil in our world. Yet, we are not to use evil to do so. Rather, we are commanded not to respond to this evil in kind, but, in the Spirit of Jesus Christ, to overcome evil with good.

1. Throughout the New Testament God tells us to follow in Jesus' steps. On this point, there can be no better pattern for the works of the Church than Jesus himself. We are called to follow in his steps.

   a. 1 Cor. 11.1

b. Eph. 5.2

c. Phil. 2.5

d. 1 John 2.6

2. As those who believe in him, we are to mimic him. Our Lord did not retaliate. He never repaid evil for evil. Vengeance belongs to God, Rom. 12.17-21.

3. We are to do good, to engage evil but to do righteousness, to engage in works of good and be willing to suffer. To engage the evil but not necessarily to win. Peter gives us the example of following in Jesus' steps as the one who prototypically gave himself even to the death on the cross, 1 Pet. 2.21-24.

Conclusion

» We are in fact to do the works of God.

» We have seen how the images of the New Testament help us to understand that role:

   » As the household of God,

   » The body of Christ,

   » The temple of the Spirit,

   » As ambassadors for Jesus, and

   » As soldiers in God's army.

» We are to do the works of God and so minister in God's name in the city and beyond.

The following questions were designed to help you review the material in the second video segment. Comprehending the nature and function of the Church through the lens of biblical images is a well attested and solid method to recognize the Church's work. Our study has concentrated on a series of images which highlight the intimate relationship the Church has with the Lord himself, with the world, and with Christ's enemy, the devil. Each image provides us with a rich theological conception of what the Church is to do as God's own people in the world. Answer these questions, therefore, carefully, giving special attention to how they help us understand better what the Church is to be and do. Be clear and concise in your answers, and where possible, support with Scripture!

Segue 2

Student Questions and Response

page 260 12

1. Why is it a legitimate practice to understand the nature and function of the Church through the lens of images of the Church in the New Testament? What kind of things ought we to be aware of when we engage in this kind of study?

2. What limits (if any) should be placed on doing study in this way, that is, through the lens of metaphor and analogy? How may we best use this method to take full advantage of the ways in which the Spirit instructs us through these analogies about the identity of Church?

3. What do we learn about the Church's work through the biblical image of the Church as the "household" or "family" of God? How does this help us understand what the Church should be doing in its relationships, especially among its members?

4. How does the image of the "body of Christ" help us comprehend what the Church is supposed to be doing in the world?

5. What do we learn about the Church's work in the world through the idea of the Church as "the temple of the Holy Spirit?" What does this image do to instruct us about the Church's role in the world?

6. Describe some of the various duties, responsibilities, and roles that are attached to the idea of being an ambassador? How does this lively image help us understand what the Church is to do in the world, as a representative of Jesus Christ?

7. What insights do we glean about the nature of the Church's work through the image of the Church as God's soldier, or army? How can this image help us to equip our members, organize and deploy our resources, and plan our activities consistent with the image?

Summary of Key Concepts

This lesson focuses upon comprehending the nature and function of the Church's work through certain marks of the Nicene Creed, the teaching of the Reformation, and the rule of St. Vincent. We also sought to understand the work and ministry of the Church through lens of certain select images which highlight the relationship of the Church to each of the members of the Trinity, to the world, and to the devil and his spiritual forces of darkness. In a world where so many professing Christians and congregations are claiming intimate relationship with God, it is imperative that Christian leaders understand what constitutes true Christian community, and be able to defend and articulate this in the midst of other disciples. Carefully reconsider these critical concepts, thinking how they enable us to properly understand the Church's work in the world.

- One of the most important and accepted criteria for understanding the nature and function of the Church is contained in the marks according to the Nicene Creed: "We believe in one, holy, catholic and apostolic Church." The true Church is one, set apart for God's possession and use, universal and global, and apostolic in origin and identity.

- The Reformation Marks of the Church concentrates on the biblical, sacramental, and procedural criteria for the Church: "The Church exists where the Word is rightly preached, the sacraments are rightly administered, and discipline is rightly ordered."

- The rule of St. Vincent (or the Vincentian Rule) concentrates on discovering the standards by which we can judge some idea or truth to be authoritative within the Church. It reads: "What has been believed everywhere, always, and by all." This rule provides a sure way whereby we can determine whether some teaching or practice conforms to the teaching of the "Great Tradition" of the one, true Church of Jesus Christ.

- By understanding and studying various images of the Church in the New Testament we can discover much about the nature and function of the Church, its mission and work in the world.

- The primary work of the Church is to give evidence of God's work in its community life: the Church's first work is to declare the excellencies of God in its life and relationships. Its critical identity is found in *being something*, not in merely *doing something*; the Church, as God's people, is called to display a quality of life that reflects the glory of him who created her in the first place.

- Through the image of the Church as the family and household of God, we see that we are to live as brothers and sisters in unity as God's own dear family.

- As Christ's body in the world, the Church is to incarnate Jesus' life in our relationships among its members and its neighbors.

- The Church is the temple of the Holy Spirit, a holy people called to pursue the works of holiness and obedience as a sacred place where God's name is known and glorified.

- As Christ's ambassadors, the Church is called to represent the authority and reign of God in the world, called to display the Kingdom's righteous rule through its works of freedom, wholeness, and justice.

- The Church is described as the army of God, giving insight in its responsibility to do battle as soldiers of God in the Lambs's war, by proclaiming the truth of God in Christ, by laboring with the Word to destroy the devil's work, and by overcoming evil with good.

Student Application and Implications

page 260 13

Now is the time for you to discuss with your fellow students your questions about your understanding of the identity and work of the Church. Your own life and ministry are deeply affected by your perspective on the role and resources of the Church. It is critical that you fully appreciate the rich truths associated with the Church. As leaders, our task is to help others in the Church discover their gift and role in the body, so that we may grow up in all things in Christ as each functions in their proper place. It is simply impossible to help others understand the significance of the Church if you yourself have a low or incorrect view of her identity and task in the world. Develop your own list of specific questions which can help you come to a richer and fuller understanding of the role of the Church in the world. What particular questions do you have in light of the material you have just studied? Maybe some of the questions below might help you form your own, more specific and critical questions.

* To what extent is it necessary to apply ourselves to these "extra-biblical" criteria about the Church (i.e., the Nicene, Reformation, and Vincentian standards and rules)? How are we to understand and appreciate the relationship of these criteria to what the Bible teaches directly about the role and work of the Church?

* What is the best way for us to teach these criteria and rules to others within the congregations we serve? How important is it for us to instruct our members in the "Great Tradition," the teachings and traditions of the larger Christian body?

* Do some of the criteria and images of the Church and its work apply to the city more than others? Explain.

* Is it possible, even using these criteria and images, to discern a "true church" or "true congregation?" What is the best way to use these criteria in helping Christians and congregations to grow into God's will for their lives?

* What is the significance of the Lord providing us with so many images of the Church in the Old Testament and New Testament? What should we seek to do in dealing with so many pictures of the Church-were they meant to be integrated into each other or understood on their own, or both?

* How do we employ these images in our preaching, teaching, and discipling that provide those we lead with the best possible image of the Church?

CASE STUDIES

Only Us and We Alone

page 261 14

One congregation, after forming through a hurtful and painful church split, is struggling with its relationship with other churches. While its leadership has not altogether abandoned the idea of forming relationships with other churches for fellowship and service, they are deeply concerned about the need to grow and stabilize the membership of the new congregation. It has been over 10 months since the split, and in all that time there has not been a single event where the new congregation could meet with other Christians for fellowship and growth. Some in the congregation are beginning to question the leader's decision about the need to stabilize by isolating the church from other congregations. How do the criteria and images we learned in this week's lesson relate to the struggle this fledgling congregation is experiencing now? What should they do in light of the criteria and images?

Christians Don't Do War

With the youth group going through a curriculum emphasizing spiritual warfare and our identity as soldiers of God, some of the parents have begun to worry about all of the vocabulary and imagery of war, and how it is or could adversely affect the kids in the youth group. Images of guerilla warfare, bombs, swords, shields, forces of darkness, and etc. have become the concern of some of the parents, who wonder whether or not the youth pastor is simply taking his read of the biblical metaphor of the Church as the army of God a little too far. What guidelines should we use to determine when we have gone too far in our use of an image in the Bible to determine our teaching, identity, and activities in the Church? Be specific.

I Don't See the Trinity in the Bible

In sharing his faith at work with a person of the Unitarian religion, Ralph was stunned when, in sharing about God's love in Jesus Christ, the person he was talking to abruptly said, "So many of you in the regular church are completely confused. You talk about God, Jesus, and the Holy Spirit as a Trinity. I have read through the Bible at least six times, and I have never come across any teaching about the Trinity. The word "Trinity" isn't even mentioned in the Bible. You claim to represent the Bible, but I don't see the Trinity in the Bible!" How would/could/should you use the criteria of the Nicene Creed, Reformation marks, or the Vincentian Rule to help them understand why the Church's view of the Trinity is not only biblical but also consistent with the tradition of the Church?

We Are Not of This World

After hearing the pastor's series on the Church as an ambassador of Christ in the world, one of the young lawyers in the congregation who was thinking about running for City Councilman is considering taking his name from the ballot. Being powerfully persuaded by the pastor's sermons that Christians are aliens, strangers, and sojourners in this world, the young candidate wonders whether or not participation in secular government positions is simply too involved with the world. After all, if we are meant to be in the world but not of it, maybe running for office and sitting on the City Council is simply too worldly in its overall involvement. If this candidate asked you for your opinion, what would you suggest to him?

Restatement of the Lesson's Thesis

Historically, three critical sources have been especially helpful in the Church to make sense of its true character and function in the world. First, the marks of the Church according to the Nicene Creed emphasize its oneness, holiness, apostleship, and universality. The definition of Church according to the teaching of the Reformation emphasized the preaching of the Word, the observance of the sacraments and the right order of discipline. In regard to doctrinal truth, the rule of St. Vincent emphasizes those things which have been believed everywhere, always, and by all. The Church's character and works can also be understood by exploring various images of the Church mentioned in the New Testament. We see the Church's intimate relationship with God through the images of the household of God, the body of Christ, and temple of the Holy Spirit. We comprehend the Church as agent of the Kingdom of God through the lens of the Church as ambassador of Christ. Finally, we see the Church as doing battle in the Lamb's war as God's engaging army.

Resources and Bibliographies

If you are interested in pursuing some of the ideas of *The Church at Work*, you might want to give these books a try:

> Bonhoeffer, Dietrich. *Life Together*. San Francisco: Harper Collins Publishers, 1954.
>
> Ellis, Carl F., Jr. *Beyond Liberation*. Downers Grove: InterVarsity Press, 1983.
>
> Ortiz, Juan Carlos. *Disciple: A Handbook for New Believers*. Orlando: Creation House Publishers, 1995.
>
> Perkins, John. *Let Justice Roll Down*. Ventura, CA: Regal Books, 1976.
>
> Sider, Ronald J. *Cry Justice: The Bible Speaks on Hunger and Poverty*. Downers Grove: InterVarsity Press, 1980.

Ministry Connections

page 261 15

You will be responsible to now apply the insights of your module in a practicum that you and your Mentor agree to. The ramifications of this module on the Church are numerous and rich: think of all the ways that this teaching can influence your devotional life, your prayers, your response to your church, your attitude at work, and on and on and on. What you must be aware of now, as you begin to make connections of these truths with your own life and ministry, is the direct and indirect links that are present. These truths about the nature and function of the Church have direct application for your life as a maturing disciple in your church;

God wants to use you as one who helps others to understand the nature of true Church life, even in your congregation. The better you see the truths, the better you will be able to articulate them to others, and flesh them out in your lifestyle and service to the other believers in your Christian assembly. As in every aspect of growth and ministry, it will be very significant that you seek to correlate this teaching with all your life and work.

This is precisely the importance of your ministry project. It was deliberately designed with these concerns in mind, and in the next days you will have the opportunity to share these insights in real-life, actual ministry situations. Pray that God will give you insight into his ways as you share your insights in your projects.

As a member of the body, and as a leader in the Church, you must ask the Lord for his insight, wisdom, and power to apply these truths to your life, and through you to those whom God wants you to share them with. Are there any issues, persons, situations, or opportunities that need to be prayed for as a result of your studies in this lesson? What particular issues or people has God laid upon your heart that require focused supplication and prayer for in this lesson? Take the time to ponder this, and receive the necessary support in counsel and prayer for what the Spirit has shown you. Pray specifically about how the criteria and images of the Church can become real in your own experience of Christian community, and how then God might want to help you communicate the truth about his people with others.

Counseling and Prayer

ASSIGNMENTS

No assignment due.

Scripture Memory

No assignment due.

Reading Assignment

By this time, you should have worked out all the details with your Mentor regarding your selections for your ministry and exegetical projects. They should now be outlined, determined, and accepted by your instructor. If for any reason you have not communicated the specifics of your project with your instructor, do so as soon as possible. Make sure that you plan ahead in your work regarding them, so that none of your work or assignments will be docked because you turned them in late.

Other Assignments

page 262 16

Final Exam Notice

The final will be a take home exam, and will include questions taken from the first three quizzes, new questions on material drawn from this lesson, and essay questions which will ask for your short answer responses to key integrating questions. Also, you should plan on reciting or writing out the verses memorized for the course on the exam. When you have completed your exam, please notify your mentor and make certain that they get your copy.

Please note: Your module grade cannot be determined if you do not take the final exam and turn in all outstanding assignments to your mentor (ministry project, exegetical project, and final exam).

The Last Word about this Module

The Lord Jesus has been gathering out of the earth a people which one day will be his very own bride, a beautiful new humanity united to God by faith in him, to live glorified as his servants in a new heavens and new earth. While our little evangelistic gatherings, Bible studies, cell groups, worship services, and other meetings may not appear to be the kind of meetings which reflect God's new humanity, the truth of the matter is that the we belong to God. We will live forever in a new city, built by the hands of the Master, where God will be glorified forever, in midst of an earth which shall be restored to its Edenic splendor. We are a part of the forever family of God, and our task is to represent Christ and his Kingdom with all the dignity, excellence, and clarity he deserves. May the Lord God use the truths of this module to help prepare a people worthy of the love and grace he has showered upon us through his Son. "Oh when the saints come marching in . . ."

Appendices

151   Appendix 1: **The Nicene Creed** *(with Scripture memory passages)*

152   Appendix 2: **We Believe: Confession of the Nicene Creed (8.7.8.7. meter)**

153   Appendix 3: **The Story of God: Our Sacred Roots**

154   Appendix 4: **The Theology of Christus Victor**

155   Appendix 5: **Christus Victor: An Integrated Vision for the Christian Life**

156   Appendix 6: **Old Testament Witness to Christ and His Kingdom**

157   Appendix 7: **Summary Outline of the Scriptures**

159   Appendix 8: **From Before to Beyond Time**

161   Appendix 9: **There Is a River**

162   Appendix 10: **A Schematic for a Theology of the Kingdom and the Church**

163   Appendix 11: **Living in the Already and the Not Yet Kingdom**

164   Appendix 12: **Jesus of Nazareth: The Presence of the Future**

165   Appendix 13: **Traditions**

173   Appendix 14: **A Theology of the Church in Kingdom Perspective**

174   Appendix 15: **Salvation as Joining the People of God**

179   Appendix 16: **A Theology of the Church**

198   Appendix 17: **The Lord's Supper: Four Views**

199   Appendix 18: **Perception and Truth**

200   Appendix 19: **Documenting Your Work**

APPENDIX 1
The Nicene Creed

Memory Verses ⇩

Rev. 4.11 (ESV) *Worthy are you, our Lord and God, to receive glory and honor and power, for you created all things, and by your will they existed and were created.*

John 1.1 (ESV) *In the beginning was the Word, and the Word was with God, and the Word was God.*

1 Cor.15.3-5 (ESV) *For what I received I passed on to you as of first importance: that Christ died for our sins according to the Scriptures, that he was buried, that he was raised on the third day according to the Scriptures, and that he appeared to Peter, and then to the Twelve.*

Rom. 8.11 (ESV) *If the Spirit of him who raised Jesus from the dead dwells in you, he who raised Christ Jesus from the dead will also give life to your mortal bodies through his Spirit who dwells in you.*

1 Pet. 2.9 (ESV) *But you are a chosen race, a royal priesthood, a holy nation, a people for his own possession, that you may proclaim the excellencies of him who called you out of darkness into his marvelous light.*

1 Thess. 4.16-17 (ESV) *For the Lord himself will descend from heaven with a cry of command, with the voice of an archangel, and with the sound of the trumpet of God. And the dead in Christ will rise first. Then we who are alive, who are left, will be caught up together with them in the clouds to meet the Lord in the air, and so we will always be with the Lord.*

We believe in one God,   *(Deut. 6.4-5; Mark 12.29; 1 Cor. 8.6)*
    the Father Almighty,   *(Gen. 17.1; Dan. 4.35; Matt. 6.9; Eph. 4.6; Rev. 1.8)*
    Maker of heaven and earth   *(Gen 1.1; Isa. 40.28; Rev. 10.6)*
    and of all things visible and invisible.   *(Ps. 148; Rom. 11.36; Rev. 4.11)*

We believe in one Lord Jesus Christ, the only Begotten Son of God,
    begotten of the Father before all ages,
    God from God, Light from Light, True God from True God,
    begotten not created,
    of the same essence as the Father,   *(John 1.1-2; 3.18; 8.58; 14.9-10; 20.28; Col. 1.15, 17; Heb. 1.3-6)*
    through whom all things were made.   *(John 1.3; Col. 1.16)*

Who for us men and for our salvation came down from heaven
    and was incarnate by the Holy Spirit and the virgin Mary
    and became human.   *(Matt. 1.20-23; John 1.14; 6.38; Luke 19.10)*
    Who for us too, was crucified under Pontius Pilate,
    suffered, and was buried.   *(Matt. 27.1-2; Mark 15.24-39, 43-47; Acts 13.29; Rom. 5.8; Heb. 2.10; 13.12)*
    The third day he rose again
    according to the Scriptures,   *(Mark 16.5-7; Luke 24.6-8; Acts 1.3; Rom. 6.9; 10.9; 2 Tim. 2.8)*
    ascended into heaven,
    and is seated at the right hand of the Father.   *(Mark 16.19; Eph. 1.19-20)*
    He will come again in glory
    to judge the living and the dead,
    and his Kingdom will have no end.
      (Isa. 9.7; Matt. 24.30; John 5.22; Acts 1.11; 17.31; Rom. 14.9; 2 Cor. 5.10; 2 Tim. 4.1)

We believe in the Holy Spirit, the Lord and life-giver,
    (Gen. 1.1-2; Job 33.4; Ps. 104.30; 139.7-8; Luke 4.18-19; John 3.5-6; Acts 1.1-2; 1 Cor. 2.11; Rev. 3.22)
    who proceeds from the Father and the Son,   *(John 14.16-18, 26; 15.26; 20.22)*
    who together with the Father and Son
    is worshiped and glorified,   *(Isa. 6.3; Matt. 28.19; 2 Cor. 13.14; Rev. 4.8)*
    who spoke by the prophets.   *(Num. 11.29; Mic. 3.8; Acts 2.17-18; 2 Pet. 1.21)*

We believe in one holy, catholic, and apostolic Church.
    (Matt. 16.18; Eph. 5.25-28; 1 Cor. 1.2; 10.17; 1 Tim. 3.15; Rev. 7.9)

We acknowledge one baptism for the forgiveness of sin,   *(Acts 22.16; 1 Pet. 3.21; Eph. 4.4-5)*
    And we look for the resurrection of the dead
    And the life of the age to come.   *(Isa. 11.6-10; Mic. 4.1-7; Luke 18.29-30; Rev. 21.1-5; 21.22-22.5)*

Amen.

APPENDIX 2

We Believe: Confession of the Nicene Creed (8.7.8.7. meter*)

Rev. Dr. Don L. Davis, 2007. All Rights Reserved.

* This song is adapted from the Nicene Creed, and set to 8.7.8.7. meter, meaning it can be sung to tunes of the same meter, such as: Joyful, Joyful, We Adore Thee; I Will Sing of My Redeemer; What a Friend We Have in Jesus; Come, Thou Long Expected Jesus

Father God Almighty rules, the Maker of both earth and heav'n.
All things seen and those unseen, by him were made, by him were giv'n!
We believe in Jesus Christ, the Lord, God's one and only Son,
Begotten, not created, too, he and our Father God are one!

Begotten from the Father, same, in essence, as both God and Light;
Through him by God all things were made, in him all things were giv'n life.
Who for us all, for our salvation, did come down from heav'n to earth,
Incarnate by the Spirit's pow'r, and through the Virgin Mary's birth.

Who for us too, was crucified, by Pontius Pilate's rule and hand,
Suffered, and was buried, yet on the third day, he rose again.
According to the Sacred Scriptures all that happ'ned was meant to be.
Ascended high to God's right hand, in heav'n he sits in glory.

Christ will come again in glory to judge all those alive and dead.
His Kingdom rule shall never end, for he will rule and reign as Head.
We worship God, the Holy Spirit, Lord and the Life-giver known;
With Fath'r and Son is glorified, Who by the prophets ever spoke.

And we believe in one true Church, God's holy people for all time,
Cath'lic in its scope and broadness, built on the Apostles' line!
Acknowledging that one baptism, for forgiv'ness of our sin,
And we look for Resurrection, for the dead shall live again.

Looking for unending days, the life of the bright Age to come,
When Christ's Reign shall come to earth, the will of God shall then be done!
Praise to God, and to Christ Jesus, to the Spirit–triune Lord!
We confess the ancient teachings, clinging to God's holy Word!

APPENDIX 3
The Story of God: Our Sacred Roots
Rev. Dr. Don L. Davis

The Alpha and the Omega	Christus Victor	Come, Holy Spirit	Your Word Is Truth	The Great Confession	His Life in Us	Living in the Way	Reborn to Serve
The LORD God is the source, sustainer, and end of all things in the heavens and earth. All things were formed and exist by his will and for his eternal glory, the triune God, Father, Son, and Holy Spirit, Rom. 11.36.							
The Triune God's Unfolding Drama God's Self-Revelation in Creation, Israel, and Christ				**The Church's Participation in God's Unfolding Drama** Fidelity to the Apostolic Witness to Christ and His Kingdom			
The Objective Foundation: The Sovereign Love of God God's Narration of His Saving Work in Christ				**The Subjective Practice: Salvation by Grace through Faith** The Redeemed's Joyous Response to God's Saving Work in Christ			
The Author of the Story	*The Champion of the Story*	*The Interpreter of the Story*	*The Testimony of the Story*	*The People of the Story*	*Re-enactment of the Story*	*Embodiment of the Story*	*Continuation of the Story*
The Father as Director	Jesus as Lead Actor	The Spirit as Narrator	Scripture as Script	As Saints, Confessors	As Worshipers, Ministers	As Followers, Sojourners	As Servants, Ambassadors
Christian Worldview	Communal Identity	Spiritual Experience	Biblical Authority	Orthodox Theology	Priestly Worship	Congregational Discipleship	Kingdom Witness
Theistic and Trinitarian Vision	Christ-centered Foundation	Spirit-Indwelt and -Filled Community	Canonical and Apostolic Witness	Ancient Creedal Affirmation of Faith	Weekly Gathering in Christian Assembly	Corporate, Ongoing Spiritual Formation	Active Agents of the Reign of God
Sovereign Willing	Messianic Representing	Divine Comforting	Inspired Testifying	Truthful Retelling	Joyful Excelling	Faithful Indwelling	Hopeful Compelling
Creator True Maker of the Cosmos	Recapitulation Typos and Fulfillment of the Covenant	Life-Giver Regeneration and Adoption	Divine Inspiration God-breathed Word	The Confession of Faith Union with Christ	Song and Celebration Historical Recitation	Pastoral Oversight Shepherding the Flock	Explicit Unity Love for the Saints
Owner Sovereign Disposer of Creation	Revealer Incarnation of the Word	Teacher Illuminator of the Truth	Sacred History Historical Record	Baptism into Christ Communion of Saints	Homilies and Teachings Prophetic Proclamation	Shared Spirituality Common Journey through the Spiritual Disciplines	Radical Hospitality Evidence of God's Kingdom Reign
Ruler Blessed Controller of All Things	Redeemer Reconciler of All Things	Helper Endowment and the Power	Biblical Theology Divine Commentary	The Rule of Faith Apostles' Creed and Nicene Creed	The Lord's Supper Dramatic Re-enactment	Embodiment Anamnesis and Prolepsis through the Church Year	Extravagant Generosity Good Works
Covenant Keeper Faithful Promisor	Restorer Christ, the Victor over the powers of evil	Guide Divine Presence and Shekinah	Spiritual Food Sustenance for the Journey	The Vincentian Canon Ubiquity, antiquity, universality	Eschatological Foreshadowing The Already/Not Yet	Effective Discipling Spiritual Formation in the Believing Assembly	Evangelical Witness Making Disciples of All People Groups

APPENDIX 4
The Theology of Christus Victor
A Christ-Centered Biblical Motif for Integrating and Renewing the Urban Church
Rev. Dr. Don L. Davis

	The Promised Messiah	The Word Made Flesh	The Son of Man	The Suffering Servant	The Lamb of God	The Victorious Conqueror	The Reigning Lord in Heaven	The Bridegroom and Coming King
Biblical Framework	Israel's hope of Yahweh's anointed who would redeem his people	In the person of Jesus of Nazareth, the Lord has come to the world	As the promised king and divine Son of Man, Jesus reveals the Father's glory and salvation to the world	As Inaugurator of the Kingdom of God, Jesus demonstrates God's reign present through his words, wonders, and works	As both High Priest and Paschal Lamb, Jesus offers himself to God on our behalf as a sacrifice for sin	In his resurrection from the dead and ascension to God's right hand, Jesus is proclaimed as Victor over the power of sin and death	Now reigning at God's right hand till his enemies are made his footstool, Jesus pours out his benefits on his body	Soon the risen and ascended Lord will return to gather his Bride, the Church, and consummate his work
Scripture References	Isa. 9.6-7￼Jer. 23.5-6￼Isa. 11.1-10	John 1.14-18￼Matt. 1.20-23￼Phil. 2.6-8	Matt. 2.1-11￼Num. 24.17￼Luke 1.78-79	Mark 1.14-15￼Matt. 12.25-30￼Luke 17.20-21	2 Cor. 5.18-21￼Isa. 52-53￼John 1.29	Eph. 1.16-23￼Phil. 2.5-11￼Col. 1.15-20	1 Cor. 15.25￼Eph. 4.15-16￼Acts. 2.32-36	Rom. 14.7-9￼Rev. 5.9-13￼1 Thess. 4.13-18
Jesus' History	The pre-incarnate, only begotten Son of God in glory	His conception by the Spirit, and birth to Mary	His manifestation to the Magi and to the world	His teaching, exorcisms, miracles, and mighty works among the people	His suffering, crucifixion, death, and burial	His resurrection, with appearances to his witnesses, and his ascension to the Father	The sending of the Holy Spirit and his gifts, and Christ's session in heaven at the Father's right hand	His soon return from heaven to earth as Lord and Christ: the Second Coming
Description	The biblical promise for the seed of Abraham, the prophet like Moses, the son of David	In the Incarnation, God has come to us; Jesus reveals to humankind the Father's glory in fullness	In Jesus, God has shown his salvation to the entire world, including the Gentiles	In Jesus, the promised Kingdom of God has come visibly to earth, demonstrating his binding of Satan and rescinding the Curse	As God's perfect Lamb, Jesus offers himself up to God as a sin offering on behalf of the entire world	In his resurrection and ascension, Jesus destroyed death, disarmed Satan, and rescinded the Curse	Jesus is installed at the Father's right hand as Head of the Church, Firstborn from the dead, and supreme Lord in heaven	As we labor in his harvest field in the world, so we await Christ's return, the fulfillment of his promise
Church Year	Advent	Christmas	Season after Epiphany￼Baptism and Transfiguration	Lent	Holy Week￼Passion	Eastertide￼Easter, Ascension Day, Pentecost	Season after Pentecost￼Trinity Sunday	Season after Pentecost￼All Saints Day, Reign of Christ the King
	The Coming of Christ	*The Birth of Christ*	*The Manifestation of Christ*	*The Ministry of Christ*	*The Suffering and Death of Christ*	*The Resurrection and Ascension of Christ*	*The Heavenly Session of Christ*	*The Reign of Christ*
Spiritual Formation	As we await his Coming, let us proclaim and affirm the hope of Christ	O Word made flesh, let us every heart prepare him room to dwell	Divine Son of Man, show the nations your salvation and glory	In the person of Christ, the power of the reign of God has come to earth and to the Church	May those who share the Lord's death be resurrected with him	Let us participate by faith in the victory of Christ over the power of sin, Satan, and death	Come, indwell us, Holy Spirit, and empower us to advance Christ's Kingdom in the world	We live and work in expectation of his soon return, seeking to please him in all things

APPENDIX 5
Christus Victor
An Integrated Vision for the Christian Life
Rev. Dr. Don L. Davis

For the Church
- The Church is the primary extension of Jesus in the world
- Ransomed treasure of the victorious, risen Christ
- *Laos:* The people of God
- God's new creation: presence of the future
- Locus and agent of the Already/Not Yet Kingdom

For Theology and Doctrine
- The authoritative Word of Christ's victory: the Apostolic Tradition: the Holy Scriptures
- Theology as commentary on the grand narrative of God
- *Christus Victor* as core theological framework for meaning in the world
- The Nicene Creed: the Story of God's triumphant grace

For Spirituality
- The Holy Spirit's presence and power in the midst of God's people
- Sharing in the disciplines of the Spirit
- Gatherings, lectionary, liturgy, and our observances in the Church Year
- Living the life of the risen Christ in the rhythm of our ordinary lives

For Gifts
- God's gracious endowments and benefits from *Christus Victor*
- Pastoral offices to the Church
- The Holy Spirit's sovereign dispensing of the gifts
- Stewardship: divine, diverse gifts for the common good

Christus Victor
Destroyer of Evil and Death
Restorer of Creation
Victor o'er Hades and Sin
Crusher of Satan

For Worship
- People of the Resurrection: unending celebration of the people of God
- Remembering, participating in the Christ event in our worship
- Listen and respond to the Word
- Transformed at the Table, the Lord's Supper
- The presence of the Father through the Son in the Spirit

For Evangelism and Mission
- Evangelism as unashamed declaration and demonstration of *Christus Victor* to the world
- The Gospel as Good News of kingdom pledge
- We proclaim God's Kingdom come in the person of Jesus of Nazareth
- The Great Commission: go to all people groups making disciples of Christ and his Kingdom
- Proclaiming Christ as Lord and Messiah

For Justice and Compassion
- The gracious and generous expressions of Jesus through the Church
- The Church displays the very life of the Kingdom
- The Church demonstrates the very life of the Kingdom of heaven right here and now
- Having freely received, we freely give (no sense of merit or pride)
- Justice as tangible evidence of the Kingdom come

APPENDIX 6
Old Testament Witness to Christ and His Kingdom
Rev. Dr. Don L. Davis

Christ Is Seen in the OT's:	Covenant Promise and Fulfillment	Moral Law	Christophanies	Typology	Tabernacle, Festival, and Levitical Priesthood	Messianic Prophecy	Salvation Promises
Passage	Gen. 12.1-3	Matt. 5.17-18	John 1.18	1 Cor. 15.45	Heb. 8.1-6	Mic. 5.2	Isa. 9.6-7
Example	The Promised Seed of the Abrahamic covenant	The Law given on Mount Sinai	Commander of the Lord's army	Jonah and the great fish	Melchizedek, as both High Priest and King	The Lord's Suffering Servant	Righteous Branch of David
Christ As	Seed of the woman	The Prophet of God	God's present Revelation	Antitype of God's drama	Our eternal High Priest	The coming Son of Man	Israel's Redeemer and King
Where Illustrated	Galatians	Matthew	John	Matthew	Hebrews	Luke and Acts	John and Revelation
Exegetical Goal	To see Christ as heart of God's sacred drama	To see Christ as fulfillment of the Law	To see Christ as God's revealer	To see Christ as antitype of divine typos	To see Christ in the Temple *cultus*	To see Christ as true Messiah	To see Christ as coming King
How Seen in the NT	As fulfillment of God's sacred oath	As *telos* of the Law	As full, final, and superior revelation	As substance behind the historical shadows	As reality behind the rules and roles	As the Kingdom made present	As the One who will rule on David's throne
Our Response in Worship	God's veracity and faithfulness	God's perfect righteousness	God's presence among us	God's inspired Scripture	God's ontology: his realm as primary and determinative	God's anointed servant and mediator	God's resolve to restore his kingdom authority
How God Is Vindicated	God does not lie: he's true to his word	Jesus fulfills all righteousness	God's fulness is revealed to us in Jesus of Nazareth	The Spirit spoke by the prophets	The Lord has provided a mediator for humankind	Every jot and tittle written of him will occur	Evil will be put down, creation restored, under his reign

APPENDIX 7
Summary Outline of the Scriptures
Rev. Dr. Don L. Davis

1. GENESIS - Beginnings
   a. Adam
   b. Noah
   c. Abraham
   d. Isaac
   e. Jacob
   f. Joseph

2. EXODUS - Redemption, (out of)
   a. Slavery
   b. Deliverance
   c. Law
   d. Tabernacle

3. LEVITICUS - Worship and Fellowship
   a. Offerings, sacrifices
   b. Priests
   c. Feasts, festivals

4. NUMBERS - Service and Walk
   a. Organized
   b. Wanderings

5. DEUTERONOMY - Obedience
   a. Moses reviews history and law
   b. Civil and social laws
   c. Palestinian Covenant
   d. Moses' blessing and death

6. JOSHUA - Redemption (into)
   a. Conquer the land
   b. Divide up the land
   c. Joshua's farewell

7. JUDGES - God's Deliverance
   a. Disobedience and judgment
   b. Israel's twelve judges
   c. Lawless conditions

8. RUTH - Love
   a. Ruth chooses
   b. Ruth works
   c. Ruth waits
   d. Ruth rewarded

9. 1 SAMUEL - Kings, Priestly Perspective
   a. Eli
   b. Samuel
   c. Saul
   d. David

10. 2 SAMUEL - David
    a. King of Judah (9 years - Hebron)
    b. King of all Israel (33 years - Jerusalem)

11. 1 KINGS - Solomon's Glory, Kingdom's Decline
    a. Solomon's glory
    b. Kingdom's decline
    c. Elijah the prophet

12. 2 KINGS - Divided Kingdom
    a. Elisha
    b. Israel (N. Kingdom falls)
    c. Judah (S. Kingdom falls)

13. 1 CHRONICLES - David's Temple Arrangements
    a. Genealogies
    b. End of Saul's reign
    c. Reign of David
    d. Temple preparations

14. 2 CHRONICLES - Temple and Worship Abandoned
    a. Solomon
    b. Kings of Judah

15. EZRA - The Minority (Remnant)
    a. First return from exile - Zerubbabel
    b. Second return from exile - Ezra (priest)

16. NEHEMIAH - Rebuilding by Faith
    a. Rebuild walls
    b. Revival
    c. Religious reform

17. ESTHER - Female Savior
    a. Esther
    b. Haman
    c. Mordecai
    d. Deliverance: Feast of Purim

18. JOB - Why the Righteous Suffer
    a. Godly Job
    b. Satan's attack
    c. Four philosophical friends
    d. God lives

19. PSALMS - Prayer and Praise
    a. Prayers of David
    b. Godly suffer; deliverance
    c. God deals with Israel
    d. Suffering of God's people - end with the Lord's reign
    e. The Word of God (Messiah's suffering and glorious return)

20. PROVERBS - Wisdom
    a. Wisdom versus folly
    b. Solomon
    c. Solomon - Hezekiah
    d. Agur
    e. Lemuel

21. ECCLESIASTES - Vanity
    a. Experimentation
    b. Observation
    c. Consideration

22. SONG OF SOLOMON - Love Story

23. ISAIAH - The Justice (Judgment) and Grace (Comfort) of God
    a. Prophecies of punishment
    b. History
    c. Prophecies of blessing

24. JEREMIAH - Judah's Sin Leads to Babylonian Captivity
    a. Jeremiah's call; empowered
    b. Judah condemned; predicted Babylonian captivity
    c. Restoration promised
    d. Prophesied judgment inflicted
    e. Prophesies against Gentiles
    f. Summary of Judah's captivity

25. LAMENTATIONS - Lament over Jerusalem
    a. Affliction of Jerusalem
    b. Destroyed because of sin
    c. The prophet's suffering
    d. Present desolation versus past splendor
    e. Appeal to God for mercy

26. EZEKIEL - Israel's Captivity and Restoration
    a. Judgment on Judah and Jerusalem
    b. Judgment on Gentile nations
    c. Israel restored; Jerusalem's future glory

27. DANIEL - The Time of the Gentiles
    a. History; Nebuchadnezzar, Belshazzar, Daniel
    b. Prophecy

28. HOSEA - Unfaithfulness
    a. Unfaithfulness
    b. Punishment
    c. Restoration

29. JOEL - The Day of the Lord
    a. Locust plague
    b. Events of the future day of the Lord
    c. Order of the future day of the Lord

30. AMOS - God Judges Sin
    a. Neighbors judged
    b. Israel judged
    c. Visions of future judgment
    d. Israel's past judgment blessings

31. OBADIAH - Edom's Destruction
    a. Destruction prophesied
    b. Reasons for destruction
    c. Israel's future blessing

32. JONAH - Gentile Salvation
    a. Jonah disobeys
    b. Other suffer
    c. Jonah punished
    d. Jonah obeys; thousands saved
    e. Jonah displeased, no love for souls

33. MICAH - Israel's Sins, Judgment, and Restoration
    a. Sin and judgment
    b. Grace and future restoration
    c. Appeal and petition

34. NAHUM - Nineveh Condemned
    a. God hates sin
    b. Nineveh's doom prophesied
    c. Reasons for doom

35. HABAKKUK - The Just Shall Live by Faith
    a. Complaint of Judah's unjudged sin
    b. Chaldeans will punish
    c. Complaint of Chaldeans' wickedness
    d. Punishment promised
    e. Prayer for revival; faith in God

36. ZEPHANIAH - Babylonian Invasion Prefigures the Day of the Lord
    a. Judgment on Judah foreshadows the Great Day of the Lord
    b. Judgment on Jerusalem and neighbors foreshadows final judgment of all nations
    c. Israel restored after judgments

37. HAGGAI - Rebuild the Temple
    a. Negligence
    b. Courage
    c. Separation
    d. Judgment

38. ZECHARIAH - Two Comings of Christ
    a. Zechariah's vision
    b. Bethel's question; Jehovah's answer
    c. Nation's downfall and salvation

39. MALACHI - Neglect
    a. The priest's sins
    b. The people's sins
    c. The faithful few

Summary Outline of the Scriptures (continued)

1. MATTHEW - Jesus the King
   a. The Person of the King
   b. The Preparation of the King
   c. The Propaganda of the King
   d. The Program of the King
   e. The Passion of the King
   f. The Power of the King

2. MARK - Jesus the Servant
   a. John introduces the Servant
   b. God the Father identifies the Servant
   c. The temptation initiates the Servant
   d. Work and word of the Servant
   e. Death, burial, resurrection

3. LUKE - Jesus Christ the Perfect Man
   a. Birth and family of the Perfect Man
   b. Testing of the Perfect Man; hometown
   c. Ministry of the Perfect Man
   d. Betrayal, trial, and death of the Perfect Man
   e. Resurrection of the Perfect Man

4. JOHN - Jesus Christ is God
   a. Prologue - the Incarnation
   b. Introduction
   c. Witness of Jesus to his Apostles
   d. Passion - witness to the world
   e. Epilogue

5. ACTS - The Holy Spirit Working in the Church
   a. The Lord Jesus at work by the Holy Spirit through the Apostles at Jerusalem
   b. In Judea and Samaria
   c. To the uttermost parts of the Earth

6. ROMANS - The Righteousness of God
   a. Salutation
   b. Sin and salvation
   c. Sanctification
   d. Struggle
   e. Spirit-filled living
   f. Security of salvation
   g. Segregation
   h. Sacrifice and service
   i. Separation and salutation

7. 1 CORINTHIANS - The Lordship of Christ
   a. Salutation and thanksgiving
   b. Conditions in the Corinthian body
   c. Concerning the Gospel
   d. Concerning collections

8. 2 CORINTHIANS - The Ministry in the Church
   a. The comfort of God
   b. Collection for the poor
   c. Calling of the Apostle Paul

9. GALATIANS - Justification by Faith
   a. Introduction
   b. Personal - Authority of the Apostle and glory of the Gospel
   c. Doctrinal - Justification by faith
   d. Practical - Sanctification by the Holy Spirit
   e. Autographed conclusion and exhortation

10. EPHESIANS - The Church of Jesus Christ
    a. Doctrinal - the heavenly calling of the Church
       A Body
       A Temple
       A Mystery
    b. Practical - The earthly conduct of the Church
       A New Man
       A Bride
       An Army

11. PHILIPPIANS - Joy in the Christian Life
    a. Philosophy for Christian living
    b. Pattern for Christian living
    c. Prize for Christian living
    d. Power for Christian living

12. COLOSSIANS - Christ the Fullness of God
    a. Doctrinal - In Christ believers are made full
    b. Practical - Christ's life poured out in believers, and through them

13. 1 THESSALONIANS - The Second Coming of Christ:
    a. Is an inspiring hope
    b. Is a working hope
    c. Is a purifying hope
    d. Is a comforting hope
    e. Is a rousing, stimulating hope

14. 2 THESSALONIANS - The Second Coming of Christ
    a. Persecution of believers now; judgment of unbelievers hereafter (at coming of Christ)
    b. Program of the world in connection with the coming of Christ
    c. Practical issues associated with the coming of Christ

15. 1 TIMOTHY - Government and Order in the Local Church
    a. The faith of the Church
    b. Public prayer and women's place in the Church
    c. Officers in the Church
    d. Apostasy in the Church
    e. Duties of the officer of the Church

16. 2 TIMOTHY - Loyalty in the Days of Apostasy
    a. Afflictions of the Gospel
    b. Active in service
    c. Apostasy coming; authority of the Scriptures
    d. Allegiance to the Lord

17. TITUS - The Ideal New Testament Church
    a. The Church is an organization
    b. The Church is to teach and preach the Word of God
    c. The Church is to perform good works

18. PHILEMON - Reveal Christ's Love and Teach Brotherly Love
    a. Genial greeting to Philemon and family
    b. Good reputation of Philemon
    c. Gracious plea for Onesimus
    d. Guiltless illustration of Imputation
    e. General and personal requests

19. HEBREWS - The Superiority of Christ
    a. Doctrinal - Christ is better than the Old Testament economy
    b. Practical - Christ brings better benefits and duties

20. JAMES - Ethics of Christianity
    a. Faith tested
    b. Difficulty of controlling the tongue
    c. Warning against worldliness
    d. Admonitions in view of the Lord's coming

21. 1 PETER - Christian Hope in the Time of Persecution and Trial
    a. Suffering and security of believers
    b. Suffering and the Scriptures
    c. Suffering and the sufferings of Christ
    d. Suffering and the Second Coming of Christ

22. 2 PETER - Warning Against False Teachers
    a. Addition of Christian graces gives assurance
    b. Authority of the Scriptures
    c. Apostasy brought in by false testimony
    d. Attitude toward Return of Christ: test for apostasy
    e. Agenda of God in the world
    f. Admonition to believers

23. 1 JOHN - The Family of God
    a. God is Light
    b. God is Love
    c. God is Life

24. 2 JOHN - Warning against Receiving Deceivers
    a. Walk in truth
    b. Love one another
    c. Receive not deceivers
    d. Find joy in fellowship

25. 3 JOHN - Admonition to Receive True Believers
    a. Gaius, brother in the Church
    b. Diotrephes
    c. Demetrius

26. JUDE - Contending for the Faith
    a. Occasion of the epistle
    b. Occurrences of apostasy
    c. Occupation of believers in the days of apostasy

27. REVELATION - The Unveiling of Christ Glorified
    a. The person of Christ in glory
    b. The possession of Jesus Christ - the Church in the World
    c. The program of Jesus Christ - the scene in Heaven
    d. The seven seals
    e. The seven trumpets
    f. Important persons in the last days
    g. The seven vials
    h. The fall of Babylon
    i. The eternal state

APPENDIX 8

From Before to Beyond Time:
The Plan of God and Human History

Adapted from: Suzanne de Dietrich. ***God's Unfolding Purpose****. Philadelphia: Westminster Press, 1976.*

I. Before Time (Eternity Past) 1 Cor. 2.7
   A. The Eternal Triune God
   B. God's Eternal Purpose
   C. The Mystery of Iniquity
   D. The Principalities and Powers

II. Beginning of Time (Creation and Fall) Gen. 1.1
   A. Creative Word
   B. Humanity
   C. Fall
   D. Reign of Death and First Signs of Grace

III. Unfolding of Time (God's Plan Revealed Through Israel) Gal. 3.8
   A. Promise (Patriarchs)
   B. Exodus and Covenant at Sinai
   C. Promised Land
   D. The City, the Temple, and the Throne (Prophet, Priest, and King)
   E. Exile
   F. Remnant

IV. Fullness of Time (Incarnation of the Messiah) Gal. 4.4-5
   A. The King Comes to His Kingdom
   B. The Present Reality of His Reign
   C. The Secret of the Kingdom: the Already and the Not Yet
   D. The Crucified King
   E. The Risen Lord

V. The Last Times (The Descent of the Holy Spirit) Acts 2.16-18
   A. Between the Times: the Church as Foretaste of the Kingdom
   B. The Church as Agent of the Kingdom
   C. The Conflict Between the Kingdoms of Darkness and Light

VI. The Fulfillment of Time (The Second Coming) Matt. 13.40-43
   A. The Return of Christ
   B. Judgment
   C. The Consummation of His Kingdom

VII. Beyond Time (Eternity Future) 1 Cor. 15.24-28
   A. Kingdom Handed Over to God the Father
   B. God as All in All

From Before to Beyond Time
Scriptures for Major Outline Points

I. Before Time (Eternity Past)

1 Cor. 2.7 (ESV) - But we impart a secret and hidden wisdom of God, *which God decreed before the ages* for our glory (cf. Titus 1.2).

II. Beginning of Time (Creation and Fall)

Gen. 1.1 (ESV) - *In the beginning*, God created the heavens and the earth.

III. Unfolding of Time (God's Plan Revealed Through Israel)

Gal. 3.8 (ESV) - And the Scripture, foreseeing that God would justify the Gentiles by faith, *preached the Gospel beforehand to Abraham*, saying, "In you shall all the nations be blessed" (cf. Rom. 9.4-5).

IV. Fullness of Time (The Incarnation of the Messiah)

Gal. 4.4-5 (ESV) - *But when the fullness of time had come*, God sent forth his Son, born of woman, born under the law, to redeem those who were under the law, so that we might receive adoption as sons.

V. The Last Times (The Descent of the Holy Spirit)

Acts 2.16-18 (ESV) - But this is what was uttered through the prophet Joel: "'*And in the last days it shall be*,' God declares, 'that I will pour out my Spirit on all flesh, and your sons and your daughters shall prophesy, and your young men shall see visions, and your old men shall dream dreams; even on my male servants and female servants in those days I will pour out my Spirit, and they shall prophesy.'"

VI. The Fulfillment of Time (The Second Coming)

Matt. 13.40-43 (ESV) - Just as the weeds are gathered and burned with fire, *so will it be at the close of the age*. The Son of Man will send his angels, and they will gather out of his kingdom all causes of sin and all lawbreakers, and throw them into the fiery furnace. In that place there will be weeping and gnashing of teeth. Then the righteous will shine like the sun in the Kingdom of their Father. He who has ears, let him hear.

VII. Beyond Time (Eternity Future)

1 Cor. 15.24-28 (ESV) - Then comes the end, when he delivers the Kingdom to God the Father after destroying every rule and every authority and power. For he must reign until he has put all his enemies under his feet. The last enemy to be destroyed is death. For "God has put all things in subjection under his feet." But when it says, "all things are put in subjection," it is plain that he is excepted who put all things in subjection under him. When all things are subjected to him, then the Son himself will also be subjected to him who put all things in subjection under him, that God may be all in all.

APPENDIX 9
"There Is a River"
Identifying the Streams of a Revitalized Authentic Christian Community in the City[1]
Rev. Dr. Don L. Davis • Psalm 46.4 (ESV) - There is a river whose streams make glad the city of God, the holy habitation of the Most High.

Tributaries of Authentic Historic Biblical Faith			
Recognized Biblical Identity	*Revived Urban Spirituality*	*Reaffirmed Historical Connectivity*	*Refocused Kingdom Authority*
The Church Is **One**	The Church Is **Holy**	The Church Is **Catholic**	The Church Is **Apostolic**
A Call to Biblical Fidelity *Recognizing the Scriptures as the anchor and foundation of the Christian faith and practice*	A Call to the Freedom, Power, and Fullness of the Holy Spirit *Walking in the holiness, power, gifting, and liberty of the Holy Spirit in the body of Christ*	A Call to Historic Roots and Continuity *Confessing the common historical identity and continuity of authentic Christian faith*	A Call to the Apostolic Faith *Affirming the apostolic tradition as the authoritative ground of the Christian hope*
A Call to Messianic Kingdom Identity *Rediscovering the story of the promised Messiah and his Kingdom in Jesus of Nazareth*	A Call to Live as Sojourners and Aliens as the People of God *Defining authentic Christian discipleship as faithful membership among God's people*	A Call to Affirm and Express the Global Communion of Saints *Expressing cooperation and collaboration with all other believers, both local and global*	A Call to Representative Authority *Submitting joyfully to God's gifted servants in the Church as undershepherds of true faith*
A Call to Creedal Affinity *Embracing the Nicene Creed as the shared rule of faith of historic orthodoxy*	A Call to Liturgical, Sacramental, and Catechetical Vitality *Experiencing God's presence in the context of the Word, sacrament, and instruction*	A Call to Radical Hospitality and Good Works *Expressing kingdom love to all, and especially to those of the household of faith*	A Call to Prophetic and Holistic Witness *Proclaiming Christ and his Kingdom in word and deed to our neighbors and all peoples*

[1] *This schema is an adaptation and is based on the insights of the* **Chicago Call** *statement of May 1977, where various leading evangelical scholars and practitioners met to discuss the relationship of modern evangelicalism to the historic Christian faith.*

APPENDIX 10

A Schematic for a Theology of the Kingdom and the Church

The Urban Ministry Institute

The Reign of the One, True, Sovereign, and Triune God, the LORD God, Yahweh, God the Father, Son, and Holy Spirit

	The Father	**The Son**	**The Spirit**
	Love - 1 John 4.8 Maker of heaven and earth and of all things visible and invisible	Faith - Heb. 12.2 Prophet, Priest, and King	Hope - Rom. 15.13 Lord of the Church
	Creation All that exists through the creative action of God.	**Kingdom** The Reign of God expressed in the rule of his Son Jesus the Messiah.	**Church** The one, holy, apostolic community which functions as a witness to (Acts 28.31) and a foretaste of (Col. 1.12; James 1.18; 1 Pet. 2.9; Rev. 1.6) the Kingdom of God.
Rom. 8.18-21 →	The eternal God, sovereign in power, infinite in wisdom, perfect in holiness, and steadfast in love, is the source and goal of all things.	**Freedom** (Slavery) Jesus answered them, "Truly, truly, I say to you, everyone who commits sin is a slave to sin. The slave does not remain in the house forever; the son remains forever. So if the Son sets you free, you will be free indeed." - John 8.34-36 (ESV)	*The Church is an Apostolic Community Where the Word is Rightly Preached. Therefore it is a Community of:* **Calling** - For freedom Christ has set us free; stand firm therefore, and do not submit again to a yoke of slavery. - Gal. 5.1 (ESV) (cf. Rom. 8.28-30; 1 Cor. 1.26-31; Eph. 1.18; 2 Thess. 2.13-14; Jude 1.1) **Faith** - ". . . for unless you believe that I am he you will die in your sins". . . . So Jesus said to the Jews who had believed in him, "If you abide in my word, you are truly my disciples, and you will know the truth, and the truth will set you free." - John 8.24b, 31-32 (ESV) (cf. Ps. 119.45; Rom. 1.17; 5.1-2; Eph. 2.8-9; 2 Tim. 1.13-14; Heb. 2.14-15; James 1.25) **Witness** - The Spirit of the Lord is upon me, because he has anointed me to proclaim good news to the poor. He has sent me to proclaim liberty to the captives and recovering of sight to the blind, to set at liberty those who are oppressed, to proclaim the year of the Lord's favor. - Luke 4.18-19 (ESV) (cf. Lev. 25.10; Prov. 31.8; Matt. 4.17; 28.18-20; Mark 13.10; Acts 1.8; 8.4, 12; 13.1-3; 25.20; 28.30-31)
Rev. 21.1-5 →	O, the depth of the riches and wisdom and knowledge of God! How unsearchable are his judgments, and how inscrutable his ways! For who has known the mind of the Lord, or who has been his counselor? Or who has ever given a gift to him, that he might be repaid?" For from him and through him and to him are all things. To him be glory forever! Amen! - Rom. 11.33-36 (ESV) (cf. 1 Cor. 15.23-28; Rev.)	**Wholeness** (Sickness) But he was wounded for our transgressions; he was crushed for our iniquities; upon him was the chastisement that brought us peace, and with his stripes we are healed. - Isa. 53.5 (ESV)	*The Church is One Community Where the Sacraments are Rightly Administered. Therefore it is a Community of:* **Worship** - You shall serve the Lord your God, and he will bless your bread and your water, and I will take sickness away from among you. - Exod. 23.25 (ESV) (cf. Ps. 147.1-3; Heb. 12.28; Col. 3.16; Rev. 15.3-4; 19.5) **Covenant** - And the Holy Spirit also bears witness to us; for after saying, "This is the covenant that I will make with them after those days, declares the Lord: I will put my laws on their hearts, and write them on their minds," then he adds, "I will remember their sins and their lawless deeds no more." - Heb. 10.15-17 (ESV) (cf. Isa. 54.10-17; Ezek. 34.25-31; 37.26-27; Mal. 2.4-5; Luke 22.20; 2 Cor. 3.6; Col. 3.15; Heb. 8.7-13; 12.22-24; 13.20-21) **Presence** - In him you also are being built together into a dwelling place for God by his Spirit. - Eph. 2.22 (ESV) (cf. Exod. 40.34-38; Ezek. 48.35; Matt. 18.18-20)
Isa. 11.6-9 →		**Justice** (Selfishness) Behold, my servant whom I have chosen, my beloved with whom my soul is well pleased. I will put my Spirit upon him, and he will proclaim justice to the Gentiles. He will not quarrel or cry aloud, nor will anyone hear his voice in the streets; a bruised reed he will not break, and a smoldering wick he will not quench, until he brings justice to victory. - Matt. 12.18-20 (ESV)	*The Church is a Holy Community Where Discipline is Rightly Ordered. Therefore it is a Community of:* **Reconciliation** - For he himself is our peace, who has made us both one and has broken down in his flesh the dividing wall of hostility by abolishing the law of commandments and ordinances, that he might create in himself one new man in place of the two, so making peace, and might reconcile us both to God in one body through the cross, thereby killing the hostility. And he came and preached peace to you who were far off and peace to those who were near. For through him we both have access in one Spirit to the Father. - Eph. 2.14-18 (ESV) (cf. Exod. 23.4-9; Lev. 19.34; Deut. 10.18-19; Ezek. 22.29; Mic. 6.8; 2 Cor. 5.16-21) **Suffering** - Since therefore Christ suffered in the flesh, arm yourselves with the same way of thinking, for whoever has suffered in the flesh has ceased from sin, so as to live for the rest of the time in the flesh no longer for human passions but for the will of God. - 1 Pet. 4.1-2 (ESV) (cf. Luke 6.22; 10.3; Rom. 8.17; 2 Tim. 2.3; 3.12; 1 Pet. 2.20-24; Heb. 5.8; 13.11-14) **Service** - But Jesus called them to him and said, "You know that the rulers of the Gentiles lord it over them, and their great ones exercise authority over them. It shall not be so among you. But whoever would be great among you must be your servant, and whoever would be first among you must be your slave even as the Son of Man came not to be served but to serve, and to give his life as a ransom for many." - Matt. 20.25-28 (ESV) (cf. 1 John 4.16-18; Gal. 2.10)

APPENDIX 11
Living in the Already and the Not Yet Kingdom
Rev. Dr. Don L. Davis

The Spirit: The pledge of the inheritance (***arrabon***)
The Church: The foretaste (***aparche***) of the Kingdom
"In Christ": The rich life (***en Christos***) we share as citizens of the Kingdom

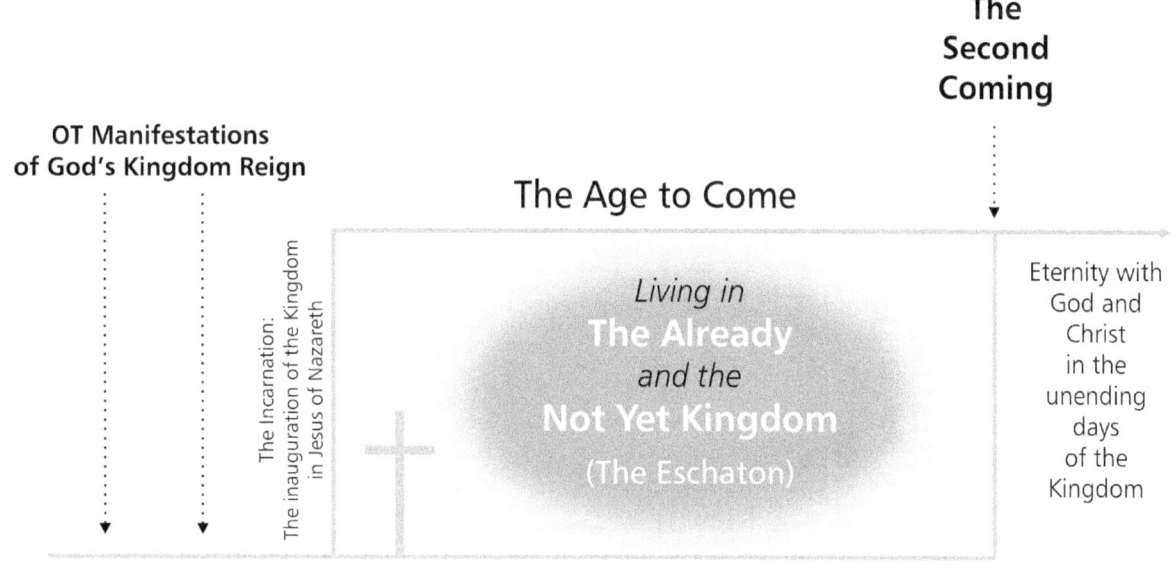

Internal enemy: The flesh (*sarx*) and the sin nature
External enemy: The world (*kosmos*) the systems of greed, lust, and pride
Infernal enemy: The devil (*kakos*) the animating spirit of falsehood and fear

Jewish View of Time

This Present Age   The Age to Come

The Coming of Messiah
The restoration of Israel
The end of Gentile oppression
The return of the earth to Edenic glory
Universal knowledge of the Lord

APPENDIX 12

Jesus of Nazareth: The Presence of the Future

Rev. Dr. Don L. Davis

Creation: The Reign of Almighty God

The Fall
- Creation
- Curse (Death)
- Slavery
- Selfishness
- Sickness

The Divine Promise
- Covenant
- Abraham
- Isaac
- Jacob
- Judah
- David

The Cross: The Center of Revelation and Redemption

- The Incarnation
- "The Kingdom is at hand!"
- Invasion of Satan's Dominion
- Rescinding of the Curse
- Emblems of the Age to Come
- Promise of the Holy Spirit
- Defeat of the Powers and Principalities

The Church
- The Spirit of God

Between the Times
- "The Age of the Spirit"
- Sign and Foretaste
- Prophetic Witness
- The Promise Fulfilled

- Church
- Consummation

Glorification: New Heavens and New Earth

APPENDIX 13

Traditions
(Paradosis)

Dr. Don L. Davis and Rev. Terry G. Cornett

Strong's Definition

Paradosis. Transmission, i.e. (concretely) a precept; specifically, the Jewish traditionary law

Vine's Explanation

denotes "a tradition," and hence, by metonymy, (a) "the teachings of the rabbis," . . . (b) "apostolic teaching," . . . of instructions concerning the gatherings of believers, of Christian doctrine in general . . . of instructions concerning everyday conduct.

1. **The concept of tradition in Scripture is essentially positive.**

   Jer. 6.16 (ESV) - Thus says the Lord: "Stand by the roads, and look, and ask for the ancient paths, where the good way is; and walk in it, and find rest for your souls. But they said, 'We will not walk in it'" (cf. Exod. 3.15; Judg. 2.17; 1 Kings 8.57-58; Ps. 78.1-6).

   2 Chron. 35.25 (ESV) - Jeremiah also uttered a lament for Josiah; and all the singing men and singing women have spoken of Josiah in their laments to this day. They made these a rule in Israel; behold, they are written in the Laments (cf. Gen. 32.32; Judg. 11.38-40).

   Jer. 35.14-19 (ESV) - The command that Jonadab the son of Rechab gave to his sons, to drink no wine, has been kept, and they drink none to this day, for they have obeyed their father's command. I have spoken to you persistently, but you have not listened to me. I have sent to you all my servants the prophets, sending them persistently, saying, 'Turn now every one of you from his evil way, and amend your deeds, and do not go after other gods to serve them, and then you shall dwell in the land that I gave to you and your fathers.' But you did not incline your ear or listen to me. The sons of Jonadab the son of Rechab have kept the command that their father gave them, but this people has not obeyed me. Therefore, thus says the

Traditions (continued)

Lord, the God of hosts, the God of Israel: Behold, I am bringing upon Judah and all the inhabitants of Jerusalem all the disaster that I have pronounced against them, because I have spoken to them and they have not listened, I have called to them and they have not answered." But to the house of the Rechabites Jeremiah said, "Thus says the Lord of hosts, the God of Israel: Because you have obeyed the command of Jonadab your father and kept all his precepts and done all that he commanded you, therefore thus says the Lord of hosts, the God of Israel: Jonadab the son of Rechab shall never lack a man to stand before me."

2. **Godly tradition is a wonderful thing, but not all tradition is godly.**

   Any individual tradition must be judged by its faithfulness to the Word of God and its usefulness in helping people maintain obedience to Christ's example and teaching.[1] In the Gospels, Jesus frequently rebukes the Pharisees for establishing traditions that nullify rather than uphold God's commands.

   Mark 7.8 (ESV) - You leave the commandment of God and hold to the tradition of men" (cf. Matt. 15.2-6; Mark 7.13).

   Col. 2.8 (ESV) - See to it that no one takes you captive by philosophy and empty deceit, according to human tradition, according to the elemental spirits of the world, and not according to Christ.

3. **Without the fullness of the Holy Spirit, and the constant edification provided to us by the Word of God, tradition will inevitably lead to dead formalism.**

   Those who are spiritual are filled with the Holy Spirit, whose power and leading alone provides individuals and congregations a sense of freedom and vitality in all they practice and believe. However, when the practices and teachings of any given tradition are no longer infused by the power of the Holy Spirit and the Word of God, tradition loses its effectiveness, and may actually become counterproductive to our discipleship in Jesus Christ.

   Eph. 5.18 (ESV) - And do not get drunk with wine, for that is debauchery, but be filled with the Spirit.

---

[1] "All Protestants insist that these traditions must ever be tested against Scripture and can never possess an independent apostolic authority over or alongside of Scripture." (J. Van Engen, "Tradition," *Evangelical Dictionary of Theology*, Walter Elwell, Gen. ed.) We would add that Scripture is itself the "authoritative tradition" by which all other traditions are judged. See "Appendix A, The Founders of Tradition: Three Levels of Christian Authority," p. 4.

Traditions (continued)

> Gal. 5.22-25 (ESV) - But the fruit of the Spirit is love, joy, peace, patience, kindness, goodness, faithfulness, gentleness, self-control; against such things there is no law. And those who belong to Christ Jesus have crucified the flesh with its passions and desires. If we live by the Spirit, let us also walk by the Spirit.

> 2 Cor. 3.5-6 (ESV) - Not that we are sufficient in ourselves to claim anything as coming from us, but our sufficiency is from God, who has made us competent to be ministers of a new covenant, not of the letter but of the Spirit. For the letter kills, but the Spirit gives life.

4. **Fidelity to the Apostolic Tradition (teaching and modeling) is the essence of Christian maturity.**

   > 2 Tim. 2.2 (ESV) - and what you have heard from me in the presence of many witnesses entrust to faithful men who will be able to teach others also.

   > 1 Cor. 11.1-2 (ESV) - Be imitators of me, as I am of Christ. Now I commend you because you remember me in everything and maintain the traditions even as I delivered them to you (cf. 1 Cor. 4.16-17, 2 Tim. 1.13-14, 2 Thess. 3.7-9, Phil. 4.9).

   > 1 Cor. 15.3-8 (ESV) - For I delivered to you as of first importance what I also received: that Christ died for our sins in accordance with the Scriptures, that he was buried, that he was raised on the third day in accordance with the Scriptures, and that he appeared to Cephas, then to the twelve. Then he appeared to more than five hundred brothers at one time, most of whom are still alive, though some have fallen asleep. Then he appeared to James, then to all the apostles. Last of all, as to one untimely born, he appeared also to me.

5. **The Apostle Paul often includes an appeal to the tradition for support in doctrinal practices.**

   > 1 Cor. 11.16 (ESV) - If anyone is inclined to be contentious, we have no such practice, nor do the churches of God (cf. 1 Cor. 1.2, 7.17, 15.3).

Traditions (continued)

> 1 Cor. 14.33-34 (ESV) - For God is not a God of confusion but of peace. As in all the churches of the saints, the women should keep silent in the churches. For they are not permitted to speak, but should be in submission, as the Law also says.

6. When a congregation uses received tradition to remain faithful to the "Word of God," they are commended by the apostles.

> 1 Cor. 11.2 (ESV) - Now I commend you because you remember me in everything and maintain the traditions even as I delivered them to you.

> 2 Thess. 2.15 (ESV) - So then, brothers, stand firm and hold to the traditions that you were taught by us, either by our spoken word or by our letter.

> 2 Thess. 3.6 (ESV) - Now we command you, brothers, in the name of our Lord Jesus Christ, that you keep away from any brother who is walking in idleness and not in accord with the tradition that you received from us.

Appendix A

The Founders of Tradition: Three Levels of Christian Authority

Exod. 3.15 (ESV) - God also said to Moses, "Say this to the people of Israel, 'The Lord, the God of your fathers, the God of Abraham, the God of Isaac, and the God of Jacob, has sent me to you.' This is my name forever, and thus I am to be remembered throughout all generations."

1. The Authoritative Tradition: the Apostles and the Prophets (The Holy Scriptures)

Eph. 2.19-21 (ESV) - So then you are no longer strangers and aliens, but you are fellow citizens with the saints and members of the household of God, built on the foundation of the apostles and prophets, Christ Jesus himself being the cornerstone, in whom the whole structure, being joined together, grows into a holy temple in the Lord.

~ The Apostle Paul

Traditions (continued)

Those who gave eyewitness testimony to the revelation and saving acts of Yahweh, first in Israel, and ultimately in Jesus Christ the Messiah. This testimony is binding for all people, at all times, and in all places. It is the authoritative tradition by which all subsequent tradition is judged.

2. The Great Tradition: the Ecumenical Councils and their Creeds[2]

What has been believed everywhere, always, and by all.

~ Vincent of Lerins

[2] See Appendix B, "Defining the Great Tradition."

The Great Tradition is the core dogma (doctrine) of the Church. It represents the teaching of the Church as it has understood the Authoritative Tradition (the Holy Scriptures), and summarizes those essential truths that Christians of all ages have confessed and believed. To these doctrinal statements the whole Church, (Catholic, Orthodox, and Protestant)[3] gives its assent. The worship and theology of the Church reflects this core dogma, which finds its summation and fulfillment in the person and work of Jesus Christ. From earliest times, Christians have expressed their devotion to God in its Church calendar, a yearly pattern of worship which summarizes and reenacts the events of Christ's life.

[3] Even the more radical wing of the Protestant reformation (Anabaptists) who were the most reluctant to embrace the creeds as dogmatic instruments of faith, did not disagree with the essential content found in them. "They assumed the Apostolic Creed–they called it 'The Faith,' *Der Glaube*, as did most people." See John Howard Yoder, *Preface to Theology: Christology and Theological Method.* Grand Rapids: Brazos Press, 2002. pp. 222-223.

3. Specific Church Traditions: the Founders of Denominations and Orders

The Presbyterian Church (U.S.A.) has approximately 2.5 million members, 11,200 congregations and 21,000 ordained ministers. Presbyterians trace their history to the 16th century and the Protestant Reformation. Our heritage, and much of what we believe, began with the French lawyer John Calvin (1509-1564), whose writings crystallized much of the Reformed thinking that came before him.

~ The Presbyterian Church, U.S.A.

Christians have expressed their faith in Jesus Christ in various ways through specific movements and traditions which embrace and express the Authoritative Tradition and the Great Tradition in unique ways. For instance,

Traditions (continued)

Catholic movements have arisen around people like Benedict, Francis, or Dominic, and among Protestants people like Martin Luther, John Calvin, Ulrich Zwingli, and John Wesley. Women have founded vital movements of Christian faith (e.g., Aimee Semple McPherson of the Foursquare Church), as well as minorities (e.g., Richard Allen of the African Methodist Episcopal Church or Charles H. Mason of the Church of God in Christ, who also helped to spawn the Assemblies of God), all which attempted to express the Authoritative Tradition and the Great Tradition in a specific way consistent with their time and expression.

The emergence of vital, dynamic movements of the faith at different times and among different peoples reveal the fresh working of the Holy Spirit throughout history. Thus, inside Catholicism, new communities have arisen such as the Benedictines, Franciscans, and Dominicans; and outside Catholicism, new denominations have emerged (Lutherans, Presbyterians, Methodists, Church of God in Christ, etc.). Each of these specific traditions have "founders," key leaders whose energy and vision helped to establish a unique expression of Christian faith and practice. Of course, to be legitimate, these movements must adhere to and faithfully express both the Authoritative Tradition and the Great Tradition. Members of these specific traditions embrace their own unique practices and patterns of spirituality, but these unique features are not necessarily binding on the Church at large. They represent the unique expressions of that community's understanding of and faithfulness to the Authoritative and Great Traditions.

Specific traditions seek to express and live out this faithfulness to the Authoritative and Great Traditions through their worship, teaching, and service. They seek to make the Gospel clear within new cultures or sub-cultures, speaking and modeling the hope of Christ into new situations shaped by their own set of questions posed in light of their own unique circumstances. These movements, therefore, seek to contextualize the Authoritative tradition in a way that faithfully and effectively leads new groups of people to faith in Jesus Christ, and incorporates those who believe into the community of faith that obeys his teachings and gives witness of him to others.

Traditions (continued)

Appendix B

Defining the "Great Tradition"

The Great Tradition (sometimes called the "classical Christian tradition") is defined by Robert E. Webber as follows:

> *[It is] the broad outline of Christian belief and practice developed from the Scriptures between the time of Christ and the middle of the fifth century*
>
> ~ Webber. **The Majestic Tapestry**.
> Nashville: Thomas Nelson Publishers, 1986. p. 10.

This tradition is widely affirmed by Protestant theologians both ancient and modern.

> *Thus those ancient Councils of Nicea, Constantinople, the first of Ephesus, Chalcedon, and the like, which were held for refuting errors, we willingly embrace, and reverence as sacred, in so far as relates to doctrines of faith, for they contain nothing but the pure and genuine interpretation of Scripture, which the holy Fathers with spiritual prudence adopted to crush the enemies of religion who had then arisen.*
>
> ~ John Calvin. **Institutes**. IV, ix. 8.

> *. . . most of what is enduringly valuable in contemporary biblical exegesis was discovered by the fifth century.*
>
> ~ Thomas C. Oden. **The Word of Life**.
> San Francisco: HarperSanFrancisco, 1989. p. xi

> *The first four Councils are by far the most important, as they settled the orthodox faith on the Trinity and the Incarnation.*
>
> ~ Philip Schaff. **The Creeds of Christendom**. Vol. 1.
> Grand Rapids: Baker Book House, 1996. p. 44.

Our reference to the Ecumenical Councils and Creeds is, therefore, focused on those Councils which retain a widespread agreement in the Church among Catholics, Orthodox, and Protestants. While Catholic and Orthodox share common agreement on the first seven councils, Protestants tend to affirm and use primarily the first four. Therefore, those councils which continue to be shared by the whole Church are completed with the Council of Chalcedon in 451.

Traditions (continued)

It is worth noting that each of these four Ecumenical Councils took place in a pre-European cultural context and that none of them were held in Europe. They were councils of the whole Church and they reflected a time in which Christianity was primarily an eastern religion in it's geographic core. By modern reckoning, their participants were African, Asian, and European. The councils reflected a church that ". . . has roots in cultures far distant from Europe and preceded the development of modern European identity, and [of which] some of its greatest minds have been African" (Oden, *The Living God*, San Francisco: HarperSanFrancisco, 1987, p. 9).

Perhaps the most important achievement of the Councils was the creation of what is now commonly called the Nicene Creed. It serves as a summary statement of the Christian faith that can be agreed on by Catholic, Orthodox, and Protestant Christians.

The first four Ecumenical Councils are summarized in the following chart:

Name/Date/Location	Purpose
First Ecumenical Council 325 A.D. Nicea, Asia Minor	Defending against: *Arianism* Question answered: *Was Jesus God?* Action: *Developed the initial form of the Nicene Creed to serve as a summary of the Christian faith*
Second Ecumenical Council 381 A.D. Constantinople, Asia Minor	Defending against: *Macedonianism* Question answered: *Is the Holy Spirit a personal and equal part of the Godhead?* Action: *Completed the Nicene Creed by expanding the article dealing with the Holy Spirit*
Third Ecumenical Council 431 A.D. Ephesus, Asia Minor	Defending against: *Nestorianism* Question answered: *Is Jesus Christ both God and man in one person?* Action: *Defined Christ as the Incarnate Word of God and affirmed his mother Mary as* **theotokos** *(God-bearer)*
Fourth Ecumenical Council 451 A.D. Chalcedon, Asia Minor	Defending against: *Monophysitism* Question answered: *How can Jesus be both God and man?* Action: *Explained the relationship between Jesus' two natures (human and Divine)*

APPENDIX 14
A Theology of the Church in Kingdom Perspective
Don Davis and Terry Cornett

APPENDIX 15
Salvation as Joining the People of God
Terry Cornett

I. The Most Significant Way to Define Salvation in the Biblical Context Is to Describe it as Being Joined to the People of God.

A. Old Testament

1. The prototype Old Testament image of salvation is the Exodus where God "saved" his people from bondage and slavery in Egypt.

   a. To be saved meant to be joined to the people of God who were being delivered together out of bondage and placed directly under God's lordship, laws, protection, provision, and presence.

   b. Exod. 6.7 (ESV) - *I will take you as my own people*, and I will be your God. Then you will know that I am the LORD your God, who brought you out from under the yoke of the Egyptians (cf. Lev. 26.12; Deut. 4.20, Hos. 13.4).

2. God's selection of Israel as "his people" gave them a unique position among all the peoples of the earth.

   a. Deut. 7.6 (ESV) - For you are a people holy to the LORD your God. *The LORD your God has chosen you out of all the peoples on the face of the earth to be his people, his treasured possession* (cf. Deut. 14.2, 26.18, 33.29).

   b. Deut. 27.9 (ESV) - Then Moses and the priests, who are Levites, said to all Israel, "Be silent, O Israel, and listen! *You have now become the people of the LORD your God.*"

3. The means of salvation for anyone outside of Israel was to join themselves to the people of God.

   a. Exod. 12.37-38, 48a (ESV) - The Israelites journeyed from Rameses to Succoth. There were about six hundred thousand men on foot, besides women and children. *Many other people went up with*

Salvation as Joining the People of God (continued)

them, as well as large droves of livestock, both flocks and herds. . . . "An alien living among you who wants to celebrate the LORD'S Passover must have all the males in his household circumcised; then he may take part like one born in the land."

b. Isa. 56.3-8 (ESV) - *Let no foreigner who has bound himself to the LORD say, "The LORD will surely exclude me from his people."* And let not any eunuch complain, "I am only a dry tree." For this is what the LORD says: "To the eunuchs who keep my Sabbaths, who choose what pleases me and hold fast to my covenant-to them I will give within my temple and its walls a memorial and a name better than sons and daughters; I will give them an everlasting name that will not be cut off. And foreigners who bind themselves to the LORD to serve him, to love the name of the LORD, and to worship him, *all who keep the Sabbath without desecrating it and who hold fast to my covenant-these I will bring to my holy mountain and give them joy in my house of prayer. Their burnt offerings and sacrifices will be accepted on my altar;* for my house will be called a house of prayer for all nations." *The Sovereign LORD declares-he who gathers the exiles of Israel: "I will gather still others to them besides those already gathered."*

4. The New Testament suggests that even Moses (an ethnic Hebrew but raised culturally as an Egyptian and therefore a foreigner) had to make a conscious choice to join himself to the people of God in faith so that he could experience salvation.

   Heb. 11.25 (ESV) - *He* [Moses] *chose to be mistreated along with the people of God* rather than to enjoy the pleasures of sin for a short time.

5. Summary: [In the Old Testament] salvation came, not by the man's mere merit, but because the man belonged to a nation peculiarly chosen by God ("Salvation," *International Standard Bible Encyclopedia* [Electronic ed.]. Cedar Rapids: Parsons Technology, 1998.).

Salvation as Joining the People of God (continued)

B. New Testament

". . . who gave himself for us to redeem us from all wickedness *and to purify for himself a people that are his very own, eager to do what is good*" (Titus 2.14).

1. Both Peter and Paul suggest that the New Testament view of salvation is equally concerned as the Old Testament with God calling out a people but that the people "called out" are bound to Christ and his Church rather than to a political or ethnic "nation."

    a. 1 Pet. 2.9-10 (ESV) - *But you are a chosen people, a royal priesthood, a holy nation, a people belonging to God*, that you may declare the praises of him who called you out of darkness into his wonderful light. *Once you were not a people, but now you are the people of God; once you had not received mercy, but now you have received mercy.*

    b. Acts 15.14 (ESV) - Simon has described to us how God at first showed his concern *by taking from the Gentiles a people for himself.*

    c. Eph. 2.13, 19 (ESV) - But now in Christ Jesus you who once were far away have been brought near through the blood of Christ. . . . Consequently, you are no longer foreigners and aliens, *but fellow citizens with God's people* and members of God's household.

    d. Rom. 9.24-26 (ESV) - Even us, whom he also called, *not only from the Jews but also from the Gentiles?* As he says in Hosea: *"I will call them 'my people' who are not my people*; and I will call her 'my loved one' who is not my loved one," and, *"It will happen that in the very place where it was said to them, 'You are not my people,' they will be called 'sons of the living God.'"*

2. "On the other hand, while the [Gospel] message involved in every case is strict individual choice, yet the individual who accepted it entered into social relations with the others who had so chosen. *So salvation involved admission to a community of service* (Mark 9.35, etc.)" (*International Standard Bible Encyclopedia* [Electronic Edition]).

Salvation as Joining the People of God (continued)

II. The Metaphors of Salvation: Joined to a People.

In human society, belonging to a "people" (family, clan, nation) happens through either:

- birth,
- adoption, or
- marrying into a family group

Thus, the New Testament language of salvation draws from these three primary metaphors to describe what happens at salvation.

A. Birth

1. John 1.12-13 (ESV) - Yet to all who received him, to those who believed in his name, he gave the right to become children of God - *children born not of natural descent*, nor of human decision or a husband's will, *but born of God.*

2. John 3.3 (ESV) - In reply Jesus declared, "I tell you the truth, *no one can see the Kingdom of God unless he is born again.*"

3. 1 Pet. 1.23 (ESV) - *For you have been born again*, not of perishable seed, but of imperishable, through the living and enduring word of God.

4. 1 Pet. 1.3 (ESV) - Praise be to the God and Father of our Lord Jesus Christ! *In his great mercy he has given us new birth* into a living hope through the resurrection of Jesus Christ from the dead.

B. Adoption

1. Rom. 8.23 (ESV) - Not only so, but we ourselves, who have the firstfruits of the Spirit, groan inwardly *as we wait eagerly for our adoption as sons*, the redemption of our bodies.

2. Eph. 1.4-6 (ESV) - For he chose us in him before the creation of the world to be holy and blameless in his sight. *In love he predestined us to be adopted as his sons through Jesus Christ*, in accordance with his pleasure and will - to the praise of his glorious grace, which he has freely given us in the One he loves.

Salvation as Joining the People of God (continued)

    3. Gal. 4.4-7 (ESV) - But when the time had fully come, God sent his Son, born of a woman, born under law, to redeem those under law, *that we might receive the full rights of sons.* Because you are sons, God sent the Spirit of his Son into our hearts, the Spirit who calls out, "Abba, Father." *So you are no longer a slave, but a son; and since you are a son, God has made you also an heir.*

C. Marriage

    1. John 3.29 (ESV) - *The bride belongs to the bridegroom.* The friend who attends the bridegroom waits and listens for him, and is full of joy when he hears the bridegroom's voice. That joy is mine, and it is now complete. *[Spoken by John the Baptist in reference to Christ.]*

    2. Eph. 5.31-32 (ESV) - "For this reason *a man will leave his father and mother and be united to his wife, and the two will become one flesh.*" This is a profound mystery - *but I am talking about Christ and the Church.*

    3. Rev. 19.7 (ESV) - Let us rejoice and be glad and give him glory! *For the wedding of the Lamb has come, and his bride has made herself ready.*

APPENDIX 16

A Theology of the Church

Don L. Davis and Terry Cornett ©1996 World Impact Press

The Church Is an Apostolic Community Where the Word Is Rightly Preached

I. **A Community of Calling**

   A. The essential meaning of Church is *Ekklesia*: those who have been "*called out*" in order to be "*called to*" a New Community.

   1. Like the Thessalonians, the Church is called out from idolatry to serve the living God and *called to* wait for his Son from heaven.

   2. The Church is *called out* in order that it may belong to Christ (Rom. 1.6). Jesus speaks of the Church as "my *ekklesia*" that is the "called out ones" who are his unique possession (Matt. 16.18; Gal. 5.24; James 2.7).

   3. The components of God's call:

      a. The foundation is God's desire to save (John 3.16, 1 Tim. 2.4).

      b. The message is the good news of the Kingdom (Matt. 24.14).

      c. The recipients are "whosoever will" (John 3.15).

      d. The method is through faith in the shed blood of Christ and acknowledgment of his lordship (Rom. 3.25; 10.9-10; Eph. 2.8).

      e. The result is regeneration and placement into the body of Christ (2 Cor. 5.17; Rom. 12.4-5; Eph. 3.6; 5.30).

   B. The Church is *called out*.

   1. Called out of the world:

      a. The world is under Satan's dominion and stands in opposition to God.

      b. Conversion and incorporation in Christ's Church involves repentance (*metanoia*) and a transfer of kingdom allegiances.

A Theology of the Church (continued)

    c. The Church exists as strangers and aliens who are "in" but not "of" this world system.

2. Called out from sin:

    a. Those in the Church are being sanctified, set apart for holy action, so that they may live out their calling as saints of God (1 Cor. 1.2; 2 Tim. 1.9, 1 Pet. 1.15).

    b. The Church must be available for God's purpose and use (Rom. 8.28-29; Eph. 1.11; Rom. 6.13).

    c. The Church must bring glory to God alone (Isa. 42.8; John 13.31-32; 17.1; Rom. 15.6; 1 Pet. 2.12).

    d. The Church must now be characterized by obedience to God (2 Thess. 1.8; Heb. 5.8-9; 1 John 2.3).

C. The Church is *called to*:

1. Salvation and new life

    a. Forgiveness and cleansing from sin (Eph. 1.7; 5.26; 1 John 1.9).

    b. Justification (Rom. 3.24; 8.30; Titus 3.7) in which God pronounces us guiltless as to the penalty of his divine law.

    c. Regeneration (John 3.5-8; Col. 3.9-10) by which a "new self" is birthed in us through the Spirit.

    d. Sanctification (John 17.19; 1 Cor. 1.2) in which we are "set apart" by God for holiness of life.

    e. Glorification and Life Eternal (Rom. 8.30, 1 Tim. 6.12; 2 Thess. 2.14) in which we are changed to be like Christ and prepared to live forever in the presence of God (Rom. 8.23; 1 Cor. 15.51-53; 1 John 3.2).

A Theology of the Church (continued)

2. Participation in a new community of God's chosen people (1 Pet. 2.9-10)

   a. Members of Christ's body (1 Cor. 10.16-17; 12.27).

   b. Sheep of God's flock under one Shepherd (John 10; Heb. 13.20; 1 Pet. 5.2-4).

   c. Members of God's family and household (Gal. 6.10; 1 Tim. 3.15).

   d. Children of Abraham and recipients of covenant promise (Rom. 4.16; Gal. 3.29; Eph. 2.12).

   e. Citizens of the New Jerusalem (Phil. 3.20; Rev. 3.12).

   f. The firstfruits of the Kingdom of God (Luke 12.32; James 1.18).

3. Freedom (Gal. 5.1, 13)

   a. Called out of the dominion of darkness which suppresses freedom (Col. 1.13-14).

   b. Called away from sin which enslaves (John 8.34-36).

   c. Called to God the Father who is the Liberator of his people (Exod. 6.6).

   d. Called to God the Son who gives the truth which sets free (John 8.31-36).

   e. Called to God the Spirit whose presence creates liberty (2 Cor. 3.17).

II. **A Community of Faith**

   A. The Church is a community of faith, which has, by faith, confessed Jesus as Lord and Savior.

   Faith refers both to *the content of our belief* and to *the act of believing* itself. Jesus is the object (content) of our faith and his life is received through faith (our belief) in him and his word. In both of these senses, the Church is a community of faith.

A Theology of the Church (continued)

1. The Church places its faith:

    a. in the Living Word (Jesus the Messiah),

    b. who is revealed in the written Word (Sacred Scripture),

    c. and who is now present, teaching and applying his Word to the Church (through the ministry of the Holy Spirit).

2. The Church guards the deposit of faith, given by Christ and the apostles, through sound teaching and the help of the Holy Spirit who indwells its members (2 Tim. 1.13-14).

B. Because it is a community of faith, the Church is also a community of grace.

   1. The Church exists by grace-through faith rather than through human merit or works (Gal. 2.21; Eph. 2.8).

   2. The Church announces, in faith, the grace of God to all humanity (Titus 2.11-15).

   3. The Church lives by grace in all actions and relationships (Eph. 4.1-7).

C. The Church is a community where the Scriptures are preached, studied, meditated upon, memorized, believed, and obeyed (Ezek. 7.10; Jos. 1.8; Ps. 119; Col. 3.16; 1 Tim. 4.13; James 1.22-25).

   1. The Church preaches the Gospel of the Kingdom, as revealed in Scripture, and calls people to repentance and faith which leads to obedience (Matt. 4.17; 28.19-20; Acts 2.38-40).

   2. The Church studies and applies the Scriptures through teaching, rebuking, correcting, and training in righteousness so that all members of the community are equipped to live godly lives characterized by good works (2 Tim. 3.16-17; 4.2).

   3. The Church intentionally reflects on the Scriptures in light of reason, tradition, and experience, learning and doing theology as a means of more fully understanding and acting upon truth (Ps. 119.97-99; 1 Tim. 4.16; 2 Tim. 2.15).

A Theology of the Church (continued)

    4. The Church functions as a listening community which is aware of the Spirit's presence and relies upon him to interpret and apply the Scriptures to the present moment (John 14.25-26).

D. The Church contends for the faith that was once for all entrusted to the saints (Jude 3).

III. A Community of Witness

A. The Church witnesses to the fact that in the incarnation, life, teaching, death and resurrection of Jesus the Christ, God's Kingdom has begun (Mark 1.15; Luke 4.43; 6.20; 11.20; Acts 1.3; 28.23; 1 Cor. 4.20; Col. 1.12-13).

    1. The Church proclaims Jesus as *Christus Victor* whose reign will:

        a. Rescind the curse over creation and humankind (Rev. 22.3).

        b. Defeat Satan and the powers and destroy their work (1 John 3.8).

        c. Reverse the present order by defending and rewarding the meek, the humble, the despised, the lowly, the righteous, the hungry, and the rejected (Luke 1.46-55; 4.18-19; 6.20-22).

        d. Propitiate God's righteous anger (Gal. 3.10-14; 1 John 2.1-2).

        e. Create a new humanity (1 Cor. 15.45-49; Eph. 2.15; Rev. 5.9-10).

        f. Destroy the last enemy- death (1 Cor. 15.26).

    2. Ultimately, the very Kingdom itself will be turned over to God the Father, and the freedom, wholeness, and justice of the Lord will abound throughout the universe (Isa. 10.2-7; 11.1-9; 53.5; Mic. 4.1-3; 6.8; Matt. 6.33; 23.23; Luke 4.18-19; John 8.34-36; 1 Cor. 15.28; Rev. 21).

A Theology of the Church (continued)

    B. The Church witnesses by:

        1. Functioning as a sign and foretaste of the Kingdom of God; the Church is a visible community where people see that:

            a. Jesus is acknowledged as Lord (Rom. 10.9-10).

            b. The truth and power of the Gospel is growing and producing fruit among every kindred, tribe, and nation (Acts 2.47; Rom. 1.16; Col. 1.6; Rev. 7.9-10).

            c. The values of God's Kingdom are accepted and acted upon (Matt. 6.33).

            d. God's commands are obeyed on earth as they are in heaven (Matt. 6.10; John 14.23-24).

            e. The presence of God is experienced (Matt. 18.20; John 14.16-21).

            f. The power of God is demonstrated (1 Cor. 4.20).

            g. The love of God is freely received and given (Eph. 5.1-2; 1 John 3.18; 4.7-8).

            h. The compassion of God is expressed in bearing each other's burdens, first within the Church, and then, in sacrificial service to the whole world (Matt. 5.44-45; Gal. 6.2, 10; Heb. 13.16).

            i. The redemptiveness of God transcends human frailty and sin so that the treasure of the Kingdom is evident in spite of being contained in earthen vessels (2 Cor. 4.7).

        2. Performing signs and wonders which confirm the Gospel (Mark 16.20; Acts 4.30; 8.6,13; 14.3; 15.12; Rom. 15.18-19; Heb. 2.4)

        3. Accepting the call to mission

            a. Going into all the world to preach the Gospel (Matt. 24.14; 28.18-20; Acts 1.8, Col. 1.6).

            b. Evangelizing and making disciples of Christ and his Kingdom (Matt. 28.18-20; 2 Tim. 2.2).

A Theology of the Church (continued)

    c. Establishing churches among those unreached by the Gospel (Matt. 16.18; 28.19; Acts 2.41-42; 16.5; 2 Cor. 11.28; Heb. 12.22-23).

    d. Displaying the excellencies of Christ's Kingdom by engendering freedom, wholeness, and justice in his Name (Isa. 53.5; Mic. 6.8; Matt. 5.16; 12.18-20; Luke 4.18-19; John 8.34-36; 1 Pet. 3.11).

4. Acting as a prophetic community

    a. Speaking the Word of God into situations of error, confusion, and sin (2 Cor. 4.2; Heb. 4.12; James 5.20; Titus 2.15).

    b. Speaking up for those who cannot speak up for themselves so that justice is defended (Prov. 31.8-9).

    c. Announcing judgment against sin in all its forms (Rom. 2.5; Gal. 6.7-8; 1 Pet. 4.17).

    d. Announcing hope in situations where sin has produced despair (Jer. 32.17; 2 Thess. 2.16; Heb. 10.22-23; 1 Pet. 1.3-5).

    e. Proclaiming the return of Jesus, the urgency of the hour, and the reality that soon every knee will bow and every tongue confess that Jesus is Lord to the glory of God the Father (Matt. 25.1-13; Phil. 2.10-11; 2 Tim. 4.1, Titus 2.12-13).

The Church Is One Community
Where the Sacraments Are Rightly Administered

IV. A Community of Worship

A. The Church recognizes that worship is the primary end of all creation.

1. The worshiper adores, praises, and gives thanks to God for his character and actions, ascribing to him the worth and glory due his Person. This worship is directed to:

    a. The Father Almighty who is the Maker of all things visible and invisible.

A Theology of the Church (continued)

      b. The Son who by his incarnation, death, and resurrection accomplished salvation and who is now glorified at the Father's right hand.

      c. The Spirit who is the Lord and Giver of Life.

  2. Worship is the primary purpose of the material heavens and earth, and all life therein (Pss. 148-150; Luke 19.37-40; Rom. 11.36; Rev. 4.11; 15.3-4).

  3. Worship is the central activity of the angelic hosts who honor God in his presence (Isa. 6; Rev. 5).

  4. Worship is the chief vocation of the "community of saints," all true Christians, living and dead, who seek to glorify God in all things (Ps. 29.2; Rom. 12.1-2; 1 Cor. 10.31; Col. 3.17).

B. The Church offers acceptable worship to God. This means:

  1. The worshipers have renounced all false gods or belief systems that lay claim to their allegiance and have covenanted to serve and worship the one true God (Exod. 34.14; 1 Thess. 1.9-10).

  2. The worshipers worship:

      a. In Spirit - as regenerated people who, through saving faith in Jesus Christ, are filled with the Holy Spirit and under his direction.

      b. In Truth - understanding God as he is revealed in Scripture and worshiping in accordance with the teaching of the Word.

      c. In Holiness - Living lives that demonstrate their genuine commitment to serve the Living God.

C. The Church worships as a royal priesthood, wholeheartedly offering up sacrifices of praise to God and employing all its creative resources to worship him with excellence.

  1. The Christian Church is a people who worship, not a place of worship.

A Theology of the Church (continued)

2. The entire congregation ministers to the Lord, each one contributing a song, a word, a testimony, a prayer, etc. according to their gifts and capacities (1 Cor. 14.26).

3. The Church worships with the full range of human emotion, intellect, and creativity:

    a. Physical expression- raising of hands, dancing, kneeling, bowing, etc.

    b. Intellectual engagement- striving to understand God's nature and works.

    c. Artistic expression- through music and the other creative arts.

    d. Celebratory expression- the Church plays in the presence of God (Prov. 8.30-31) experiencing "Sabbath rest" through festivals, celebrations, and praise.

4. The Church worships liturgically by together reenacting the story of God and his people.

    a. The Church proclaims and embodies the drama of God's redemptive action in its ritual, tradition, and order of worship.

    b. The Church, like the covenant people Israel, orders its life around the celebration of the Lord's Supper and Baptism which reenact the story of God's salvation (Deut. 16.3; Matt. 28.19; Rom. 6.4; 1 Cor. 11.23-26).

    c. The Church remembers the worship and service of saints through the ages, learning from their experiences with the Spirit of God (Deut. 32.7; Pss. 77.10-12; 143.5; Isa. 46.9; Heb. 11).

5. The Church worships in freedom:

    a. Constantly experiencing new forms and expressions of worship which honor God and allow his people to delight in him afresh (Pss. 33.3; 40.3; 96.1; 149.1; Isa. 42.9-10; Luke 5.38; Rev. 5.9).

A Theology of the Church (continued)

      b. Being led by the Spirit so that its worship is responsive to God himself (2 Cor. 3.6; Gal. 5.25; Phil. 3.3).

      c. Expressing the unchanging nature of God in forms that are conducive to the particular cultures and personalities of the worshipers (Acts 15).

  6. The Church worships in right order, making sure that each act of worship edifies the body, and stands in accordance with the Word of God (1 Cor. 14.12, 33, 40; Gal. 5.13-15, 22-25; Eph. 4.29; Phil. 4.8).

D. The Church's worship leads to wholeness:

  1. Health and blessing attend the worshiping community (Exod. 23.25; Ps. 147.1-3).

  2. The community takes on the character of the One who is worshiped (Exod. 29.37; Ps. 27.4; Jer. 2.5; 10.8; Matt. 6.21; Col. 3.1-4; 1 John 3.2).

V. A Community of Covenant

A. The Church is the gathering of those who participate in the New Covenant. This New Covenant:

  1. Is mediated by Jesus Christ, the Great High Priest, and is purchased and sealed by his blood (Matt. 26.28; 1 Tim. 2.5; Heb. 8.6; 4.14-16).

  2. Is initiated and participated in only through the electing grace of God (Rom. 8.29-30; 2 Tim. 1.9; Titus 1.1; 1 Pet. 1.1).

  3. Is a covenant of peace (*Shalom*) which gives access to God (Ezek. 34.23-31; Rom. 5.1-2; Eph. 2.17-18; Heb. 7.2-3).

  4. Is uniquely celebrated and experienced in the Lord's Supper and Baptism (Mark 14.22-25; 1 Cor. 10.16; Col. 2.12; 1 Pet. 3.21).

A Theology of the Church (continued)

    5. By faith, both imputes and imparts righteousness to the participants so that God's laws are put in the hearts and written on their minds (Jer. 31.33; Rom. 1.17; 2 Cor. 5.21; Gal. 3.21-22; Phil. 1.11; 3.9; Heb. 10.15-17; 12.10-11; 1 Pet. 2.24).

B. The Covenant enables us to understand and experience Christian sanctification:

    1. Righteousness: right relationships with God and others (Exod. 20.1-17; Mic. 6.8; Mark 12.29-31; James 2.8).

    2. Truth: right beliefs about God and others (Ps. 86.11; Isa. 45.19; John 8.31-32, 17.17; 1 Pet. 1.22).

    3. Holiness: right actions toward God and others (Lev. 11.45; 20.8; Eccles. 12.13; Matt. 7.12; 2 Cor. 7.1; Col. 3.12; 2 Pet. 3.11).

C. The purpose of the New Covenant is to enable the Church to be like Christ Jesus:

    1. Jesus is the new pattern for humanity:

        a. The second Adam (Rom. 5.12-17; 1 Cor. 15.45-49).

        b. The likeness into which the Church is fashioned (Rom. 8.29; 1 John 3.2).

        c. His life, character, and teaching are the standard for faith and practice (John 13.17; 20.21; 2 John 6, 9, 1 Cor. 11.1).

    2. This covenant is made possible by the sacrifice of Christ himself (Matt. 26.27-29; Heb. 8-10).

    3. The apostolic ministry of the new covenant is meant to conform believers to the image of Christ (2 Cor. 3; Eph. 4.12-13).

A Theology of the Church (continued)

    D. The Covenant binds us to those who have gone before.

        1. It recognizes that the Church is one (Eph. 4.4-5).

        2. It reminds us that we are surrounded by a cloud of witnesses who have participated in the same covenant (Heb. 12.1).

        3. It reminds us that we are part of a sacred chain:

                God-Christ-Apostles-Church.

        4. It reminds us that we share the same:

            a. Spiritual parentage (John 1.13; 3.5-6; 2 Cor. 1.2; Gal. 4.6; 1 John 3.9).

            b. Family likeness (Eph. 3.15; Heb. 2.11).

            c. Lord, faith and baptism (Eph. 4.5).

            d. Indwelling Spirit (John 14.17; Rom. 8.9; 2 Cor. 1.22).

            e. Calling and mission (Eph. 4.1; Heb. 3.1; 2 Pet. 1.10).

            f. Hope and destiny (Gal. 5.5; Eph. 1.18; Eph. 4.4; Col. 1.5).

        5. Causes us to understand that since we share the same covenant, administered by the same Lord, under the leadership of the same Spirit with those Christians who have come before us, we must necessarily reflect upon the creeds, the councils, and the actions of the Church throughout history in order to understand the apostolic tradition and the ongoing work of the Holy Spirit (1 Cor. 11.16).

VI. A Community of Presence

    A. "Where Jesus Christ is, there is the Church" - Ignatius of Antioch (Matt. 18.20).

A Theology of the Church (continued)

B. The Church is the dwelling place of God (Eph. 2.19-21):

1. His nation

2. His household

3. His temple

C. The Church congregates in eager anticipation of God's presence (Eph. 2.22).

1. The Church now comes into the presence of God at every gathering:

   a. Like the covenant people in the Old Testament, the Church gathers in the presence of God (Exod. 18.12; 34.34; Deut. 14.23; 15.20; Ps. 132.7; Heb. 12.18-24).

   b. The gathered Church makes manifest the reality of the Kingdom of God by being in the presence of the King (1 Cor. 14.25).

2. The Church anticipates the future gathering of the people of God when the fullness of God's presence will be with them all (Ezek. 48.35; 2 Cor. 4.14; 1 Thess. 3.13; Rev. 21.13).

D. The Church is absolutely dependent on the presence of the Spirit of Christ.

1. Without the presence of the Holy Spirit there is no Church (Acts 2.38; Rom. 8.9; 1 Cor. 12.13; Gal. 3.3; Eph. 2.22; 4.4; Phil. 3.3).

2. The Holy Spirit creates, directs, empowers, and teaches congregations of believers (John 14.16-17, 26; Acts 1.8; 2.17; 13.1; Rom. 15.13, 19; 2 Cor. 3.18).

3. The Holy Spirit gives gifts to the Church so that it can accomplish its mission, bringing honor and glory to God (Rom. 12.4-8; 1 Cor. 12.1-31; Heb. 2.4).

4. The Holy Spirit binds the Church together as the family of God and the body of Christ (2 Cor. 13.14; Eph. 4.3).

A Theology of the Church (continued)

E. The Church is a Kingdom of priests which stands in God's presence (1 Pet. 2.5, 9):

1. Ministering before the Lord (Ps. 43.4; Ps. 134.1-2).

2. Placing God's blessing on his people (Num. 6.22-27; 2 Cor. 13.14).

3. Bringing people before the attention of God (1 Thess. 1.3; 2 Tim. 1.3).

4. Offering themselves and the fruit of their ministry to God (Isa. 66.20, Rom. 12.1; 15.16).

F. The Church lives in God's presence through prayer.

1. Prayer as access to the Holy of Holies (Rev. 5.8).

2. Prayer as communion with God (Ps. 5.3; Rom. 8.26-27).

3. Prayer as intercession.

   a. For the world (1 Tim. 2.1-2).

   b. For the saints (Eph. 6.18-20, 1 Thess. 5.25).

4. Prayer as thanksgiving (Phil. 4.6; Col. 1.3).

5. Prayer as the warfare of the Kingdom.

   a. Binding and loosing (Matt. 16.19).

   b. Engaging the principalities and powers (Eph. 6.12,18).

The Church Is a Holy Community Where Discipline Is Rightly Ordered

VII. A Community of Reconciliation

A. The Church is a community that is reconciled to God: all reconciliation is ultimately dependent on God's reconciling actions toward humanity.

A Theology of the Church (continued)

1. God's desire to reconcile is evidenced by sending his prophets and in the last days by his Son (Heb. 1.1-2).

2. The incarnation, the life, the death, and the resurrection of Jesus are the ultimate acts of reconciliation from God toward humanity (Rom. 5.8).

3. The Gospel is now a message of reconciliation, made possible by Christ's death, that God offers to humanity (2 Cor. 5.16-20).

B. The Church is a community of individuals and peoples that are reconciled to each other by their common identity as one body.

1. By his death Christ united his people who are born of the same seed (1 John 3.9), reconciled as fellow citizens and members of a new humanity (Eph. 2.11-22).

2. The Church community treats all members of God's household with love and justice in spite of differences in race, class, gender, and culture because they are organically united by their participation in the body of Christ (Gal. 3.26-29; Col. 3.11).

C. The Church is a community that is concerned for reconciliation among all peoples.

1. The Church functions an ambassador that invites all people to be reconciled to God (2 Cor. 5.19-20). This task of mission lays the foundation for all the reconciling activities of the Church.

2. The Church promotes reconciliation with and between all people.

   a. Because the Church is commanded to love its enemies (Matt. 5.44-48).

   b. Because the Church is an incarnational community which seeks, like Christ, to identify with those alienated from itself.

A Theology of the Church (continued)

      c. Because the Church embodies and works for the vision of the Kingdom of God in which peoples, nations, and nature itself will be completely reconciled and at peace (Isa. 11.1-9; Mic. 4.2-4; Matt. 4.17; Acts 28.31).

      d. Because the Church recognizes the eternal plan of God to reconcile all things in heaven and on earth under one head, the Lord Jesus Christ, in order that the Kingdom may be handed over to God the Father who will be all in all (Eph. 1.10; Rom. 11.36; 1 Cor. 15.27-28; Rev. 11.15, 21.1-17).

D. The Church is a community of friendship: friendship is a key part of reconciliation and spiritual development.

  1. Spiritual maturity results in friendship with God (Exod. 33.11; James 2.23).

  2. Spiritual discipleship results in friendship with Christ (John 15.13-15).

  3. Spiritual unity is expressed in friendship with the saints (Rom. 16.5, 9, 12; 2 Cor. 7.1; Phil. 2.12; Col. 4.14; 1 Pet. 2.11; 1 John 2.7; 3 John 1.14).

VIII. A Community of Suffering

A. The Church community suffers because it exists in the world as "sheep among wolves" (Luke 10.3).

  1. Hated by those who reject Christ (John 15.18-20).

  2. Persecuted by the world system (Matt. 5.10; 2 Cor. 4.9; 2 Tim. 3.12).

  3. It is uniquely the community of the poor, the hungry, the weeping, the hated, the excluded, the insulted, and the rejected (Matt. 5.20-22).

  4. It is founded on the example and experience of Christ and the apostles (Isa. 53.3; Luke 9.22; Luke 24.46; Acts 5.41; 2 Tim. 1.8; 1 Thess. 2.2).

A Theology of the Church (continued)

B. The Church community imitates Christ in his suffering.

1. Because it purifies from sin (1 Pet. 4.1-2).

2. Because it teaches obedience (Heb. 5.8).

3. Because it allows them to know Christ more fully (Phil. 3.10).

4. Because those who share in Christ's suffering will also share in his comfort and glory (Rom. 8.17-18; 2 Cor. 1.5; 1 Pet. 5.1).

C. The Church community suffers because it identifies with those who suffer.

1. The body of Christ suffers whenever one of its members suffers (1 Cor. 12.26).

2. The body of Christ suffers because it voluntarily identifies itself with the despised, the rejected, the oppressed, and the unlovely (Prov. 29.7; Luke 7.34; Luke 15.1-2).

D. The cross of Christ is both the instrument of salvation and the pattern for Christian life. The cross embodies the values of the Church community.

1. The cross of Christ is the most fundamental Christian symbol. It serves as a constant reminder that the Church is a community of suffering.

2. The basic requirement of discipleship is a willingness to take up the cross daily and follow Jesus (Mark 8.34; Luke 9.23; Luke 14.27).

IX. **A Community of Works**

A. "Works of Service" are the hallmark of Christian congregations as they do justice, love mercy, and walk humbly with God.

1. The leadership of the Church is charged with preparing God's people for "works of service" (Eph. 4.12).

2. These good works are central to the new purpose and identity which is given us during the new birth. "For we are his workmanship, created in

A Theology of the Church (continued)

Christ Jesus for good works, which God prepared beforehand, that we should walk in them" (Eph. 2.10).

3. These works of service reveal God's character to the world and lead people to give him praise (Matt. 5.16; 2 Cor. 9.13).

B. Servanthood characterizes the Christian's approach to relationships, resources, and ministry.

1. The Church community serves based on the example of Christ who came "not to be served but to serve" (Matt. 20.25-28; Luke 22.27; Phil. 2.7).

2. The Church community serves based on the command of Christ and the apostles (Mark 10.42-45; Gal. 5.13; 1 Pet. 4.10).

3. The Church community serves, first of all, "the least of these" according to the mandates of Christ's teaching (Matt. 18.2-5; Matt. 25. 34-46; Luke 4.18-19).

C. Generosity and hospitality are the twin signs of kingdom service.

1. Generosity results in the giving of one's self and one's good for the sake of announcing and obeying Christ and his kingdom reign.

2. Hospitality results in treating the stranger, the foreigner, the prisoner, and the enemy as one of your very own people (Heb. 13.2).

3. These signs are the true fruit of repentance (Luke 3.7-14; Luke 19.8-10; James 1.27)

D. Stewardship is the foundational truth which governs the way the Church uses resources in order to do "Works of Service."

1. Our resources (time, money, authority, health, position, etc.) belong not to ourselves but to God.

A Theology of the Church (continued)

      a. We answer to God for our management of the things entrusted to us personally and corporately (Matt. 25.14-30).

      b. Money should be managed in such as way that treasures are laid up in heaven (Matt. 6.19-21; Luke 12.32-34; Luke 16.1-15; 1 Tim. 6.17-19).

      c. Seeking first the Kingdom of God is the standard by which our stewardship is measured and the basis upon which more will be entrusted (Matt. 6.33).

2. Proper stewardship should contribute to equality and mutual sharing (2 Cor. 8.13-15).

3. Greed is indicative of dishonest stewardship and a repudiation of God as the owner and giver of all things (Luke 12.15; Luke 16.13; Eph. 5.5; Col. 3.5; 1 Pet. 5.2).

E. Justice is a key goal of the Church as it serves God and others.

1. Doing justice is an essential part of fulfilling our service to God (Deut. 16.20; 27.19; Pss. 33.5; 106.3; Prov. 28.5; Mic. 6.8; Matt. 23.23).

2. Justice characterizes the righteous servant but is absent from the hypocrite and the unrighteous (Prov. 29.7; Isa. 1.17; 58.1-14; Matt. 12.18-20; Luke 11.42).

APPENDIX 17
The Lord's Supper: Four Views
Rev. Terry G. Cornett

	Transubstantiation	Consubstantiation	Reformed	Memorialist
Groups	Roman Catholic	Lutheran	Presbyterian and other Reformed Churches, Episcopalians	Baptists, Mennonites, Pentecostals
Key Person	Thomas Aquinas	Martin Luther	John Calvin	Ulrich Zwingli
Presence of Christ	After being consecrated by the priest, the bread changes into Christ's body and the wine changes into Christ's blood so that Christ is present in the elements themselves	The elements do not change but Christ is actually present in, with, and under the elements of bread and wine	Christ is not literally present in the elements since Christ's body is in heaven. Christ is spiritually present and at work in the partaking of the elements through the Holy Spirit when received in faith.	Christ is not present in the elements either literally or spiritually.
What Takes Place	Spiritual food is given to the soul which strengthens the participant spiritually and cleanses them from venial sins. Christ's sacrifice on the cross is made present anew at each mass.	Sins are forgiven and the new covenant promises are reconfirmed. Unless the elements are received in faith, the sacrament has no benefit.	As the elements are received in faith, the partaker receives spiritual nourishment which strengthens the soul, is brought close to the presence of Christ and has a renewed experience of God's grace.	Christ's command is obeyed and Christ's death is commemorated so that the partaker is reminded of the benefits of salvation accomplished by his sacrificial death. Love for God is renewed through the remembering of his love for us.
Key Verses	John 6.53-58 Matt. 26.26 1 Cor. 10.16	Matt. 26.26 1 Cor. 10.16	John 6.63; 16.7 Col. 3.1	Luke 22.19 1 Cor. 11.24-25
Term Used	Sacrament	Sacrament	Sacrament	Ordinance
Who Presides	Priest	Ordained Minister	Church Leaders (Clergy or Laity)	Church Leaders (Clergy or Laity)

APPENDIX 18

Perception and Truth

Rev. Dr. Don L. Davis

Levels of Perception

What is really happening
What is apparent
What you see
What others see
What the enemy sees
What the enemy wants you to think about what you see
What God sees
What God wants you to know about what you see

The Present Situation

What's going on here?
What does this mean?

---

① The So-Called "Facts" of the Matter

What is apparent to all of us
What we're going through
Our initial reactions and categories

② The Common Prognosis

What usually happens
What we can expect
What it feels like

③ Opinions of Key People

- Significant Others
- Leaders
- Experts
- Friends and Family

④ Your Current Spiritual, Experiential, and Psychological Predisposition ("Habits of the Heart")

Keen spiritual awareness
Spiritually alert
Sober and Ready to fight

State of unawareness
Distraction and preoccupation
Proneness to doubt

⑤ The Lying Persuasion of the Enemy ("Dirty Fighter")

Awareness of deep inadequacy
Fear of vulnerability
Impossibility of change
Certainty of chronic bondage
Prospect of failure

⑥ The Testimony of the Divine Promise

Certainty of God's supply
Assurance of safety
Possibility of radical transformation
Power of Divine deliverance
Affirmation of victory

APPENDIX 19

Documenting Your Work
A Guide to Help You Give Credit Where Credit Is Due
The Urban Ministry Institute

Avoiding Plagiarism

Plagiarism is using another person's ideas as if they belonged to you without giving them proper credit. In academic work it is just as wrong to steal a person's ideas as it is to steal a person's property. These ideas may come from the author of a book, an article you have read, or from a fellow student. The way to avoid plagiarism is to carefully use "notes" (textnotes, footnotes, endnotes, etc.) and a "Works Cited" section to help people who read your work know when an idea is one you thought of, and when you are borrowing an idea from another person.

Using Citation References

A citation reference is required in a paper whenever you use ideas or information that came from another person's work.

All citation references involve two parts:

- Notes in the body of your paper placed next to each quotation which came from an outside source.

- A "Works Cited" page at the end of your paper or project which gives information about the sources you have used

Using Notes in Your Paper

There are three basic kinds of notes: parenthetical notes, footnotes, and endnotes. At The Urban Ministry Institute, we recommend that students use parenthetical notes. These notes give the author's last name(s), the date the book was published, and the page number(s) on which you found the information. Example:

> In trying to understand the meaning of Genesis 14.1-24, it is important to recognize that in biblical stories "the place where dialogue is first introduced will be an important moment in revealing the character of the speaker . . ." (Kaiser and Silva 1994, 73). This is certainly true of the character of Melchizedek who speaks words of blessing. This identification of Melchizedek as a positive spiritual influence is reinforced by the fact that he is the King of Salem, since Salem means "safe, at peace" (Wiseman 1996, 1045).

Documenting Your Work (continued)

Creating a Works Cited Page

A "Works Cited" page should be placed at the end of your paper. This page:

- lists every source you quoted in your paper
- is in alphabetical order by author's last name
- includes the date of publication and information about the publisher

The following formatting rules should be followed:

1. **Title**

   The title "Works Cited" should be used and centered on the first line of the page following the top margin.

2. **Content**

   Each reference should list:

   - the author's full name (last name first)
   - the date of publication
   - the title and any special information (Revised edition, 2nd edition, reprint) taken from the cover or title page should be noted
   - the city where the publisher is headquartered followed by a colon and the name of the publisher

3. **Basic form**

   - Each piece of information should be separated by a period.
   - The second line of a reference (and all following lines) should be indented.
   - Book titles should be underlined (or italicized).
   - Article titles should be placed in quotes.

   Example:

   Fee, Gordon D. 1991. *Gospel and Spirit: Issues in New Testament Hermeneutics.* Peabody, MA: Hendrickson Publishers.

Documenting Your Work (continued)

4. Special Forms

A book with multiple authors:

> Kaiser, Walter C., and Moisés Silva. 1994. *An Introduction to Biblical Hermeneutics: The Search for Meaning.* Grand Rapids: Zondervan Publishing House.

An edited book:

> Greenway, Roger S., ed. 1992. *Discipling the City: A Comprehensive Approach to Urban Mission.* 2nd ed. Grand Rapids: Baker Book House.

A book that is part of a series:

> Morris, Leon. 1971. *The Gospel According to John.* Grand Rapids: Wm. B. Eerdmans Publishing Co. The New International Commentary on the New Testament. Gen. ed. F. F. Bruce.

An article in a reference book:

> Wiseman, D. J. "Salem." 1982. In *New Bible Dictionary.* Leicester, England - Downers Grove, IL: InterVarsity Press. Eds. I. H. Marshall and others.

(An example of a "Works Cited" page is located on the next page.)

Standard guides to documenting academic work in the areas of philosophy, religion, theology, and ethics include:

> Atchert, Walter S., and Joseph Gibaldi. 1985. *The MLA Style Manual.* New York: Modern Language Association.

> *The Chicago Manual of Style.* 1993. 14th ed. Chicago: The University of Chicago Press.

> Turabian, Kate L. 1987. *A Manual for Writers of Term Papers, Theses, and Dissertations.* 5th edition. Bonnie Bertwistle Honigsblum, ed. Chicago: The University of Chicago Press.

For Further Research

Works Cited

Fee, Gordon D. 1991. *Gospel and Spirit: Issues in New Testament Hermeneutics*. Peabody, MA: Hendrickson Publishers.

Greenway, Roger S., ed. 1992. *Discipling the City: A Comprehensive Approach to Urban Mission*. 2nd ed. Grand Rapids: Baker Book House.

Kaiser, Walter C., and Moisés Silva. 1994. *An Introduction to Biblical Hermeneutics: The Search for Meaning*. Grand Rapids: Zondervan Publishing House.

Morris, Leon. 1971. *The Gospel According to John*. Grand Rapids: Wm. B. Eerdmans Publishing Co. *The New International Commentary on the New Testament*. Gen. ed. F. F. Bruce.

Wiseman, D. J. "Salem." 1982. In *New Bible Dictionary*. Leicester, England-Downers Grove, IL: InterVarsity Press. Eds. I. H. Marshall and others.

Mentoring
The Capstone Curriculum

Before the Course Begins

- First, read carefully the Introduction of the Module found on page 5, and browse through the Mentor's Guide in order to gain an understanding of the content that will be covered in the course. The Student's Workbook is identical to your Mentor's Guide. Your guide, however, also contains a section of additional material and resources for each lesson, called *Mentor's Notes*. References to these instructions are indicated by a symbol in the margin: 📖. The Quizzes, Final Exam, and Answer Keys can all be found on the TUMI Satellite Gateway. (This is available to all approved satellites.)

- Second, you are strongly encouraged to view the teaching on both DVDs prior to the beginning of the course.

- Third, you should read any assigned readings associated with the curriculum, whether textbooks, articles or appendices.

- Fourth, it may be helpful to review the key theological themes associated with the course by using Bible dictionaries, theological dictionaries, and commentaries to refresh your familiarity with major topics covered in the curriculum.

- Fifth, please know that the students *are not tested on the reading assignments*. These are given to help the students get a fuller understanding of what the module is teaching, but it is not required that your students be excellent readers to understand what is being taught. For those of you who are receiving this module in any translation other than English, the required reading might not be available in your language. Please select a book or two that is available in your language - one that you think best represents what is being taught in this module - and assign that to your students instead.

- Finally, begin to think about key questions and areas of ministry training that you would like to explore with students in light of the content that is being covered.

Before Each Lesson

Prior to each lesson, you should once again watch the teaching content that is found on the DVD for that class session, and then create a *Contact* and *Connection* section for this lesson.

Review the Mentor's Guide to understand the lesson objectives and gather ideas for possible Contact activities. (Two to three Contacts are provided which you may use, or feel free to create your own, if that is more appropriate.)

Then, create a Contact section that introduces the students to the lesson content and captures their interest. As a rule, Contact methods fall into three general categories.

Attention Focusers capture student attention and introduce them to the lesson topic. Attention focusers can be used by themselves with motivated learners or combined with one of the other methods described below. Examples:

- Singing an opening song related to the lesson theme.

- Showing a cartoon or telling a joke that relates to an issue addressed by the lesson.

- Asking students to stand on the left side of the room if they believe that it is easier to teach people how to be saved from the Gospels and to stand on the right side if they believe it is easier to teach people from the Epistles.

Story-telling methods either have the instructor tell a story that illustrates the importance of the lesson content or ask students to share their experiences (stories) about the topic that will be discussed. Examples:

- In a lesson on the role of the pastor, a Mentor may tell the story of conducting a funeral and share the questions and challenges that were part of the experience.

- In a lesson about evangelism, the Mentor may ask students to describe an experience they have had of sharing the Gospel.

Problem-posing activities raise challenging questions for students to answer and lead them toward the lesson content as a source for answering those questions, or they may ask students to list the unanswered questions that they have about the topic that will be discussed. Examples:

- Presenting case studies from ministry situations that call for a leadership decision and having students discuss what the best response would be.

Preparing the Contact Section

- Problems framed as questions such as "When preaching at a funeral, is it more important for a minister to be truthful or compassionate? Why?"

Regardless of what method is chosen, the key to a successful Contact section is making a transition from the Contact to the Content of the lesson. When planning the Contact section, Mentors should write out a transition statement that builds a bridge from the Contact to the lesson content. For example, if the lesson content was on the truth that the Holy Spirit is a divine Person who is a full member of the Godhead, the Contact activity might be to have students quickly draw a symbol that best represents the Holy Spirit to them. After having them share their drawings and discuss why they chose what they did, the Mentor might make a transition statement along the following lines:

> *Because the Holy Spirit is often represented by symbols like fire or oil in Scripture rather than with a human image like the Father or the Son, it is sometimes difficult to help people understand that the Spirit is a full person within the Godhead who thinks, acts, and speaks as personally as God the Father or Jesus Christ. In this lesson, we want to establish the scriptural basis for understanding that the Spirit is more than just a symbol for "God's power" and think about ways that we can make this plain to people in our congregations.*

This is a helpful transition statement because it directs the students to what they can expect from the lesson content and also prepares them for some of the things that might be discussed in the Connection section that comes later. Although you may adapt your transition statement based on student responses during the Contact section, it is important, during the planning time, to think about what will be said.

Three useful questions for evaluating the Contact section you have created are:

- Is it creative and interesting?
- Does it take into account the needs and interests of this particular group?
- Does it focus people toward the lesson content and arouse their interest in it?

Again, review the Mentor's Guide to understand the lesson objectives and gather ideas for possible Connection activities.

Then, create a Connection section that helps students form new associations between truth and their lives (implications) and discuss specific changes in their beliefs, attitudes, or actions that should occur as a result (applications). As you plan, be a little wary of making the Connection section overly specific. Generally this lesson section should come to students as an invitation to discover, rather than as a finished product with all the specific outcomes predetermined.

At the heart of every good Connection section is a question (or series of questions) that asks students how knowing the truth will change their thinking, attitudes, and behaviors. (We have included some Connection questions in order to "prime the pump" of your students, to spur their thinking, and help them generate their own questions arising from their life experience.) Because this is theological and ministry training, the changes we are most concerned with are those associated with the way in which the students train and lead others in their ministry context. Try and focus in on helping students think about this area of application in the questions you develop.

The Connection section can utilize a number of different formats. Students can discuss the implications and applications together in a large Mentor-led group or in small groups with other students (either open discussion or following a pre-written set of questions). Case studies, also, are often good discussion starters. Regardless of the method, in this section both the Mentor and the learning group itself should be seen as a source of wisdom. Since your students are themselves already Christian leaders, there is often a wealth of experience and knowledge that can be drawn on from the students themselves. Students should be encouraged to learn from each other as well as from the Mentor.

Several principles should guide the Connection discussions that you lead:

- First, the primary goal in this section is to bring to the surface the questions that students have. In other words, the questions that occur to students during the lesson take priority over any questions that the Mentor prepares in advance–although the questions raised by an experienced Mentor will

Preparing the Connection Section

still be a useful learning tool. A corollary to this is to assume that the question raised by one student is very often the unspoken question present among the entire group.

- Second, try and focus the discussion on the concrete and the specific rather than the purely theoretical or hypothetical. This part of the lesson is meant to focus on the actual situations that are being faced by the specific students in your classroom.

- Third, do not be afraid to share the wisdom that you have gained through your own ministry experience. You are a key resource to students and they should expect that you will make lessons you have learned available to them. However, always keep in mind that variables of culture, context, and personality may mean that what has worked for you may not always work for everyone. Make suggestions, but dialogue with students about whether your experience seems workable in their context, and if not, what adaptations might be made to make it so.

Three useful questions for evaluating the Connection section you have created are:

- Have I anticipated in advance what the general areas of implication and application are likely to be for the teaching that is given in the lesson?

- Have I created a way to bring student questions to the surface and give them priority?

- Will this help a student leave the classroom knowing what to do with the truth they have learned?

Finally, because the Ministry Project is the structured application project for the entire course, it will be helpful to set aside part of the Connection section to have students discuss what they might choose for their project and to evaluate progress and/or report to the class following completion of the assignment.

Steps in Leading a Lesson

- Take attendance.

- Lead the devotion.

- Say or sing the Nicene Creed and pray.

- Administer the quiz.

- Check Scripture memorization assignment.

- Collect any assignments that are due.

- Use a Contact provided in the Mentor's Guide, or create your own.

- Present the Content of the lesson using the video teaching.

    Using the Video Segments
    Each lesson has two video teaching segments, each approximately 25 minutes in length. After teaching the Contact section (including the transition statement), play the first video segment for the students. Students can follow this presentation using their Student Workbook which contains a general outline of the material presented and Scripture references and other supplementary materials referenced by the speaker. Once the first segment is viewed, work with the students to confirm that the content was understood.

    Ensuring that the Content is Understood
    Segue
    Using the Mentor's Guide, check for comprehension by asking the questions listed in the "Student Questions and Response" section. Clarify any incomplete understandings that students may demonstrate in their answers.

    Ask students if there are any questions that they have about the content and discuss them together as a class. NOTE - The questions here should focus on

Opening Activities

Teach the Contact Section

Oversee the Content Section

understanding the content itself rather than on how to apply the learning. Application questions will be the focus of the upcoming Connection section.

Take a short class break and then repeat this process with the second video segment.

Teach the Connection Section

- Summary of Key Concepts
- Student Application and Implications
- Case Studies
- Restatement of Lesson's Thesis
- Resources and Bibliographies
- Ministry Connections
- Counseling and Prayer

Remind Students of Upcoming Assignments

- Scripture Memorization
- Assigned Readings
- Other Assignments

Close Lesson

- Close with prayer
- Be available for any individual student's questions or needs following the class

Please see the next page for an actual "Module Lesson Outline."

The quizzes, the final exam, and their answer keys are located at the back of this book.

Module Lesson Outline

    Lesson Title   Introduction

    Lesson Objectives

    Devotion

    Nicene Creed and Prayer

    Quiz

    Scripture Memorization Review

    Assignments Due

    Contact (1-3)   Contact

    Video Segment 1 Outline   Content

    Segue 1 (Student Questions and Response)

    Video Segment 2 Outline

    Segue 2 (Student Questions and Response)

    Summary of Key Concepts   Connection

    Student Application and Implications

    Case Studies

    Restatement of Lesson's Thesis

    Resources and Bibliographies

    Ministry Connections

    Counseling and Prayer

    Scripture Memorization   Assignments

    Reading Assignment

    Other Assignments

    Looking Forward to the Next Lesson

The Church Foreshadowed In God's Plan

📖 1
Page 13
Lesson Introduction

Welcome to the Mentor's Guide for Lesson 1, *The Church Foreshadowed in God's Plan*. The overall focus of the *Theology of the Church* module is to concentrate on the important truth of how the Church becomes foreshadowed in God's exalted purpose for salvation. From the beginning God determined to bring glory to himself by drawing to himself a new humanity through the covenant he would make with Abraham. This wondrous plan not only included those of Abraham's physical lineage who would come to believe in Christ, but also included the Gentiles who would come to faith. This grand mystery of his inclusion of the Gentiles in Christ Jesus has been revealed in this age and time through the apostles and the prophets. Further, the aim of this module is to detail God's intent to make this new humanity his own unique and peculiar People, the *laos* of God. Salvation, therefore, is integrally connected to one's place in the people of God, intimately tied and related to one's participation in the Church. This module is critical for developing leaders for it cements into the minds and hearts of the students the central role of the Church in God's salvific plan. Notice in the objectives that these aims are clearly stated, and you ought to emphasize them throughout the lesson, during the discussions and interaction with the students. The more you can highlight the objectives throughout the class period, the better the chances are that they will understand and grasp the magnitude of these objectives.

📖 2
Page 13
Lesson Objectives

Concentrate the entire training period on attaining the objectives. Relate all dimensions of class presentation and participation to the objectives. Do not hesitate to discuss these objectives briefly before you enter into the class period. Draw the students attention to the objectives, for, in a real sense, this is the heart of your educational aim for the class period in this lesson. Everything discussed and done ought to point back to these objectives. Find ways to highlight these at every turn, to reinforce them and reiterate them as you go. The more opportunity you have to focus upon the objectives, the better. Again, what we are seeking overall is for the students to come to appreciate the way in which God gave careful outline of the centrality of the Church in every phase of his work in history, in his work with his people, and especially in his work of salvation.

This devotion focuses on the identity of the Church as God's own holy nation. Notice the emphasis here on just how the Church reflects and displays the glory and standard of God and his Kingdom, or, at the very least, should aspire to display this grandeur in her life and work. Undoubtedly, it is a common problem among Church men and women to entertain low and ignoble thoughts about the Church. And no wonder, considering the fact that the Church has had its share of tragic expressions of sinfulness, greed, and worldliness. Churches in particular sometimes do not reflect the glory of the one, true Church, and often our students can fall prey to the habits of denouncing and rejecting the Church as necessary. Phrases like "churchianity" become derogatory, and often commentators can provide low and spiteful treatments of the role and practice of congregations whose life shows anything but what God represents and who he is. The goal of this devotion is to begin right away with a clear sense that God Almighty has selected the Church, and that the Church, as his chosen people, have an integral and important role in representing God and his interests in the world today. Truly, to be a part of the Church is to be a part of his community, and to be given the high privilege and calling to reveal him and his purposes to the world through its proclamations and practice. No one congregation can claim to fulfill this mission entirely, but this is our corporate aspiration and deepest desire.

*3
Page 13
Devotion*

The prayers in these lessons are intended to be emphasized, not merely as a formal introduction to the study of the lesson and its concepts, but as a heartfelt invitation to God to come into the midst of the students and do the work that only the Holy Spirit can. Jesus makes it clear that the teaching ministry of the Holy Spirit is a central and life-giving ministry.

*4
Page 14
Nicene Creed
and Prayer*

> John 16.13 - When the Spirit of truth comes, he will guide you into all the truth, for he will not speak on his own authority, but whatever he hears he will speak, and he will declare to you the things that are to come.

Take the time of prayer seriously, for in doing so, you will through your actions demonstrate to the students the foundational role that the Holy Spirit plays for us in the discovery of revelation in our study of the Word.

📖 **5**
Page 14
Contact

In order to make sense of the Scriptures, our students must welcome their role as scholars and theologians. In a real sense, everyone with a theological opinion about some religious matter is a theologian. The role of study is to encourage each student to become a *biblical* theologian, one who finds his or her understanding of life through a critically informed study and engagement of the Holy Scriptures. These contacts focus on some of the common kinds of questions and issues that disciples and disciple-makers of Jesus will find as they engage with others on issues related to the Word of God, and the work of the Lord in the world. Use the contacts to introduce the central themes of the lessons in such a way as to highlight and bring to clear foreground the issues you will be wrestling with as you proceed through the lesson.

📖 **6**
Page 15
Contact 2

Have the students briefly share (in groups or with the entire class) what they drew and why. Then ask the students, "Is your identity as a member of the Church of Jesus Christ, one identity among many others that make you who you are, or is your membership in the Church the key defining fact about who you are?" "At The Urban Ministry Institute, we contend that incorporation into the Church surpasses and transforms every other form of human identity. In a sense, your identity as a member of the Church is more like the paper you drew on than it is like any of the individual symbols. It is the context in which all other identities come to have their meaning. In today's lesson we will focus on the critical importance of the Church for understanding salvation and the Christian life."

📖 **7**
Page 16
Outline Point I

That all things exist for the glory of God is the core theological notion in all of Scripture. The key Hebrew term is *kabod*, while the Greek *doxa*, comes from *dokeo*, "to think" or "to seem." The word *kabod* comes from *kabed* "to be heavy", and is linked to concepts of the one possessing glory being laden with riches (Gen. 31.1), power (Isa. 8.7), position (Gen. 45.13), etc. While those who translated the Septuagint used *doxa* for *kabod*, it is clear that *kabod* had a larger meaning of carrying the idea of both honor and reputation. *Kabod* is associated with the idea of God revealing himself through displays of light or through appearances of God in human forms in Old Testament episodes, referred to as "theophanies."

The sense of God as the Possessor of divine glory, and as the One who is deserving of all praise and honor because of his own infinite perfections is a central recurring idea in all of the revelation of Scripture. Moses' desire to witness the wondrous essence and marvelous being of the Lord is summarized in his request to God to "Show me thy glory" (Exod. 33.18). Glory in this sense is not something other than the person of the Lord but a fundamental disclosure of what God is in Godself. Awkward language, but such is the wonder of the God we serve! God's glory is not something added on to himself but is a central and fundamental constituent part of who he is in his deepest self, his majesty, his splendor, his "glory." This glory may be accompanied as it was in this vision by some outward or visible sign, but should not be equated with what human beings can observe or comprehend. God's glory was displayed in the vision of Isaiah in the temple (cf. Isa. 6.1ff.), and was referenced in John 12.41, which is also in connection to Jesus Christ's person, which establishes the close relationship between Jesus and the glory of God (cf. John 1.14-18). In the New Testament, the concept of glory refers to his perfect majesty as Creator (Rom. 1.23) as well as to God's perfections, and in reference to humankind, especially God's glorious righteousness which is now displayed in his salvation in Jesus Christ (Romans 3.23). God's glory is displayed perfectly and comprehensively in the face of Jesus Christ (2 Cor. 4.6; Heb. 1.3; John 1.14-18), who himself is the perfect display of the Father's own glorious being, which cannot be witnessed by the human eye (note that the Father is referred to by Paul as the "Father of glory" in Eph. 1.17). The richness of God's glorious being, as One who is glorious and worthy therefore to be glorified, is shown in Paul's reference to God's glory in terms of wealth (Eph. 1.18; 3.16) and power and might (Col. 1.11). God displays the wonder of his great power and unlimited splendor in the resurrection of Jesus from the dead (Rom. 6.4 cf. Eph. 1.19ff.). Beyond all doubt, the God and Father of Jesus Christ is glorious and worthy of honor. This is the plain ethical mandate of all creation–to give honor to him who is worthy of all glory in all things (Rev. 4.11).

📖 **8**
Page 18
Outline Point II-C

Take special note of this distinction and truth during your discussions with the students, especially the miraculous election of the Gentiles to be included in God's kingdom and salvation plan. This will probably not hit your students with the force it ought to, but your emphasis here can reinforce the wondrous power of this selection on God's part by a brief discussion with them of the then contemporaneous understanding of the Gentiles in the mind of the faithful.

When one looks at the concept of the Gentiles in the Bible, it is easy to see why God's selection of the Gentiles is a remarkable revelation of God's lovingkindness and grace, and appears to be out of sync with the typical depiction of them in the Word. They include all the nations except the Jews (Rom. 2.9; 3.9; 9.24) and are called a number of names in the Scriptures, including (in the KJV) "heathen" (e.g., Ps. 2.1; Gal. 3.8), the "nations" (Pss. 9.20; 22.8; Isa. 9.1), the "uncircumcised" (Isa. 14.6; 52.1), and "the uncircumcision" (Rom. 2.26). The Gentiles are referred to as Greeks (Rom. 1.16; 10.12), foreigners, or strangers (Isa. 14.1; 60.10). The way in which Gentiles are characterized in Scripture would seem to indicate that they could not or would never be included in the salvific purposes of God. Not only are they chastised and punished by God (e.g., 2 Chron. 20.6; Pss. 47.8; 9.5; 94.10), but they are depicted as being ignorant of God (Rom. 1.21; 1 Thess. 4.5), gripped by a refusal to know God (Rom. 1.28), being without the covenant of Law (Rom. 2.14), and being idol worshipers full of superstitions (Rom. 1.23, 25; 1 Cor. 12.2; Deut. 18.14). Gentiles are characterized as being wicked, depraved, full of reproach, and blasphemous (Rom. 1.28-32; Eph. 4.19; Neh. 5.9), who neither know nor love the true God but show a kind of perverse fidelity to their own false gods (Jer. 2.11). Because of this evil character and idolatrous tendency, the Gentiles are portrayed as having perpetual and difficult conflicts with God's people (Esther 9.1, 5; Pss. 44.13-14; 123.3), and God's people are neither to follow their ways nor intermarry with them (cf. Lev. 18.3; Jer. 10.2; Deut. 7.3). In surveying this picture of those who are even portrayed in Scripture as dogs (cf. Matt. 15.26), it is amazing and glorious that the Lord of heaven's original and yet hidden intent was to gather both Jews and Gentiles into a new humanity which would represent his kingdom people forever (Eph. 2.11-22)!

Again, the importance of Gentile inclusion is the central truth undergirding the global and worldwide reception of Jesus among the nations. It is clear from the reading of the Scriptures that the Gentiles were to be excluded from Israel's privileges, in terms of election and covenant, at least on the face of it through the Israelite's history (Eph. 2.11-12). Gentiles were not allowed to enter the temple (see Acts 21.28-29), but were restricted to the outer court (Eph. 2.14; Rev. 11.2). Through the redemption, however, that Christ won through his death and resurrection, the Gentiles are now given as an inheritance to Christ (Ps. 2.8), who, according to prophetic testimony, shined as a light to them for their salvation (Isa. 42.6; Luke 2.32). The conversions of the Gentiles is alluded to in the Scriptures in Isaiah 2.2 and 11.10, and the distinction between Jew and Gentile is eliminated in the person of Jesus Christ (cf. Col. 3.11; Gal. 3.28). While the Gospel was not preached to them until after the Jews had heard the good news in Christ (Matt. 10.5; Luke 24.47; Acts 13.46), the Gospel did come to them, as recorded in Acts 10.34-45 and Acts 15.14. Paul identified himself in his role in the salvation scheme as the Apostle of the Gentiles in Acts 9.15 and Galatians 2.7-8. God, in his own time and manner, determined that he would not leave the Gentiles on the outskirts of his love and grace, but would include them in his salvation plan. This recognition of God's inclusion of the Gentiles lies at the very heart of our understanding of taking the Gospel into the entire world for Christ (Acts 1.8; Matt. 28.18-20).

📖 **9**
Page 20
Outline Point III-B

These questions are designed to ensure that the students understand the critical aims and facts presented in the first video segment. You will have to gauge your time well, especially if your students are intrigued with the concepts, and want to discuss their implications at length. Allow for the proper time to focus in on the main points, and still have enough time for a break before the next video segment is started.

📖 **10**
Page 22
Student Questions and Response

It is highly important that you help the students to see the radical and revolutionary character of God's love in his covenant with Abraham, as well as the revelation of the mystery to include the nations in his new people of God. The weight of this teaching cannot be measured; its implications touch on every part of our understanding of God, and correspondingly, our understanding of other peoples. Simply being spiritual does not in any way protect us from being ethnocentric, bigoted, or prejudiced against peoples who are different than us. One of the most practical ethical implications of this teaching is for leaders and congregations to imitate their God by coming to love (and not caricature) other peoples and groups which are different from us. The sin of Israel of thinking itself to be more significant than other peoples is easily transferred and reproduced in us believers who may mistakenly think that we are loved more because we believe in Christ. This is not the case; God's intent is that all people come to a knowledge of the truth, and the more we can feel the heart of God, the more we will work to see that all peoples, regardless of their background, gain an opportunity to believe in Christ for salvation.

📖 11

Page 23
Summary of
Segment 2

This video segment concentrates on understanding the meaning of salvation. Theologically it is important that students be able to describe why we need to be saved (sin has separated us from God), the objective means by which we are saved (by being united to Christ in his death and resurrection), and the biblical meaning of salvation (being joined to the people of God who inherit his Kingdom and its promises).

It is critical for a correct understanding of salvation to grasp that union with Christ cannot be separated from incorporation into the Church. The scriptural teaching is quite clear on this point. [See the Appendix to this Lesson titled "Salvation as Joining the People of God]. To be saved by Christ is to be joined to a church body of which he is the head (Col. 1.18) and to participate in his plan to call and redeem a people out of the earth (2 Cor. 6.15-16; Titus 2.14; Heb. 8.8-10) and which will literally constitute a new form of the human race (1 Cor. 15.45-49). Christ's parting words to his disciples were not only to preach the Good News to every creature but also to baptize them (Matt. 28.19) which is the clear outward sign by which individuals are identified with the people of God. Salvation always means incorporation into the Church.

Finally, it is important for students to grasp that, like the children of Israel during the Exodus who had been saved (freed from slavery in Egypt), were being saved (traveling to the Promised Land), and who would be saved (participate in the restoration of all things when the Lord's temple was raised as chief among the mountains), our salvation is also an accomplished fact, an ongoing reality, and a future hope. Therefore the Scriptures can refer to us as those who "are being saved" (1 Cor. 1.18; 2 Cor. 2.15); can speak about the "hope of salvation" (1 Thess. 5.8), of our salvation being "nearer now than when we first believed" (Rom. 13.11); of salvation as something that will be "inherited" (Heb. 1.14) and as something that Christ will bring to us when he returns (Heb. 9.28). Although the Scriptures clearly refer to salvation as both a "past" event secured by Christ on the cross (Eph. 2.5, Titus 3.4-5), and as a "present reality being worked out in those who believe" (1 Cor. 1.18; 2 Cor. 6.2), it always looks forward to the ultimate meaning of salvation as coming to us with the return of Christ to earth.

 12
Page 26
Outline Point III-A

This new relationship of being "in Christ" was first announced by the Lord to his disciples in the upper room in the statement, "Ye in me [en emoi], and I in you" (John 14.20). The new relationship of the believer in Christ is defined as a new position, "in Christ," resulting from a work of God. That it is more than merely a position created by divine reckoning is revealed by the companion revelation, "I in you." The resultant doctrine is embraced in the word union, which is commonly taken as a synonym for identification. Various figures are employed in Scripture to illustrate this union and identification. The fine and the branches is employed by Christ himself in John 15.1-6. . . . Another figure is that of the head and the body (cf. Eph. 1.22-23; 4.12-16; 5.23-30. . . . Various expressions are used to signify this identification. Most frequent is the terminology "in Christ" (en Christo), but others also are used such as "in" or "into Christ" (eis Christon), and "in the Lord" (en kyrio).

~ J. F. Walvoord. "Identification with Christ." **Evangelical Dictionary of Theology**. Grand Rapids: Baker, 1984. p. 542

📖 **13**
Page 27
Outline Point III-B

1 John 3.24a - Those who obey his commands live in him and he in them. (Cf. Eph. 1.1-14 and Col. 2.6-10 for passages that further develop the "in him" concept.)

📖 **14**
Page 31
Outline Point IV-D

Note that the following is a typological interpretation of the Scriptures. Biblical typology is based on the recognition that events, persons, and places which appear early on in salvation history become the patterns by which later events are interpreted. The Exodus (which includes the Passover, the Red Sea crossing, and the desert journey to Canaan) has a long history of being used as a type in Christian interpretation. This usage traces back to Paul himself who wrote:

> 1 Cor. 10.1-4 - For I do not want you to be ignorant of the fact, brothers, that our forefathers were all under the cloud and that they all passed through the sea. [2] They were all baptized into Moses in the cloud and in the sea. [3] They all ate the same spiritual food [4] and drank the same spiritual drink; for they drank from the spiritual Rock that accompanied them, and that Rock was Christ.

📖 **15**
Page 34
Summary of
Key Concepts

Listed in this section are the fundamental truths written in sentence form which the students should have received from this lesson, that is, from the videos and your guided discussion with them. Make sure that these concepts are clearly defined and carefully considered, for their quiz work and exams will be taken from these items directly. What is especially important is to help the students gain a working vocabulary of these ideas in order that they might become more and more familiar with them. This familiarity will be key for them as they continue to train and teach others on the nature of the Church. The clearer your students are on the nature of the Church, the better it will be for them to articulate and help define for their students the *function and ministry* of the Church. The one is directly related to the other. The more they can see the Church as God sees her, the more fluid and flexible they will be to imagine the Church in a fresher and new ministry in their own community, and the nation and world at large.

In helping your students think through their own situations, you might want to design some questions or use those provided below as water to "prime the pump" of their interests, so to speak. What is significant here is not the questions written below, but for you, in conversation with your students, to settle on a cadre of issues, concerns, questions, and ideas that flow directly from their experience, and relate to their lives and ministries. Do not hesitate to spend the majority of time on some question that arose from the video, or some special concern that is especially relevant in their ministry context right now. The goal of this section is for you to enable them to think critically and theologically in regards to their own lives and ministry contexts. Again, the questions below are provided as guides and primers, and ought not to be seen as absolute necessities. Pick and choose among them, or come up with your own.

This part of the lesson demands that you as mentor concentrate directly on the relevance of these concepts to the experience and challenges of the students in general. In other words, how do the issues of God's election of the Church and its foreshadowing in the Israel, of salvation as participation in the Church relate specifically to their context and to their questions. Without question, links can be made between these ideas and their experience, and your task is to explore ways in which these links can be identified and pursued in conversation together for understanding and edification.

📖 **16**
Page 35
Student Application and Implications

The case studies in this section are directly correlated with some of the concepts covered in the teaching portion of this lesson. These studies emphasize the need for discernment to be exercised regarding the nature of the true people of God, especially who is to be included or left out, and how we are to know what constitutes the people of God considering what has been covered in this lesson. Emphasize in your discussion with the students the need for them to be critically aware of God's radical inclusiveness when it comes to those who accept and believe in Christ for their personal salvation. Again, the tendency of even the most righteous men and women (e.g., Peter) is to limit God's lovingkindness to those who are like us, who believe in every particular thing that we do, who practice and worship as we like, and who emphasize doctrinal ideas and issues that we have found

📖 **17**
Page 37
Case Studies

convincing. God, however, has selected both Jews and Gentiles to be part of his new humanity, and established that salvation is being directly associated with his new people, even those whom we might find difficult to relate to or enjoy. The choice is not ours but the Lord's, and we are called to love and embrace all those who welcome Christ into their lives as Lord of all. Draw out from the studies these and other related ideas which might help your students identify their own bigotries and criticisms against those who might be different from them.

*18
Page 39
Ministry Connections*

A ministry connection should be the cleanest, most direct, and most personal connection that each student can make to relate these concepts to some particular experience they have, whether in their own personal lives or those whom they serve in and through their church. We tend to apply things to our lives only when we can discover the linkages and connections between the relevance and validity of the truth against the desire and/or pressing need of our lives. Seek to help the students discover the most pressing need or issue they have, and enable them to see how these truths might answer some of their questions, resolve issues, illumine experiences, or supply insight into new directions they ought to turn. Pray for your students fervently that the Lord the Spirit will instruct them through the remaining interaction you have with them, and that the students will have with each others. Again, remember what Jesus taught about the Holy Spirit and the truth:

> John 16.13 - When the Spirit of truth comes, he will guide you into all the truth, for he will not speak on his own authority, but whatever he hears he will speak, and he will declare to you the things that are to come.

Jesus will want to make the connections for each student, so be sensitive to direct them to the appropriate point of contact that might be most important for them at this time.

*19
Page 39
Counseling
and Prayer*

The close association between the ministry of the Word and prayer is affirmed in the Scriptures, especially in the ministry of the apostles in dispute over the supply to the Hellenist widows (cf. Acts 6.1ff.). When tempted to enter into the fray of conflict in the body over right allocation of goods within the body, the apostles urged the Church to select representatives spiritually worthy and mature to settle those matters, but they would concentrate on the ministry of the word and prayer (Acts 6.4 - "But we will devote ourselves to prayer and to the ministry of the word"). Actually, prayer is emphasized first in this text, suggesting that a close association exists between fervent faith-filled prayer and an effective application of the Word of God. Always leave ample time to pray with the students about the truths they have discovered in the Word. The Holy Spirit can use the prayer to cement the truth in the spirit, and ignite new and different desires and concerns in the students as a result of their listening to God in prayer. Be available, if possible, to pray with students about specific areas which might be especially relevant to them through the teaching of this lesson.

Make certain that the students understand the assignment for next week, especially the written piece. This is not difficult; the goal is that they would read the material as best as they can and write a few sentences on what they take them to mean. This is a critical intellectual skill for your students to learn, so make sure that you encourage them in this process. Of course, for those students who might find this difficult, assure them of the intent behind this assignment, and emphasize their understanding of the material being the key, not their writing skills. We want to improve their skills, but not at the expense of their encouragement and edification. Nor, however, do we want to sell them short. Strike to find the midpoint between challenge and encouragement here.

 20
Page 40 Assignments

The Church at Worship

MENTOR'S NOTES 2

📖 1
Page 43
Lesson Introduction

Welcome to the Mentor's Guide for Lesson 2, *The Church at Worship*. The goal of this lesson is to help students understand the Church as a community of people who have experienced the grace of God and who respond to this grace by engaging in worship as their duty and their delight.

The first segment will focus on the fact that salvation is all by grace since this is the starting point for a response of worship. It will also talk about the Lord's Supper and baptism as two of the most significant ways that the Church acknowledges, experiences, and responds to the grace of God. Since there are legitimate differences about the nature of the Lord's Supper and baptism among evangelical believers, please be prepared for disagreements among your students about what the Bible teaches and be ready to lead a discussion that is fair-minded and which helps students to develop their own convictions in light of Scripture and their denominations' theology.

The second segment will focus on the theology of Christian worship and the key elements that should be included in the worship of the Church. The central idea is the worthiness of God and the resulting idea that the Church is the people called to give him the glory he deserves. Ironically, the focus on the Church at worship is not upon the Church itself. In its worship of God, the Church focuses on the person and works of God. The Church worships and adores God because of the inherent majesty of his nature. We glorify God because of his solitary holiness, his infinite beauty, his incomparable glory and his matchless works. As the one, true, and living Triune God, the Church worships God through Jesus Christ. No one can approach God except through faith in the person of Jesus Christ, in the power of the Holy Spirit. Finally, the Church gives its worship offerings to God through its praise and thanksgiving and through it practice of its worship schedule (i.e., liturgy), which emphasizes the preaching of the Word and the sacraments. In one sense, all that we do as believers is a form of worship to God, and so we may also glorify God through our obedience and lifestyle as a covenant community.

Since the focus of this lesson is on worship, be sure that you cultivate "warm hearts" as well as "clear minds" on these issues. Students should be led to active thanksgiving and praise during these lessons as well as reflection on the theological issues involved. Please read the following objectives carefully. The more you can highlight the objectives throughout the class period, the better the chances are that they will understand and grasp the essential truths that underlie this lesson.

This devotion focuses on the motive of all God-honoring praise and worship: the incomparable glory of the person of God, Father, Son, and Holy Spirit. Often we may think that worship involves a certain kind of ritual action, ceremonial process, or liturgical order. The worship of God is not rooted in geography or religious orthodoxy, but, as Jesus says, in "spirit and in truth" (John 4.24). The Father cannot be approached except in the person of Jesus Christ (John 14.6), whose atoning sacrifice has brought us near to God in faith (Heb. 10.22-24). Because God has granted us entrance into his presence, even the Holy of holies through the blood of Jesus, and because God's glory is unmatched and unchanging, there remains a ready reason to give glory and honor to God. We need never wait for circumstances to be warm and wonderful in order to praise God; even in the midst of the most horrible tragedy, the severest loss, the most disarming trouble, and the greatest need, we are to give praise and glory to God. In spite of all we face and know, he is the Lord of all, perfect, glorious, majestic, full of splendor and wonder, who will never forsake us or abandon us. Regardless of how things look, God is and remains forever by our side and for our benefit. Learning to give the "sacrifice" of praise, to change the meaning of the term for a moment, is a central skill of the developing disciple of Jesus. Countless times we will face situations where there does not appear, at least on the surface of the situation, a single reason to praise. All is wrong and bleak; God appears to have vanished, either not knowing, not caring, or being unable to help. In the midst of this kind of trouble, we grab our harps and give glory to the One who gives us life and sustains our days. He is worthy because he is, for his name is "I Am that I Am." Challenge the students to their truest vocation, the unbroken and unyielding praise of Almighty God because of who he is and what he has done in Jesus Christ.

2
Page 43
Devotion

📖 3
Page 45
Scripture
Memorization
Review

The Psalmist affirms the power of the Word of God to keep our way pure (Ps. 119.9), to protect from the power of sin (Ps. 119.11), and to give life to the one who receives them (Ps. 119.93). Do not turn the Scripture memorization time into merely a class assignment drill, full of routine and boring repetition. Use this time to challenge and instruct the students on the benefit and profit of the memorized Word. Memorize the Scripture along with the students, and review with them where you are able. Discuss the Scripture's meaning, and how it relates thematically to what was covered in the lesson last week. This portion of the lesson may very well be the most important, so treat it with the requisite importance and respect. It is simply too easy to get overwhelmed and to treat the memorized Word as simply something to accomplish for the lesson's requirement. As mentor, attempt to safeguard this time from this deadly error.

📖 4
Page 45
Contact 1

Have students share briefly in groups how this realization occurred. (There is not time for everyone to give their entire testimony so make sure students hone in on the specific point of when they grasped that the could not earn salvation). Bring students back together and say "The Church exists only because of the grace of God. Today's lesson helps us understand worship as the Church's response to grace."

📖 5
Page 45
Contact 2 and 3

Both of these last two contact portions deal with a similar theme, that is, the character and quality of our worship, and what it is that God requires or demands. What is significant in considering worship here is the cultural and social norms associated with the practices and events deemed to be worship. In other words, churches are largely unaware that their worship is culturally and historically conditioned, and that worship of God, as an expression of truth and the heart, must have a deeply personal and immediate characteristic to it. It will never be worship simply to ape what others have done, expecting the feelings and affections that they had to be reproduced in us by the mere doing of their acts, the singing of their songs, or the practice of their deeds. Worship, as an expression of the Spirit, will always be dressed in cultural garments but it will also always be given to the God-above-all-cultures, the God and Father of our Lord Jesus. Gaining flexibility in worship styles and methods is directly correlated to seeing that God is a God of all humankind, and therefore can be legitimately and wonderfully glorified through the heartfelt cultural expression of any people who have repented, believed, and are following through faith, hope, and love the Son of God, Jesus Christ. Equating some cultural expression of worship with *worship itself*, that is, the way in which all worship everywhere is to be conceived and done, is a common and yet devastating error made in many congregations, and by many Christians. Allowing freedom to express our deepest gratitude and praise to God is a critical part of a leader's ministry in leading others into the presence of God.

Theologians often divide grace into descriptive categories. *Common grace* refers to God's providence over all people by which he sustains life (breath, rain, food), provides moral awareness, affords civil government, and restrains evil so that human life and culture is possible. *Special grace* refers to the grace by which God redeems, sanctifies, and glorifies his people. *Prevenient grace* refers to the grace which comes before all human effort or decisions and makes it possible for people to desire salvation and respond in faith.

📖 6
Page 47
Outline Point I-C

> *[Pelagius taught that] the power to do good resides naturally in the free will itself, apart from any gift of God to human nature, so that by following the example of Christ, the way of virtue is made clear and persons of their own will may abstain from sin. Hence there is a need not for any direct prevenient operation of the Spirit upon the human will in order for it to do good, but merely for the Spirit to operate indirectly through conscience and reason. . . Between A.D. 411 and 431, no fewer than twenty-four councils faced the question of Pelagianism. It was the burning issue of Augustine's mature life. . . .The consensual response [of the Church] was further refined at the councils of Ephesus (431) and Orange (529), which held grace to be necessary for all acts pertinent to salvation. "No branch can bear fruit by itself; it must remain in the vine. Neither can you bear fruit unless you remain in me (John 15.4; cf. 1 Cor. 12.3).*
>
> ~ Thomas C. Oden. **The Transforming Power of Grace**. Nashville: Abingdon Press, 1993. pp. 110-111.

📖 7
Page 48
Outline Point I-D-1

📖 8
Page 48
Outline Point I-D-2

Evangelical theology starts with the premise that the formula for salvation is always "by *grace* through *faith*." Make sure that every student understands this basic truth.

📖 9
Page 49
Outline Point II

Worship Defined

*The principal biblical terms, the Hebrew **saha** and the Greek **proskyneo**, emphasize the act of prostration.*

~ E. F. Harrison, "Worship." **Evangelical Dictionary of Theology.** p. 1192.

Worship is responding to God with full recognition of his rightful position as the One who is worthy of absolute adoration, obedience, service, gratitude, and praise.

> Ps. 95.6 - Come let us bow down in worship, let us kneel before the Lord our Maker (cf., Lev. 26.1; Deut. 26.10; Ps. 138.2; Matt. 4.9-10).

Some Key Assumptions

The Word basis of worship: we worship the One who is revealed to us.

Apart from the hearing of God's Word we could not worship because we would not know him. He dwells in unapproachable light. Only because he has revealed himself can we respond to him.

> John 1.18 - No one has ever seen God, but God the One and Only, who is at the Father's side, has made him known.

The covenant basis of worship: we worship by means of Christ Jesus (Hebrews). Christian worship is distinctive in that it is christocentric. The veil has been torn away. We have direct access to the Father through Christ Jesus. Giving glory to God the Father through him. (Heb. 10.20 - By a new and living way opened up for us through the curtain, that is, his body . . .)

The communal basis of worship: the holy priesthood (worship is always corporate first, individual second).

> Heb. 10.25 - Let us not give up meeting together, as some are in the habit of doing, but let us encourage one another-and all the more as you see the Day approaching.

It has been said that sacraments are like the signature on a check. They are not the same thing as the actual money in the bank or the desire of the person who writes it to see you provided for but they do make those things visible. The signature by itself would be worthless but it serves as a visible sign of what the person is providing and thus is very valuable. Likewise, a sacrament has no value in itself but has great value as the visible sign of God's promise.

📖 **10**
Page 49
Outline Point II-B

The Catholic Church recognizes seven sacraments: baptism, the Lord's Supper, confirmation, penance, holy orders (ordination), matrimony, and extreme unction (anointing of the seriously ill) in addition to many smaller acts called "sacramentals" (such as "the sign of the cross) which are also believed to confer grace.

📖 **11**
Page 50
Outline Point II-B-2

Some Pentecostal, Mennonite, and a few Baptist groups also practice foot washing as an additional ordinance (cf. John 13.14) in addition to baptism and the Lord's Supper.

📖 **12**
Page 50
Outline Point II-C-1

The common analogy would be that baptism in the New Testament doesn't automatically save a person any more than being circumcised in the Old Testament automatically saved a person. It was possible to be physically circumcised and yet choose to live as an idolatrous and unbelieving Jew. Circumcision was the sign of the Old Covenant and baptism is the sign of the new. They are both intended to show that a person is genuinely a part of God's chosen people but one must not make the mistake of assuming that baptism automatically makes a person a Christian. This is equally true whether one sees baptism as a sacrament or as an ordinance.

📖 **13**
Page 51
Outline Point III-A-2

In this sense, being baptized is no more optional than it was optional for the Hebrew people to decline eating the Passover and putting the blood on the doorpost. To disobey the command of God was to disassociate oneself from the

📖 **14**
Page 53
Outline Point III-C

people of God who were being rescued. The obedience in the Exodus story revealed that a person believed God and was committed to leaving with his people. While an extraordinary circumstance might prevent a person from being baptized (e.g. the thief on the cross) without placing that person's intentions in question, all true believers who have the opportunity to be baptized will do so because they have accepted Christ's lordship and want to obey his commands and be incorporated into his people.

📖 **15**
Page 53
Outline Point IV

If students need a resource for practical help on leading a communion service (or a baptism), *Baker's Worship Handbook*, by Paul E. Engle (Grand Rapids, MI: Baker Book House, 1998) offers a number of sample services from a wide variety of Evangelical traditions including both "sacramental" and "ordinance" perspective.

📖 **16**
Page 55
Outline Point IV-D-1

Another major difference between Catholic and Protestant theology about the Lord's Supper is the Catholics believe that Christ is sacrificed for sin each time that the Lord's Supper is reenacted. (Protestants refute this on the basis of Hebrews 7.27 and 9.25-26). Unlike Protestants, Catholics also teach that the communion elements (being the actual body and blood of Christ) are worthy of veneration. Catholics and Protestants have made progress in recent years at resolving these differences but differences still remain.

📖 **17**
Page 55
Outline Point IV-E-1

It has been held that the substance of bread and wine remain in this sacrament after consecration. But this position cannot be maintained, for in the first place it destroys the reality of this sacrament, which demands that in the sacrament there should be the true body of Christ, which was not there before consecration. . . . And this is done in the sacrament by the power of God, for the whole substance of bread is converted into the whole substance of Christ's body. Hence the conversion is properly called transubstantiation. It is obvious to our sense that after consecration all the accidents of bread and wine remain. And, by divine providence, there is good reason for this. First, because it is not normal for people to eat human flesh and to drink human blood, in fact, they are revolted by this idea. Therefore Christ's flesh and blood are set before us to be taken under the appearances of those things which are of frequent use, namely bread and wine. Secondly, if we ate our Lord under his proper appearance, this sacrament would be ridiculed by unbelievers. Thirdly, in order that, while we take the Lord's body and blood invisibly, this fact may avail toward the merit of Faith.

~ Thomas Aquinas. **Summa Theologiae** (1265).

What is true concerning Christ is also true concerning the sacrament. In order for the divinity to dwell in a human body, it is not necessary for the human nature to be transubstantiated and the divinity contained under the accidents of the human nature. Both natures are simply there in their entirety and it is true to say: 'This man is God; this God is man. . . .' In the same way it is not necessary in the sacrament that the bread and wine be transubstantiated and that Christ be contained under their accidents in order that a real body and real blood may be present. But both remain there at the same time, and it is truly said, 'This bread is my body; this wine is my blood,' and vice versa.

~ Martin Luther. **The Babylonian Captivity of the Church** (1520).

📖 **18**
Page 56
Outline Point IV-E-2

"On this we take our stand, and we also believe and teach that in the Supper we eat and take to ourselves Christ's body truly and physically." While [Luther] acknowledged the mystery, he was certain of the fact of Christ's real corporeal presence inasmuch as he had said when he instituted the Supper, "This is my body." If Scripture cannot be taken literally here, it cannot be believed anywhere, Luther held, and we are on the way to "the virtual denial of Christ, God, and everything." (Works, XXXVII, 29, 53)

~ M. E. Osterhaven. Quoting Luther in "Lord's Supper, Views of."
Evangelical Dictionary of Theology. Grand Rapids: Baker, 1984. p. 655.

In these questions, you will find the focus is upon mastering the data and the facts associated with the claims made in the first video segment. Concentrate on ensuring that the students understand the answers in light of the lesson aims of the first

📖 **19**
Page 59
Student Questions and Response

segment. Make certain that you watch the clock here, covering the questions below and those posed by your students, and watch for any tangents which may lead you from rehearsing the critical facts and main points.

📖 20
Page 61
Outline Point I

Worship of God is a central concept, and to adequately understand the Church at worship, you may refer the students to the general concepts associated with the term. Our word "worship" is taken from an English term, "worthship," which referred to the worthiness of someone to be given honor or recognition consistent with the value of their worth or place. There are a number of words used in the Scriptures in association with the idea of worship, with perhaps the most critical terms being the Hebrew term *saha* and the Greek *proskyneo*. These ideas are closely identified with the physical motion and action of being prostrate, of prostrating oneself before another, the act of doing great reverence or obeisance to another or something out of an act of deep respect, reverence, and acknowledgment. This understanding of worship in conjunction to prostrating oneself, of doing obeisance to another might have been in association with social mores or habits to provide one acknowledged as worthy their proper respect (Gen. 18.2), the exalted station someone might have in their life position (1 Kings 1.31), or the rank and/or place an individual had in the overall family situation (Gen. 49.8).

This act of obeisance, whether a physical act or a inward submission and acknowledgment, can also be applied to divine beings, whether the idols of a people or nation (e.g., Exod. 20.5) or to Yahweh God (Ps. 2; Exod. 24.1). The God of Scripture makes plain that the glory and honor due to him will never be shared or given to any other god, those which were not in fact gods at all but either the figments of the worshipers minds or demons seeking to steal the glory that belongs to God alone (Exod. 20.1-3; Isa. 14; Deut. 8.19; Isa. 42.8). To offer to false deities the glory, reverence, and obedience that God alone is worthy of is the height of pride and sinfulness; God, because of his infinite worth and their incomparable worthiness, will never stand for this kind of act, however innocently or harshly given. Above all else, God's infinite glory guarantees that he is a jealous God (Exod. 20.5), not in the sense of a small-minded, petty God who is selfish in demanding all recognition be given to him. On the contrary, God is jealous in the sense that there is no one and nothing that should ever give glory to itself or himself or herself; God's beauty and majesty are simply peerless, and to allow anyone to rob him of his acknowledgment would be the very worst kind of sin and wrong.

Of all the most perverted acts to rob God of his legitimate right to all glory, the Devil's insane attempts are to be seen to be the most egregious (Isa. 14.12-20). The Scriptures record his futile attempts to receive from Christ the praise due to God alone (Matt. 4.9), and, in the summation of this age, his representatives will seek the same foolish acclaim (cr. 2 Thess. 2 with Rev. 13.4).

Because God is infinitely glorious, his worship (i.e., his worthship) cannot be properly limited to what takes place inside the temple, or in conjunction with the Church as it honors God in its praise and thanksgiving. Not only can we include all the acts of the saints and the angels in acknowledgment of God's glory as worship (i.e., Ps. 150; 138.2; 1 Sam. 1.3), but also all the works in heaven and earth, including all the heavens, the spheres, all forms of life and creation, can therefore give God glory and worship as it fulfills the purpose for which it was created (Ps. 135.6 and Rev. 4.11).

As you will see through this lesson, God made worship of himself even more rich and revealing through the incarnation of his own glory in the person of Jesus Christ (John 9.38; 20.28; Heb. 1.6; Rev. 5.6-14). Our God, who is beyond description in terms of his beauty and majesty, is worthy to be praised in and through the person of his Son, who is to be worshiped alongside the Father as our Savior and Lord (John 5.22-23).

It might be beneficial to emphasize here that the early Church, the generation of the first Christian community in Jerusalem relied heavily upon its Jewish roots and orientation in all aspects of worship, especially in the place of the Old Testament as its authoritative Word. These early fellowships focused on the confession that Jesus of Nazareth was the promised Messiah with the salvation of God and his reign having come in his life and through his death and resurrection. (This conviction about Jesus, above all, was probably what distinguished them from their Jewish worship counterparts). The worship of the early Church, therefore, was centered in

21
Page 64
Outline Point II

different *content* (Jesus as Messiah and Savior), but very similar to Jewish *orientation*, yet including the significant and central addition of the eucharist (i.e., the Lord's Supper) at its center, (Acts 2.42, 46) along with prayers being offered to God in the name of the Lord Jesus (Acts 4.24-30). While we see evidence for their assembling to pray, fellowship, and to hear the Word of God preached and taught (e.g., Acts 2.46; 5.42), the first community changed its day for services from the Sabbath to Sunday, the first day of the week, since the Lord Jesus was raised upon the first day of the week.

While scholars disagree regarding the nature of the *form of the worship* of the first generation apostolic Church, there is consensus that the form was simple and devout. The evidence of the New Testament and the non-canonical writings reveal that while the service had no formulaic process or standard approach, the heart and center of the Christian services was the celebration of the Lord's Supper on the Lord's Day. The *Didache* (ca. 95-150), an invaluable and quite early source of evidence for Christian belief and practice of the early Church, provides us with a rich narrative of how the first Christians celebrated the eucharist, detailing the prayers they used, liturgical directions that needed to be followed, along with the forms of prayer to be prayed. Time was allowed for open-ended prayer at certain times of the service (liturgy). Before any of the believers could celebrate the Lord's Supper, confession of sin was required for all who desired to participate in their celebration (*Didache* 14.1).

The Jewishness of the service of the early Church was quite evident, and therefore, the guidelines and contours of Jewish praise and worship would have resonated in the midst of the earliest Christian assemblies.

📖 22
Page 66
Outline Point II-B

It may be interesting for you and the students to know a little about the beginnings of the concept of *liturgia*, that special order and schedule of worship structure used in many churches today worldwide. One of the early fathers of the Church, Justin Martyr, notes in his *First Apology* which he wrote near the middle of the second century, a clear description of the Christian service, with the Lord's Supper (or eucharist, "thanksgiving"), also referred to in the *Didache* (14.1). Justin describes the service of Christian worship in the second century as the readings of the "memoirs of the apostles" (that is, the Gospels), along with the Prophets (books of the Old Testament) were read aloud "as long as time allowed" (*First Apology*, 67). Justin's descriptions reveal that the churches embraced a definite order to their services due to the tradition that they shared, although it was quite simple. From evidence we also see that baptized believers assembled and celebrated the Lord's Supper, associated with a fully stocked meal to be shared by all, but the meal was separated from the celebration of the Lord's Supper very early in the Church's history (Clement of Alexandria, *Paedagogos* 2.1; *Stromata* 3.2; Tertullian, *Apology* 39; *Chaplet* 3). This meal associated with the Lord's Supper came to be called the "agape feast," i.e., love feast, but according to our records, it died out by the fourth century because of the great disorders of conduct associated with it (Augustine, *Letter to Aurelium* 22.4).

Deeply affected by the Jewish observance of festivals throughout the year, Christians gave rise early to the idea of a "Church year," analogous to the Jewish year. This was the beginnings of the modern idea of "liturgical year," which was an early Christian effort to set apart the year through a retelling of the Christian story through an ongoing succession of sacred events and celebrations. That the actual selection and inclusion of certain festivals and holidays occurred slowly over a period of time is universally acknowledged. For instance, the celebrations of Christmas and Epiphany, although a central part of the Christian story, were not added to the liturgical calendar till the fourth century, and the present calendar evolved until completion at the end of the sixth century. This emphasis on liturgy should probably be seen as a Christian reliance on Jewish roots and orientations, which serves as the ground and foundation of today's modern liturgy.

In dealing with the concepts of this discussion session, it is critical that you make certain distinctions for the students which will hopefully enable them to keep in mind the critical differences associated with the Church at worship. Underscore for the students that although the Bible refers to certain *principles* and *predispositions* associated with worshiping God, there are no formulas, fixed patterns, or mandated ritual programs connected with worship. While the Lord's Supper and baptism are

23
*Page 68
Student Questions
and Response*

connected with the Church's worship, from the very beginning of the Church's worship, she used nor sought a standardized form that was woodenly mandated for all the congregations. Although from the New Testament and the non-canonical historical writings we can detect a definite tradition emerging in the apostolic churches which gave rise to the liturgical calendar of today, there was never a time where every portion of the service was predetermined and mapped out. In your discussion, make certain that you highlight this complimentary emphasis in the Church's worship between a deeply committed allegiance to the apostles' tradition, while, at the same time, a fresh approach to freedom and spontaneity. This is critical for understanding all that the Bible describes of the Church at worship.

📖 **24**
Page 69
Summary of
Key Concepts

Make certain that you distinguish between the Church's response in its worship towards God (worship in terms of its *effect*) and the beauty of the Lord and his character and works in Jesus Christ (worship in terms of its cause). Unfortunately, some discussions of worship have become more focused on the *ways in which we worship* rather than *the reasons why we worship*. While both are important in understanding the Church's vocation as a worshiping priesthood of believers, it is imperative that the focus remain on the God whom we worship, and the clear reason why we are a worshiping community. Only when these concepts are reiterated and kept clear can we rightly consider the ways in which we are to approach God. The *why* of worship must necessarily and understandably precede the *what* and the *how* of worship. This statement ought not to be understood as an appeal to belittle the significance of discussions about human responses to God. It is, however, to underscore that worship's significance derives from the understanding that *God is worthy of our obeisance and our obedience*. Discussions of worship should begin and end in a "theocentric" vein (God-centered) not an "anthropocentric" vein (human-centered one).

📖 **25**
Page 71
Student Application
and Implications

While there are many individual and personal implications to this teaching on worship, it will be important for you as mentor to help the students retain the corporate nature of the questions and the issues. The tendency to turn the discussion about the Church at worship to "me at worship" is a strong one, and your ability in review and reflection with the students to keep them on the communal implications is important here.

These case studies highlight the concern of the nature of worship in our congregations. The need here is to enable your students to understand the general teachings, truths, and principles associated with the Church at worship, and their ability to apply these principles to real-life problems associated with the Church's worship today. Each of the following case studies can be understood through an array of perspectives and principles covered in this lesson. The aim, of course, is not to give the perfect answer in order to clarify the situation or resolved the problem, but to help the students gain skill in addressing particular existential problems and concerns while keeping specific biblical principles in mind. Armed with the truth of the Word and the experience of Christian history and tradition, the students can use their own experience and understandings to help carve new directions to understanding and address these questions. Help them apply different principles to the situations and see how those principles make clear the underlying questions or concerns which need to be addressed.

📖 **26**
Page 72
Case Studies

Always encourage the students to not simply study the word of God, making the most of their critical functions, but also to pray fervently over issues, and so exercise their spiritual gifts and capacities. All the issues we face as leaders will require our specific and ongoing intercession, and by emphasizing this in our lessons we train our students to never study the Bible without reference to the wisdom that only God can provide, the kind that will never make us ashamed but will enable us to represent God in the way he desires (James 1.5-8). Admitting that we do not understand something is never a problem to the Lord; God is beyond us and will provide us with wisdom if we search for it with all our hearts, and not simply with all our minds (Prov. 2.1-9). As the writer to the Proverbs suggests, we are never to lean on our own understanding as if we could conjure up solutions because we thought well (Prov. 3.5-6). Train the students, even after the Word has been

📖 **27**
Page 74
Counseling and Prayer

consulted, to look to God in prayer. It is not prayer or the Word, but prayer alongside the Word that characterized the ministry of the apostles, and should characterize ours (Acts 6.4). Encourage your students to seek the Lord's face in prayer and ask him for specific insights, approaches, and solutions to the issues and concerns they face, both in their personal lives as well as their ministries.

The Church as Witness

📖 1
Page 79
Lesson Introduction

Welcome to the Mentor's Guide for Lesson 3, *The Church as Witness*. The overall focus of this particular lesson of this Theology of the Church module is to enable your students to understand the various dimensions of the Church in its witness to Christ and his Kingdom. We begin this lesson by paying attention to some of the most significant aspects of the doctrine of election as it applies to Jesus Christ as the Elect Servant of God. In Jesus Christ, God has elected for himself a Savior and Lord through whom he revealed himself to the world, and redeemed a people for himself. The righteous are elected by virtue of their union with the Son of God, Jesus Christ, by faith. We will also consider specifically how God's election relates both to his chosen people Israel as well as to the Church. Using God's selection of Israel and the Church as a conceptual backdrop, we will then consider briefly the relationship of God's election of individual believers "in Christ," that is, in connection to Christ as they cling to him by faith. The second segment of this lesson focuses upon the Great Commission, the mandate that Jesus has given to the Church of this age to bear witness to him and the kingdom promise through faith in his shed blood. In that segment we will see how the Great Commission provides an overall outline for the Church's threefold witness in the world to make disciples. We'll consider how the Church fulfills Christ's commission by obeying Jesus' call to evangelize the lost, by baptizing new believers in Christ (incorporating them as members into the Church), and by teaching true converts to obey all that Christ has commanded them. The Church is called to engage in this effort until the end of the age, and Jesus has promised never to forsake us as we obey his command to make disciples worldwide. Notice in the objectives that these aims are clearly stated, and you ought to emphasize them throughout the lesson, during your discussions and interaction with the students. As has been stated before, there is no way to overestimate the importance of staying centered on the objectives as you proceed through the data and phases of the lesson. As we concentrate on these objectives, we will use every phase of our teaching and all of the information shared in the lesson to help our students understand and internalize these objectives for the sake of teaching others. We will reap what we sow here. The more time you spend understanding the objectives and leading your students to understand and attain them, the better your fruit will be for your teaching sessions specifically, and the Capstone modules generally.

This devotion focuses on the priority of Jesus' last words, and how those words exhort us to share the good news of his salvation and Kingdom to the ends of the earth. The Church of Jesus Christ has been commissioned by its Head to go and share his Gospel with all the peoples of the earth. In this sense the Church is both a redeemed community and a redemptive one, we are a saved community as well as a salvation-declaring community. We have experienced the fruits and riches of God's gracious salvation, and are likewise called to go and share with others the promise and hope of redemption in Jesus Christ. The goal here is explicit and discrete. We are to preach the Gospel to every creature; what a testament this is to God's intent to draw from every clan, group, ethnicity, nation, tongue, and group on earth a people that will belong to him and serve him forever. What a remarkable privilege we have to share this news unashamedly, with all the creativity, energy, and sincerity that God's Spirit may supply, and to resolve, deep in our hearts, never to give up until the commission is accomplished. Indeed, this was his last Word to us, and for us who belong to his Church of every new generation, this Word will and must remain the Word of our mission and life, until he comes.

*2
Page 79
Devotion*

These contacts highlight critical points, perhaps the most important being an exploration in what does it mean for God to elect and choose someone. Many conflicting views exist on this particular point when applied to the character and working of God. If God chooses one person, does that mean that he rejects another? How can God elect when the Scriptures suggest that there is no partiality with God? What about God being arbitrary–does God make decisions randomly, or if he does it with purpose, does he inform us as to what criteria or standard he was using when he made the decision? These and related questions are liable and probable to arise in this week's lesson of election. Do not be dismayed at any of these questions; we ought to engage each one with an open mind and an open Bible, seeking the best we can to wrestle with the implications of each question. We ought not, however, pretend to speak about God's inner motives with absolute certainty, especially on items or issues where he does not disclose his mind to us on things. A good principle by which we should operate is contained in a revealing text in Deuteronomy:

*3
Page 80
Contact*

> Deut. 29.29 - The secret things belong to the Lord our God, but the things that are revealed belong to us and to our children forever, that we may do all the words of this law.

As you engage these difficult concepts with the students, simply be aware that not everything God knows and thinks has been revealed in Scripture, but what he has made known provides us with an absolutely sufficient and comprehensive understanding of his will, able to help us to joyfully obey his will. We ought not to assert certainty where God has not provided it to us. Rather, we ought to sanctify our minds, explore the Word, and submit to the reality and wonder of God's mystery on issues where complete clarity is either wanting or not able to be understood fully. We do see in a glass darkly now, as Paul tells the Corinthians in 1 Corinthians 13. Humility would suggest that we not boldly assert what the limits of revelation has not taught. Psalm 131 is the central text for the humble theologian and Bible student.

> Ps. 131.1-3 - *A Song of Ascents of David*. O Lord, my heart is not lifted up; my eyes are not raised too high; I do not occupy myself with things too great and too marvelous for me. [2] But I have calmed and quieted my soul, like a weaned child with its mother; like a weaned child is my soul within me. [3] O Israel, hope in the Lord from this time forth and forevermore.

God's election of Jesus as the Messiah is a specific kind of election mentioned in Scripture, and in my mind, the most significant kind. For instance, the Scriptures make mention of a certain class of angels being elected by God, and one text actually refers to "the elect angels" (1 Tim. 5.21; cf. 1 Cor. 6.3; 2 Pet. 2.4; Jude 6). Also, God's choice of David to be the one through whom the Messiah would come and reign is highly significant in terms of God's elective purpose (1 Sam. 16.7-12; cf. 2 Sam. 7.8-16). Of course, mention is made in the New Testament of Jesus' choice of the disciples and Apostles (Luke 6.13; John 6.70; 15.16; Acts 9.15; 15.7). All of these are mentioned, along with others, but none are as significant as God's election of Messiah, and our redemption and salvation "in him." The book of Isaiah is filled with references to God's Servant, and often refers to this servant of the Lord as "My chosen one" (see Isa. 42.1; cf. Matt. 12.18). In the Synoptic Gospels (i.e., Matthew, Mark, and Luke) Luke alone names Jesus as the Chosen One (9.35; 23.35). In Peter's first Epistle, he carefully associates Jesus with another Isaiah reference (Isaiah 28.16 in 1 Peter 1.20 and 2.4, 6, speaking in regard to Jesus as the Stone of stumbling, choice selected in Zion). God's election of Jesus is the central theological idea in all of the Bible's discussion about God's choice, for through Jesus' unique and unrepeatable act as God's Messiah and our Mediator God enacts his salvific purpose through Christ for the sake of the entire world. As you will see, and should emphasize with the students, God's choice of Jesus conditions and makes possible God's choice of us in him.

It is important that you emphasize during this session that election is "election in Christ"; it includes God's act of delivering us from our own sinful bondage, the guilt we experience as a result of our own sinful conscience, and the wondrous deliverance from its power we experience through faith in Jesus Christ. That we are chosen in Christ is plain from such central texts as Ephesians 1.4-5, 11, and Romans 8.29. In some ways, it is not helpful to think of election in regards to individualism as the foundation of election; Jesus is not simply the footnote on which God demonstrates his sovereign choice of human beings to salvation. Rather, election should always be conceived as being in Christ and through Christ. God's election of humankind occurs in the person of Jesus to salvation. Jesus is the Mediator for all humankind (1 Tim. 2.5-6), and those whom God calls effectually to himself all repent and believe in Jesus Christ to salvation (1 John 5.11-13). God chooses us in Christ, who is the foundation of all that God does in terms of human salvation.

📖 5
Page 89
Outline Point II-B-3

While it is not important to linger over the long-standing historical debate of the doctrine of election, it is critical to know some of the general outlines of the discussion in the Church on election.

📖 6
Page 89
Outline Point II-C

Much dispute has arisen throughout Church history over the precise meaning of the biblical doctrine of election. The most significant clashes probably have taken place over the ideas of Pelagianism (of the 5th and 6th centuries), and during the period of the Reformation. The key to the dispute is whether or not we, as fallen human beings, possess the freedom to turn God for salvation apart from God's effective choice and supply of grace through the Spirit, or are we so depraved in our unsaved condition as to make impossible our freedom to choose or reject God's grace in Christ.

Pelagianism outlined its doctrine in this way: the will of human beings is not so damaged that we cannot respond to God's command to repent and believe. This view was perceived and understood to mean that individuals can become acceptable and righteous without God's sovereign elective grace, and had no need for his sovereign involvement through election. This doctrine of human ability was condemned at the Council of Orange (529), which also condemned a form of semi-Pelagianism, which taught that human beings could choose Christ without any sense of God's special grace. During this time, the Church in the West held to a view of election that was built on Augustine's idea of "double predestination." This doctrine taught that God chose the elect to his salvation and, that he chose the "reprobate" (that is, the lost and unsaved) to damnation.

Election as a doctrine during the Reformation was rethought and re-formed, and the issues which came out of those discussions continue to influence the wrestlings and conflicts up to the present. Many of the key Reformers held to the idea of "unconditional election," which has today been directly associated with what is known as the "Calvinist" view of election. This teaching was built on Augustine's view, and emphasized that God's election of individuals was the ground and condition of every other thing in salvation. What God does in election determines not only the first step, but the entire salvation of the elect, which God establishes by his own choice and sustains according to his own plan. This teaching emphasized God's determination before time for those who were to receive salvation as well as those appointed for damnation. God's election of the elect was based upon his mercy alone and without any reference to the merit and or worth of the chosen.

The major reaction to this teaching came in the form of a tradition today known as Arminianism. It focused especially on the idea of rejecting the view of unconditional election. Rather, this tradition taught that election was in some form "conditional," i.e., God chose those whom he foresaw would respond to the Gospel through the Holy Spirit's general call to salvation. Their perspective focuses upon human freedom and God's grace being bestowed in some measure on all human beings, which allows us to respond to God's free gift of grace. The so-called "Five Points of Calvinism" (TULIP) are a good summary of the Calvinist position, and a great way to note the distinctions between Calvinism and Arminianism. These points include the idea of total depravity, unconditional election, limited atonement, irresistible grace, and the perseverance of saints.

Today, another alternative exists in theological discussions regarding unconditional election, it is called Universalism. A common view in liberal circles, this view purports that all humankind was included in God's salvation work in Jesus Christ. All human beings are therefore God's elect, and ultimately, all human beings will be saved in the end. Perhaps the most discussed view of this in theological circles relates to Karl Barth's theology of election. Barth articulated a view that suggested that election from God is fundamentally christological (centered in the person of Jesus Christ). God does not select a group of individuals but Christ himself. He and he only is the elect one, and, correspondingly, he is the only one whom God rejected. Upon Christ fell reprobation, and now through his work, election falls upon all human beings.

It is important to note here that whatever position one takes in regard to election, the concept is clear that God's choice is not based on human works (Rom. 9.11). According to Ephesians 1.4-5, we are elected by God to be holy and blameless in his sight, adopted as children through Jesus Christ. It is not according to our efforts or will, but through the blood of Jesus Christ and in sync with the will of God himself (Eph. 1.7; John 1.12-13).

📖 **7**
Page 89
Outline Point II-C-1

Please emphasize with your students that God's elective choice does not make missions and evangelism unnecessary, rather, it confirms it. God assuring us that those who repent and believe shall be saved does not cancel our responsibility to tell the world about Jesus and his love. God's elective choice includes not only the salvation of God's own, but includes the means by which these would be saved.

📖 **8**
Page 92
Outline Point III-C

God's election of the saved in Jesus Christ assumes that they have heard the good news of the Gospel, and responded to the Gospel in repentance and faith. We are saved through the sanctifying work of the Holy Spirit and through belief in the truth of the Gospel; we must hear and believe in order to be saved (2 Thess. 2.13). From this and many other passages, it is clear, then that the preaching and teaching of the truth of Christ is critical for salvation, and therefore for making sure God's call of election (Rom. 10.14-17; cf. Acts 18.9-11).

📖 9
Page 92
Outline Point III-D

One of the critical issues dealing with the doctrine of election (as well as its sister idea "reprobation," or God's rejection of those who have not been elected) is whether or not the election of God is corporate and communal, individual and personal, or some kind of hybrid election in between. We emphasize throughout this lesson that we are elected in Christ, and that this sense of election is both practically and spiritually the heart of the doctrine. Texts in the New Testament support claims on both sides, that election has both an individual as well as a communal aspect.

For instance, the plain statements of Ephesians suggests that the election is in some sense communal, shown by Paul's references to "us" and "we" (1.4-5, 12). Furthermore, in one of the most often quoted texts in reference here, Romans 8.28-30, Paul uses a plural pronouns, "those," whom God foreknew, were the ones that he predestined, called, justified, and glorified. Again, Romans 9 speaks to election in terms of Israel's election, and personal election as an element within it. This assertion, though, is set against Paul's statement in Romans 9.8 where he indicates that "not all who are descended from Israel are Israel" (9.6, 8), and then masterfully argues the point in an individual example of Jacob and Esau (9.7, 11-13). Those who would argue strongly for individual election would cite a number of verses, including such texts as John 6.37-40; 10.14-16, 26-29; 17.2, 6, 9, 24. Again, for the sake of our lesson, we are emphasizing the need to focus on the Christ centered nature of election, and our election in Christ.

In these questions, you will find the focus is upon mastering the data and the facts associated with the claims made in the first video segment. The doctrine of election is a significant concept related to the Church, and it is possible to become distracted on many apparently important and related discussions about it. What is critical in this discussion is to highlight the way in which the students understand God's election *in Christ*, that is some sense God has effected his election of us in Jesus Christ. Focus on this idea, and seek to ensure that the students understand the answers in light of this critical idea, as well as the other lesson aims of this first segment.

> 📖 **10**
> Page 93
> Student Questions and Response

The Great Commission serves as the heart of Jesus' biblical injunction to the Church to preach the good news of his salvation to the entire world, making disciples of him in every place. This mandate to go and make disciples of Jesus among all the people groups of the earth is emphasized prophetically in the Old Testament (Isa. 45.22; cf. Gen. 12.3) and realized and reaffirmed in the New Testament (Matt. 9.37-38; 28.19; Acts 1.8). The heart of disciple-making is making plain for those who have never heard the story of Jesus of Nazareth, including the truths of his life, ministry and his passion, but especially the facts and meaning of his crucifixion on Calvary as both substitute for sin and champion over the devil (1 Cor. 15.3; Col. 2.14-15). This proclamation also includes testimony regarding Christ's resurrection from among the dead, his ascension into heaven at the right hand of God (Luke 24.46-48; Rom. 4.25; 1 Cor. 15. 3-4; Eph. 1.20-23), and the hope of the consummation of his work at the *Parousia* or Jesus' Second Coming (Acts 3.19-21).

> 📖 **11**
> Page 95
> Summary of Segment 2

In teaching the students make plain that the underlying motive for Christ's commandment for mission is the constraining love that Christ has revealed in his acts for us (2 Cor. 5.14-21). The mystery and depth of the Incarnation reveals the wonder and scope of God's love for humankind (John 3.16). In sharing the Good News, those who proclaim the Good News are constrained, determined, ruled by the richness of God's love in Christ. Jesus as God's Son, the Author of life (Acts 3.15) and the Lord of glory (1 Cor. 2.8), now has been granted all authority in heaven and earth. It is this risen and conquering Lord who commands his Church to make disciples among all nations (Matt. 28.18-19).

In a real sense, making disciples in obedience to the Great Commission is merely following through on the work that Christ himself began through his proclamation of the Kingdom on earth. It is the testimony of the apostles that Jesus went about overcoming the devil's work and doing good (Acts 10.38), proclaiming the inauguration of the Kingdom of God (Mark 1.14-15), and coming to seek and save those who were lost, those who needed to experience the saving grace of God available only in him (Luke 19.10).

The nature of the commission will be important for you to emphasize, that is, the different elements of the Commission and how they relate to our obedience to it. The Good News of Christ is to be linked to making disciples of Jesus among all the nations. We are to seek to make followers of Christ among all peoples, beginning in Jerusalem and Judea, proceeding to nearby Samaria, and finally going to the very ends of the earth (Luke 24.47-48; Acts 1.8). All classes and ethnicities of people are to be targeted in our efforts, including both Jews (Acts 2.5-11) and Gentiles (Acts 13.46; Rom. 1.16). The Holy Spirit of God will provide us with the power to attain this work: he is the one who convicts the world of sin, righteousness, and judgment (John 16.8-11), illumines the mind of those who hear the truth of Jesus Christ (1 Cor. 2.9-15), and regenerates the soul with Christ's own life (Titus 3.5). We are to engage in this effort until all have heard, until the very coming of Christ (Matt. 24.14).

 12
*Page 105
Summary of
Key Concepts*

In reviewing the concepts of this lesson, it is important that your review the lesson aims. In some way, the breadth of subjects covered in this lesson mandate that you pay careful attention to the lesson aims so that you do not become overly distracted on tangential issues. While you should not hesitate to discuss thoroughly the kinds questions your students may have on difficult-to-understand concepts, you want to make sure they have a general comprehension of the concepts below. Especially take note of the relationship between the doctrine of election and its correlation with our responsibility to make disciples worldwide by obeying the Great

Commission. As much as possible, enable the students to understand the correlation between the themes.

While concentrating on general themes, take special note in this section of the questions and concerns of the students. Undoubtedly, many questions could have emerged from the discussion on the nuances of the doctrine of election, and now allow for ample time to wrestle with the various implications of the different positions. Especially in the doctrine of election, there are a number of issues which beg for critical reflection and discussion, and some of them can even cause varying degrees of distress. It is important to emphasize the role of mystery and finiteness in all theological education. God has supplied us with insight that is both comprehensive and beyond our understanding, but he has not provided us with exhaustive understanding. We need to be humble enough to admit that there are genuine limits to our understanding of God's intentions and motives, and we ought to be careful in our assertions about what God knows absolutely and unconditionally. Through your answers and your demeanor model for your students what it means to be secure in accepting God's mysteries. The things revealed belong to us and the things hidden belong to the Lord (Deut. 29.29). Most of our error in theological speculation often arises from our pride in assuming that we can know everything possible about God and his works in the world. We cannot. We therefore should engage in our questions with humility and openness. The Holy Spirit is our teacher and we can rely on him as we continue our studies together (1 John 2.27).

 13
Page 106
Student Application and Implications

These case studies are designed to enable the students to apply the difficult and yet refreshing truth about election and the Commission to real life situations. It is important to know that in many situations, as we apply the Word of God, there are often times when our best reflection and most biblical sentiments will not yield easy answers to our dilemmas. What we seek here is an openness and fairness to read the facts of the situation carefully, and relate the Word of the God to the situations as intuitively and wisely as possible. There may be more than a single right answer in a

 14
Page 107
Case Studies

situation, and we must help our students to be biblical without being legalistic, wooden, or strained. In order to be a good student of Scripture our students must be able to "rightly divide the Word of God" (2 Tim. 2.15), making the kind of fine and important discriminations necessary in these cases. In your discussions of these case studies, help your students look at them from every vantage point in order to best discover options within them.

📖 **15**
Page 109
Ministry Connections

The breadth of application possible here is plain, but one of the central connections that can be made is the sovereignty of God both in election and mission. Our God is in control, Jesus Christ is Lord of all, and we can know that we never encounter anything in any way that our God is not able to provide us with the requisite knowledge and power to fulfill his will. Highlight this central truth as you help students make the connections of these truths to their personal lives and ministries.

📖 **16**
Page 111
Assignments

You should now have communicated well with the students regarding the timing of their assignments due soon. For instance, by the end of the second class session, you should have emphasized the need for them to have done the spadework and thought out precisely how they intend on carrying out their Ministry Project. Also, by this time, the end of the third lesson, you should have emphasized their selection of the passage they will study for their Exegetical Project. Both will be done with far better thought and excellence the earlier the students begin to think through them and decide what they want to do. Do not fail to emphasize this, for, as in all study, at the end of the course many things become due, and the students will begin to feel the pressure of getting a number of assignments in at the same time. Any way that you can remind them of the need for advanced planning will be wonderfully helpful for them, whether they realize it immediately or not.

Because of this, we advocate that you consider docking a modest amount of points for late papers, exams, and projects. While the amount may be nominal, your enforcement of your rules will help them to learn to be efficient and on time as they continue in their studies.

The Church at Work

📖 1
Page 115
Lesson Introduction

Welcome to the Mentor's Guide for Lesson 4, *The Church at Work*. The overall focus of this lesson of the Capstone module *Theology of the Church* is to enable your students comprehend clearly and be able to explain to others the various dimensions and elements of the Church, describing how we may detect authentic Christian community through the Church's actions and lifestyle. We will be looking at the identity and works of the Church through the marks provided in the Nicene Creed, the Reformation's teaching, and St. Vincent's rule. Through these sources we can come to understand and evaluate traditions and teachings claiming to speak about the nature of the Church and Christian doctrines. We will also explore the character of the Church's works in the world by exploring various images of the Church mentioned in the New Testament. Through the lens of images of the household of God, the body of Christ, and temple of the Holy Spirit, the ambassadorship of the Church as the agent of the Kingdom of God, and the Church as God's army, we'll comprehend what the Church is called to be and do in the world.

As in your leading of the previous lessons, note here again how critical it is to orient your class session around the learning objectives of the class. Your responsibility as mentor is to emphasize the ideas coming through the objectives in such a way that they provide clear targets and goals for you throughout the lesson. Emphasize the objectives throughout the time, but especially during the discussions and interaction with the students. The more you can highlight the objectives throughout the class period, the better the chances are that they will understand and grasp the magnitude of these objectives.

📖 2
Page 115
Devotion

This devotion focuses on the privilege the Church has in representing the soon-and-coming Kingdom of our Lord Jesus in what it does and says in the world. Jesus commands us to allow our lights to so shine, both personally and communally, that our works would be seen by our neighbors, and for them through those works to glorify God the Father, who is in heaven (Matt. 5.14-16). To represent another is to stitch their reputation to your actions, to force them to be seen in the light of what you do (or fail to do). As the agent and representative of Christ, we reveal him through what we do, how we conduct ourselves in the world, and the way in which we function in this age. Help the students recognize better the remarkable opportunity they have as individuals and members of assemblies to reflect, like moons, the glorious rays of the Son of God. To fulfill this mandate, they must both be aware of it, as well as embrace it. The first steps is welcoming the challenge and the opportunity of representing him before others.

One of the signs of this current age is the proliferation and growth of cults, sects, and false religions. It is important for students in the city to be able to identify, understand, and refute the doctrines and practices of false religious groups. The despair and difficulty of urban life can make people in the city especially susceptible and vulnerable to the groups which prey on the poor and the broken. In the following contacts you can see the emphasis on identifying the authentic among those who claim to belong to Christ and represent him. It is critical for the students to be highly motivated to know the various elements of the true Church, what she believes and does, in order to detect false and unconvincing portrayals of the Church in the neighborhood. Please emphasize with your students in your brief discussion here that Christian leaders must be able to create convincing arguments for and defend the historic orthodox faith against attack. Not all churches claiming to represent Christ and his Kingdom are legitimate; their role, as budding leaders, is to be able to help their congregations grow more and more into the vision that God desires, that all of us grow to full maturity in Jesus Christ (Eph. 4.9-15; 2 Pet. 3.18).

3
Page 117
Contact

In light of the widespread disunity and disarray among churches today, the unity of the Church is a central theme for us to emphasize in Christian leadership development. Like all the apostles, Paul warns early Christian congregations against the temptation of schisms, divisions, and conflicts in 1 Corinthians 1.10-30, and exhorts them to be unified in faith, mission, and fellowship. In his extended section on the body, Paul emphasizes in 1 Corinthians 12 that the Holy Spirit disperses various expressions of God's grace among the members of the Church, but does it in order that the same level of care and love may be in operation among all the believers. In other words, there are many members in the body of Christ, but only one body exists (cf. Rom. 12.3-8). Regardless of Christians who have believed

4
Page 119
Outline Point I-A

throughout the ages in various places, Jesus can state that together believers make up one shepherd with one flock (John 10.16), and he prays explicitly for our unity in his high priestly prayer during his passion (17.20-26). In Colossians 3.11 and Galatians 3.27-28 we see that the Church is not known by categories; everyone who believes in Jesus Christ has become one, and none possess distinction based on gender, race, ethnicity, social status, or history. Being one in Christ by faith, however, does not mean that believers will conform woodenly to the same uniform expressions. The Jerusalem Council of Acts 15 ensures that Christian belief need not slavishly conform to Jewish tradition or Gentile sentiment. Churches gather according to the locales, according to different languages and cultures. From the beginning, churches (gatherings) have possessed their own characters, worship, opportunities for mission, persecutions and perils, and expressions. We hold today to the same challenge that churches have felt throughout the age: believers are to live together with love and unity regarding the heart of our faith in Christ, without demanding that all assemblies imitate our expressions of worship, mission, teaching, and structure. Please emphasize with your students that God's elective choice of his members includes all the branches of the Vine, of which Jesus himself is the Taproot for all of us (John 15.4-5).

5
Page 120
Outline Point I-B

While every individual Christian assembly could point to its own share of division, conflict, or struggle, God calls his people holy. How so? The biblical language regarding holiness does relate directly to the actual character of holiness which we seek to demonstrate in our personal and corporate purity (e.g., 1 Thess. 4.1-8). But, it also refers to the state or status of being separated from the unclean, the impure, and the profane in order to be separated unto the possession, pleasure, and purpose of God. The fact that the Church is holy, then, does not mean that the Church (nor all the churches and assemblies making up the Church) is free from all forms of sin or immorality. It means, rather, that the Church has, through God's elective purpose, been set aside for his possession and use, and that she should seek to become all that she is and has been called to through God's calling. This is completely in sync and illustrated by Paul's discussion of his own desire to glorify God in Philippians 3.12 where he suggests that at the present, he was neither altogether perfect or having attained the high calling of God in Christ. Even the Corinthian assembly is called holy, and the members are "saints" (cf. 1 Cor. 1.2). We as congregations are holy, at least in the sense that we have been set apart by God for his possession, pleasure, and use (2 Thess. 2.13; Col. 3.12, etc.).

In using the term "catholic," we are not suggesting that the Roman Catholic form and structure of the Church is authoritative and correct, or even primary. What we do mean here, however, is that the Church includes all the believing, living, dead, and yet unborn, who make up the one multi-national, multi-era, universal community of God. The term itself is based on the Latin terms *catholicus*, a term connected to the Greek *katholikos* which means "universal." The concept is shown to be biblical, although cognates of these actual terms are nowhere cited in the New Testament. A simple way of understanding the concept of catholicity of the Church is to think in terms of the whole Church or the entire people of God, of all ages, times, clans, kindreds, tongues, lands, and languages. It also reflects equally on the unity of the Church, which means that we have a single purpose, identity, mission, and destiny in all the various forms and structures which represent the one true Church.

📖 **6**
*Page 120
Outline Point I-C*

It will be important in your discussion of this material to explore some of the implications of this truth, which is to say that every association of churches which profess and live Jesus as Lord and Savior must be seen as equal. No section, sector, era, or tradition of the Church, therefore, should pretend to be more important or authoritative than any other. The urban churches, therefore, should strive to find its special place in influencing others for Christ. Urban Christianity need not be overly dependent or intimidated at other forms, since they are a part of the one true, catholic Church.

The idea that the Church is apostolic is built on the idea that the heart and soul of the Church's faith and practice is built upon the apostles' testimony and teaching. This is plainly taught by Paul in Ephesians:

📖 **7**
*Page 121
Outline Point I-D*

Eph. 2.19-22 - So then you are no longer strangers and aliens, but you are fellow citizens with the saints and members of the household of God, [20] built on the foundation of the apostles and prophets, Christ Jesus himself being the cornerstone, [21] in whom the whole structure, being joined together, grows into a holy temple in the Lord. [22] In him you also are being built together into a dwelling place for God by the Spirit.

The high place that the apostles hold in the history and development of the Church is based on their eyewitness testimony about the person and work of Jesus Christ, especially his resurrection, as well as their authoritative revelation as to the meaning of Jesus' life and ministry for humankind and the Church. In one sense, the apostles have become the standard for the entire vision of the Church: their opinion form the basis for the canonization of the New Testament writings, the legitimacy of Church leadership and doctrine, and the heart of the norms which establish our credibility as true believers. To reject the apostles is to deny the Christ; the Church, therefore, is apostolic to its very foundation.

8
Page 123
Outline Point II-B

A sacrament can be defined as a rite or ceremony, whether instituted by Jesus Christ or through Church history, which is understood to be a means of grace or a memorial or token of Christian belief and practice. Some believers, especially Protestants, would limit the term to those rites and ceremony instituted by Jesus Christ himself. The two recognized by all traditions of the Church are baptism and the Lord's Supper. These two sacraments are mentioned in the New Testament by Jesus, and both held a significant role and place in the life and community of the first believers (Acts 2.41-42; 10.47; 20.7, 11). While the Catholic Church and others traditions have extended the sacraments to include a number of rites and ceremonies, both baptism and the Lord's Supper are directly associated with the person and work of Jesus Christ, especially in connection with his death and resurrection, and with his coming again (Matt. 28.19-20; Acts 2.38; Rom. 6.3-5; 1 Cor. 11.23-27; Col. 2.11-12).

These questions are designed to highlight the main points associated with the first video segment. Again, we are using the various marks of the Nicene Creed, the Reformation teaching, and the Vincentian Rule to discern what are the most effective and biblically convincing marks of the true Church. As you discuss these marks, make sure that you cover how a mark may or may not reflect the Bible's teaching on the nature of the Church. While these and other extra-biblical sources (that is, sources other than the Scriptures themselves) are important, they cannot eclipse or be seen as critical as the biblical witness itself on the nature of the Church. Therefore, make certain that you undergird all discussions about the true marks with reference to the Scriptures.

 9
Page 129
Student Questions and Response

The method that we are employing to discover the work of the Church (i.e., looking at images of the Church in the New Testament and drawing conclusions from them), deserves some explanation. Even a cursory glance at the various images of the Church in the New Testament reveals that a multiplicity of images and concepts exist, and these all possess different and correlated understandings of what the Church is and what the Church does. In a remarkable and important work on the Church, *Images of the Church in the New Testament*, Paul Minear identifies 96 different images of the Church in the New Testament. Among these, Minear categorizes these into five categories he calls minor images, the people of God, the new creation, the fellowship in faith, and the body of Christ. The richness of these images suggest that a tremendous wealth of insight waits to be mined in these images. To study the Church through this great diversity of images is the task of the serious Bible student. There will be many images which unfortunately will not receive any of the attention they so richly deserve: people of God's possession, the salt of the earth, holy nation, epistle of Christ, branches of the vine, the elect lady, the bride of the Lamb, sojourners and exiles, the priesthood of God, the new creation, the sanctified slaves, friends, and the pillar and ground of the truth. Suffice it to say that God gave us these rich images that we might engage in serious and continuous study to understand his people *through* them. This rich company of images makes it both necessary and desirable to discern the nature of the Church *indirectly* through the concrete image we study. We encourage all students of

 10
Page 130
Summary of Segment 2

Scripture to pursue this method, not only to understand the Church, but all of the great doctrines of Scripture.

📖 11
Page 135
Outline Point III

Believers do battle against the devil, the first of God's angelic creatures who in pride and lust for God's glory, rebelled against the Lord Almighty and became the enemy of God and humankind. Many connect the person of Satan with Isaiah 14.12-14 and Ezekiel 28.12-15, which describe this great angelic being as "Lucifer" and as "the Anointed Cherub" before his rebellion and fall. In John's Revelation, Satan is seen to have led vast numbers of other spirits after him in rebellion against God (Rev. 12.4), one of many instances which show him to live up to the name of "the Evil One" and "the Tempter." According to Scripture, the devil initiated, through his lying deception, the fall of humankind as "the Serpent" (Gen. 3). In what theologians call the *protoevangelium*, the devil's ultimate destruction through God's anointed seed is prophesied (Gen. 3.15), which was accomplished through the work of Jesus Christ on the cross, as *Christus Victor* (i.e., Christ the Victor) where he defeated the devil and his minions, and inaugurated the "beginning of the end" of the rule of the devil and the establishment of the Kingdom of God (John 12.13-33 cf. Col. 2.15).

Believers have been delivered from the kingdom of darkness to the Kingdom of light through Jesus Christ (Col. 1.13), and have been "drafted" into the army of God as soldiers in the cosmic battle of God to reclaim the universe for him and his people. Even though the devil has been judged and defeated soundly through the blood of the cross (Col. 2.15), the devil continues to operate in this age and in this realm as a deceiver of those who do not believe (2 Cor. 4.4), accusing the saints before the Lord (Rev. 12.10), and tempting humankind through his complete and entire control of the world (1 John 2.15-17; 5.19). Believers are to be vigilant and sober for the devil seeks those who are not aware to destroy them, and to undermine God's work at every turn (1 Pet. 5.8). This work of tempting, accusation, deception, and destruction is worldwide and systemic, coordinated both in the world system and through his network of demons who function under his authority along with those who do not believe (Isa. 14.12-17; 2 Cor. 4.3-4; Eph. 2.2; Col. 1.13).

A significant part of the work of the Church is to fight the enemy, the devil, through a proclamation of the Word of God. We remain in continuous battle with the devil and his minions (Eph. 6.11-18), who seek to render us ineffective through direct attack, lies, deception, and oppression, both physically and spiritually (1 Cor. 5.5; 1 John 5.16). We overcome all of the satanic and demonic fury through the blood of the Lamb and the word of our testimony (Rev. 12.11), as we take up the armor of God and stand against his wiles in the evil time (Eph. 6.11-18).

Discussion of these important images of the Church will demand an efficient and effective use of time. All of the images allow for a wide berth of angles and issues to be explored, so for the sake of time stewardship, it will be necessary to determine how much time you will give to each image. It can easily be argued that the Holy Spirit provides us with a diversity and variety of images in order that we might derive a maximum amount of insight from each image. The apostles did not feel the need to share each image with each congregation or group of congregations in every letter. Rather, they employed the images to counsel and to instruct the churches about various dimensions of their unique and particular community life, and what they needed to change or do in order to remedy a particular problem, or resolve some relational tension. Use the times of discussion to show your students how to analyze and reflect on the images in order to fulfill pastoral and counselor responsibility. This is *how* the apostles thought, and you can use your discussions of these images to think their thoughts after them–or at least, imitate their methods.

📖 12
*Page 140
Student Questions
and Response*

In discussing the student application and implication questions, it will be important to help the students understand the wisdom of the Spirit's providing us with a diversity of images. There is no attempt by the apostles to harmonize them or classify them; they use them freely to address issues or needs, or simply provide us with richer insight into the nature of God's community. As you answer questions with the students, help them understand how these marks and images can be an invaluable resource to understand the nature of the Church. Focus carefully on the

📖 13
*Page 142
Student Application
and Implications*

student questions, while at the same time, using the moments as an opportunity to help them understand the apostles' use of the "marks" and "images."

📖 **14**
Page 143
Case Studies

What is significant in the application of the Word of God to specific situations is the ability to be flexible and open in how we handle Scripture, while, at the same time, respecting it enough to exegete it with care and reverence. In considering the various experiences and situations of these case studies, it is helpful to think of how you may enable the students to think of the marks and images of the Church at work as a reference library of images to deal with specific ailments and challenges. Each mark and image allows for its own rich reservoir of meanings, interpretations, and connotations, all of which can help us understand who we are and are supposed to be in a particular situation. Being a Christian congregation is to live out an identity, one which the Holy Spirit has provided to us through the multiple images of the Church in the New Testament. As you consider these studies carefully, think of how the marks and the images can allow you and your students to think creatively and expressively about how to identify and address problems or issues in church planting and church growth through a fresh reading of the biblical images of the Church.

📖 **15**
Page 145
Ministry Connections

As much as any lesson in the Capstone curriculum, this lesson emphasizes a key skill that all leaders must have to function effectively in the Church. The images and marks that God provides us of the true identity and authentic work of the Church are not merely for the sake of discussion and reflection. On the contrary, these images make up a collage, a mosaic of meanings which define the very nature of the character of the Church. Christian leaders are to understand and apply these meanings in every level of their local congregational ministries, including their preaching, teaching, counseling, administrating, and leading. As you enable your students to make connections between this material and their ministries, reiterate to them the need for them to become expert in their knowledge of the images of the Church, as well as in their ability to apply the meaning of those images to every phase and stage of the Church's development and life. As you discuss with them their own applications, reemphasize this key role of Christian leadership, and challenge them again to discover ways they can master these concepts and apply them practically as often as they can.

Congratulations! You have now come to the end of the module on the Church. It is now that your responsibility as an instructor and grader begins in earnest. Make sure that you have commitments for the ministry projects, exegetical projects, and other data together as this will be important for you to determine the student's overall grade. Again, your discretion regarding late work can easily determine whether you dock students of points, resulting in letter grade changes, or give students an "Incomplete" until the work is finished. However you adopt your standard regarding their work, remember that our courses are not primarily about the grades that the students receive, but the spiritual nourishment and training these courses provide. Also, however, remember that helping our students strive for excellence is an integral part of our instruction.

In every respect, make certain that your students prepare well for the remaining work and that they do not become complacent or lazy at this phase of the course. It is always difficult to finish strong, but that is exactly the challenge for them. They will reap a harvest of blessing, if they do not quit and give up (Gal. 6.9). Exhort them to complete their work with vigor and excellence, and model the same for them in the way you treat their material and exams.

16
*Page 146
Assignments*

www.ingramcontent.com/pod-product-compliance
Lightning Source LLC
Chambersburg PA
CBHW080731300426
44114CB00019B/2552